# MINIATURES AT KENWOOD

## *The Draper Gift*

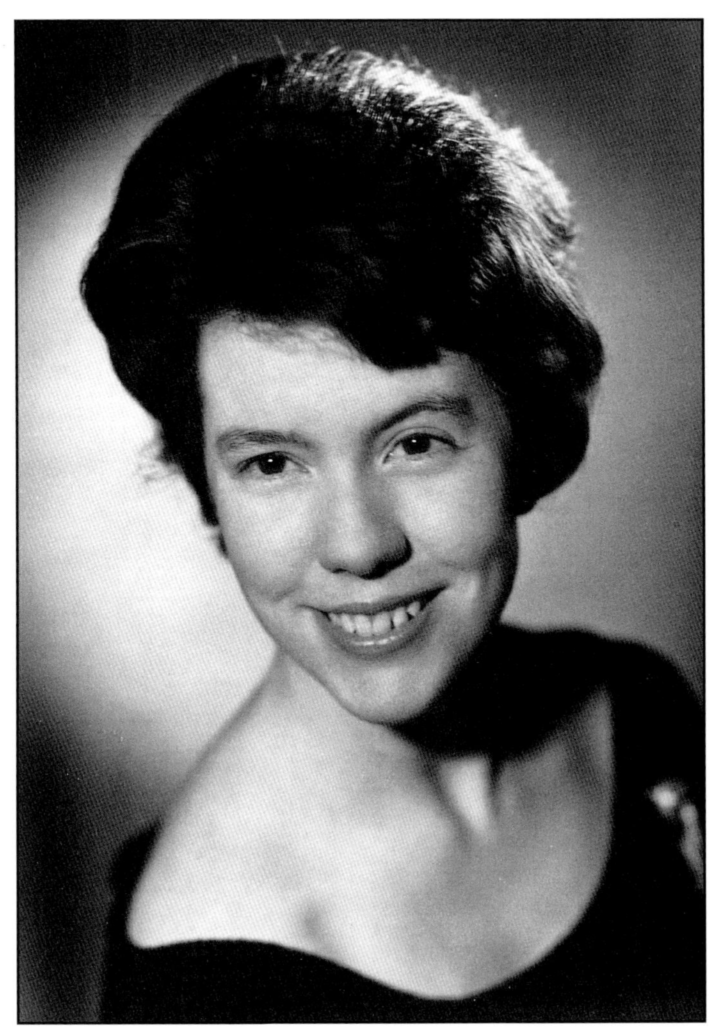

*Marie Elizabeth Jane Irving Draper (1940–87)*

# MINIATURES AT KENWOOD
## *The Draper Gift*

ENGLISH HERITAGE

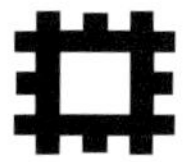

1997

Edited by Katy Carter

Designed by Nick Cannan

Indexed by Lesley Adkins


Copyright © 1997 English Heritage


First published 1997 by English Heritage

23 Savile Row, London W1X 1AB


A catalogue record for this book is available from the British Library


Printed in the European Union


ISBN 1 85074 664 8

# Contents

## Preface: The Draper Gift

Every curator dreams of the day when an unknown benefactor walks into the museum and offers to help form a collection. Such good fortune befell Kenwood in 1988, and since then over one hundred portrait miniatures have been acquired to complement the British paintings in the Iveagh Bequest. This catalogue celebrates the formation of a collection of enduring value to specialists as a source of reference, and of sheer pleasure and enlightenment to London's residents and visitors, particularly those who have enjoyed the outstanding miniatures in the Wallace Collection and the Victoria and Albert Museum. It also commemorates the late Marie Jane Draper, whose discerning eye formed the nucleus of twenty miniatures bequeathed to Kenwood. This gift so kindled the enthusiasm of her mother (and executrix) and the curators that the collection has grown to its present scale at an exhilarating pace, largely financed from Marie's estate.

Since the 1970s, Kenwood has been home to the Lady Maufe Collection of Georgian Shoe Buckles and to the Hull Grundy Bequest of costume jewellery. The gift of Marie Draper's collection gave an appropriate means of linking these less familiar aspects of the museum with Lord Iveagh's celebrated society portraits by Reynolds, Gainsborough, Romney, Raeburn and others through the acquisition of further miniatures. Whereas these jewellery collections were formed by private individuals to satisfy their own tastes and ambitions, the expansion of the Draper Gift has been steered by curatorial interests.

For the Draper Gift to make a lasting contribution to its field, it would be as a coherent reference collection where most, if not all, faces would be backed up by a firm attribution to an artist, ideally with a signature or monogram and date, and wherever possible the name of the sitter. These aims, combined with a continuance of Marie's known liking for interesting people, faces, attires and settings, ensure that many of the portraits, acquired initially for relatively modest sums, record faces of real character, and something of the true physiognomy of the Georgian era, rather than the fashionable beauties who tend to monopolise the walls of the world's art galleries.

The variety of ways in which miniatures were mounted, from rings, brooches, bracelets and pendants backed often with ornately plaited samples of the sitter's hair, to boxes, *souvenirs d'amitié*, etc have also been valued to illustrate the medium's varied role as portable social tools akin to jewellery. Likewise, this theme grew out of the original group of twenty portraits.

The choice of historical period mirrors that of the Iveagh Bequest, broadly from the mid-eighteenth century to the early Victorian era. But inevitably, as opportunities have arisen, so the limits have been stretched to embrace a fine likeness, such as those by Snelling, Lens and Zincke. The earlier examples help to indicate the technical development of the art form, while the later miniatures show its subsequent competition with early photography. However, no attempt has been made to provide a comprehensive survey by including the great early masters, such as Hilliard and Oliver.

Portrait miniatures have long been part of the history of Kenwood. The museum collection includes two enamels (cats 64, 65) by William Russell Birch of *William Murray, 1st Earl of Mansfield*, painted after Reynolds' portrait of the Lord Chief Justice who commissioned fellow Scotsman Robert Adam to remodel the villa between 1764 and 1779. Birch painted thirteen miniatures of Mansfield, presumably for his sitter to give to his family and many political admirers. The artist became a regular visitor to Kenwood, recording many vivid vignettes of daily life at the house in his autobiography. The 2nd Earl of Mansfield was a patron of Richard Cosway, and John Linnell was commissioned to visit Kenwood in 1820 and 1823 to copy miniatures of the third Earl's four daughters. The museum has recently acquired miniatures of relevance to the history of the house, including a copy of Batoni's portrait of the second Earl (cat. 71) and portraits of the second Earl's agent, Nathaniel Parker Forth and his family (cats 72, 50, 105). But perhaps the strongest links between the Draper Gift and the

Iveagh Bequest lie in the sitters themselves, some of whom would have known each other, and in the artists: two sitters (*Mrs Crouch* by Romney and *Mrs Johnstone* by Raeburn) are shown holding portrait miniatures.

Marie Elizabeth Jane Irving Draper (1940–87) lived in Hampstead at 110 Heath Street, and 5 Hampstead Square, and first came to Kenwood when the house was closed to the public during the war. She came from a family involved with aspects of art and artefacts. She was educated at Channing School in Highgate village and at the Sorbonne and travelled widely abroad before working as an Approved School housemistress and then at St Bartholomew's and St Mary's hospitals.

Her love of portrait miniatures began as a small child on regular visits to the National Maritime Museum with her naval officer uncle, who taught history at the Royal Naval College, Greenwich. Of Huguenot descent, she spoke French fluently, and the gift from her stepfather of a biography of Isabey revealed to her the full potential of portrait miniatures when painted by the French master. She became a regular visitor to the Wallace Collection and the Victoria and Albert Museum. Her first miniature (by Guy Head) was purchased in about 1970 from Asprey's.

Her love of the genre took on new importance after a severe injury and major surgery in 1969. The following year she was found to have pigmented glaucoma, with advanced tunnel vision, a disability which only confirmed and heightened her love of miniatures. Her mother recalls how she had to focus closely on a miniature in her hand as though peering at it through a key hole. She then saw it with great clarity. This illness led to her forming a small but highly choice collection of her own. At that time is was possible to become a serious collector with only modest means, and Marie Draper earned and benefited from the interest and generosity of the leading expert dealers of her day. She also formed a small collection of

Georgian jewellery and presented various items to the Bethnal Green Museum of Childhood. Her harp by Sebastian Erard, 1811, decorated like that of the Empress Josephine, now stands in the Music Room at Kenwood.

The goodwill and support that Marie Draper enjoyed from the fine art trade continued after her death in 1987, following the decision to form the collection for Kenwood from her estate. Haydn Williams of Sotheby's, Alexandra Fennell of Christie's, Claudia Hill of Bonham's, the late Mrs Bette Viner and her husband Brigadier Gordon Viner, and the late Robert Bayne-Powell have all given generously of their time and expertise in advising both on the 'shopping list' and on individual purchases. Mr Bayne-Powell indeed donated a miniature from his own exceptional collection (cat. 57). English Heritage is also most grateful to Graham Reynolds and Aileen Ribeiro for their contributions to this catalogue, which do much to put the collection in its art historical and social context. It was Sebastian Edwards who, as Assistant Curator of Kenwood, had charge of the miniatures, their records, their display in the newly formed 'little gallery', and liaison regarding them generally and over acquisitions. To Sebastian fell the responsibility for compiling this catalogue, the completion and editing of which was taken up by Ian Dejardin, the region's Senior Curator of Collections, after Sebastian's departure from English Heritage.

Whilst not aspiring to provide more than an introduction to its subject, to the artists and works of art, this catalogue does seek to convey something of the personalities behind the faces that gaze out from the following pages. In this way it should help satisfy the curiosity that is invariably aroused by the sense of immediacy peculiar to portraiture in miniature.


**Julius Bryant**
Director of Museums and Collections
English Heritage

# Introduction

Throughout the sixteenth and seventeenth centuries English miniature painters were the dominant masters of this type of portraiture in the Western world. The achievements of Hans Holbein, Nicholas Hilliard, Isaac Oliver, John Hoskins and Samuel Cooper were admired throughout Europe and, although emulated, were not excelled. By the beginning of the eighteenth century the rich vein of native talent which had maintained this excellence had temporarily been exhausted. The miniaturists who eventually followed them had to assimilate two changes in technique which profoundly altered the character of the art.

The earlier masters had painted their small portraits in watercolour on vellum, a method adopted from the practice of the artists who illuminated manuscripts. The first innovation lay in the use of pigments fused into enamel on metal. Since enamel painting is a ceramic process akin to the decoration of porcelain, it encouraged the use of strong colours and a technique of modelling with little points of pigment. This method had the merit of combining brilliance with permanence of colour, and the virtual monology achieved in the medium of the Court of Louis XIV by Jean Petitot ensured its wide use on the Continent. So, when foreign artists were attracted to England from the end of the seventeenth century to meet the unabated demand for miniatures, enamellists such as Charles Boit and Christian Friedrich Zincke were among the most prominent.

The second technical change was introduced in the first decade of the eighteenth century, when the Venetian artist Rosalba Carriera began to use ivory in place of vellum as the ground on which her watercolour miniatures were painted. This practice took hold rather slowly, but by the second half of the century ivory had replaced vellum as a painting ground. At the same time it mainly restricted the use of enamel to the reproduction of oil paintings. When in the 1780s Lord Mansfield required small replicas of his portrait by Reynolds he had them made in enamel by William Birch.

As the technique of painting on ivory became fully understood the artists of the second half of the eighteenth century were able to make full use of its unique quality – the luminosity of colour achieved by the reflection of light through the thin pigment on its polished white surface.

The collection of miniatures at Kenwood illustrates the course of events by which the methods introduced from the Continent were taken over by artists working in England in the eighteenth century, and became the foundation of a second flowering of the art in this country.

The miniatures produced in England in the first years of the eighteenth century bear marks of their Continental antecedents. Charles Boit had been trained in Stockholm and Paris. His enamels, of which the portrait of *James FitzJames, Duke of Berwick* (cat. 4) is a characteristic example, offer much the same stolid assessments of their subjects as those of his Swedish compatriot Michael Dahl, who shared with Sir Godfrey Kneller the main patronage of large-scale portraiture at the time. Christian Friedrich Zincke came from a German artistic background, and learned enamelling as Boit's assistant. However, his immense technical facility was pervaded by mannerism, and he was quizzed in his own day for the similarity of his female portraits.

Whilst these enamel painters were prospering, a less accomplished attempt to naturalise painting on ivory was being made by Bernard Lens, the first English-born miniaturist to emerge in the new century. He became drawing master to George II's daughters, Princess Mary and Princess Louisa, and his portraits of them in this collection (1739, cats 6, 7) show that although his skills were unassuming he could achieve a pleasing decorative effect.

The next generation consolidated the transition from enamel to ivory. Both Nathaniel Hone and Gervase Spencer practised each method. Whilst doing so they inaugurated a more recognisably national style of miniature portraiture, reflecting the truly British vision of which Hogarth was such a powerful advocate. They and their contemporaries produced miniatures which are modest in scale and conception. Their size, small even in the context of the miniature, was influenced by the fashion for wearing miniatures as bracelets, a practice exemplified here by the setting of Thomas Redmond's portrait of a woman (1762, cat. 32). Amongst the painters of these agreeably unpretentious works are artists with distinctive styles, seen in the rococo charm of Luke Sullivan (cats 15, 16) and the quiet *naïveté* of Penelope Carwardine (cat. 20).

This modest school of miniaturists paved the way for a transformation which became noticeable in the 1760s and gathered strength till the end of the century. The harbinger of this robust epoch was Jeremiah Meyer. He came to England from Germany as a child and after tuition from the ageing Zincke began his career as an enamellist. But his strength as a draughtsman and his mastery of a clear decisive line led him to work more and more on ivory. He pioneered the increased size of the miniature, which by the 1770s was often over 3 inches (7.5 cm) in height. Whether he was working on the large scale of his royal portraits or in the smaller format seen in the Kenwood collection (cats 28, 29), he was the master of a linear elegance which matches the oils of Reynolds and Gainsborough. He introduced into his portraits a nobility of demeanour lacking in his homelier predecessors. His eminence was marked by his election as a founder member of the Royal Academy in 1769, the only miniaturist to be so honoured.

The increased prestige which Meyer bestowed upon the art was consolidated by four artists who were all born in 1742: Richard Cosway, John Smart, Ozias Humphry and Richard Crosse. They were its acknowledged leaders till the end of the century and they were supplemented by a large number of lesser artists who, as this collection shows, had individual styles and did not lack for patronage. The ambitions and range of these miniaturists were encouraged by the spread of public exhibitions such as those of the Society of Arts and later the Royal Academy, in which their works could be compared with large-scale portraiture and assessed alongside those of their rivals. It was a period of growing demand. Already in the 1760s it was possible to make a choice from more than two dozen miniature painters, and each decade brought a substantial increase in the number of practitioners. Those who were at the top of the profession were kept well employed; for instance, Richard Crosse frequently painted about one hundred miniatures a year, and he was not exceptionally prolific.

The most prominent masters, such as Meyer, Cosway and Smart, have distinctive and easily discriminated styles. The enlargement of the surface on which they worked provided scope for increased virtuosity. Cosway took advantage of this to create his likenesses with the utmost economy of means, virtually sketching the image on to the ivory with restrained colour and grey tonality. His work has often been likened to Gainsborough's in the way he achieves a portrait by suggestion rather than by elaboration of detail. John Smart, in contrast, aimed at a high degree of finish which recalls the enamels which such miniatures on ivory had replaced. Ozias Humphry had some early encouragement from Sir Joshua Reynolds and an echo of that painter's Venetian colouring may be seen in his miniatures.

The exertions of these four leading masters were supplemented by scores of other able miniaturists. Amongst those represented at Kenwood with a marked individuality of touch are Samuel Cotes, Samuel Collins, James Scouler and William Wood. Another prominent contemporary was Samuel Shelley. When the American miniaturist Edward Malbone visited in 1801 he thought Shelley to be the equal of Cosway. Shelley wished to make subject pictures in little rather than confining himself to portraiture, and took a leading role in the watercolour societies which sprang up at the time. Andrew Plimer was Cosway's pupil, and in the late nineteenth century was thought to be almost his master's equal. His portrait here of Elizabeth Farren (1790s, cat. 49) at the height of her fame as a leading actress at the Drury Lane and Haymarket theatres is a product of his earlier period, before he fell into the habit of making stereotyped images.

Though London was the focus for wealth and society it was not the only centre to attract a body of miniature painters. Bath provided employment for Samuel Collins, Ozias Humphry, Abraham Daniel and Charles Jagger. The Irish-born George Place, Charles Robertson and John Comerford worked in Dublin, and the Scots John Bogle and Alexander Gallaway in Edinburgh. Hope of the riches to be found in India attracted a number of artists, some of whom, such as John Smart, Ozias Humphry, Charles Shirreff and George Chinnery, had begun to make their reputation in England.

The close of the eighteenth century is memorable for the immense output of George Engleheart. In a single year he recorded the production of 228 miniatures, and during his long working life he painted over 5,000 such portraits. Since there were at least sixty other artists making a living out of miniature painting at the time, these figures give an idea of the widespread demand at the end of the century for these precious tokens of esteem. This heyday of the miniature was encouraged by a number of interrelated factors. The population was growing, and wealth was becoming more widely spread. In consequence the demand for portraiture as record and remembrance came from a wider section of society than in earlier times, when it was largely confined to the court and nobility. In the collection at Kenwood the range of sitters extends from the Princesses Mary and Louisa, the Duke of Berwick and Elizabeth Farren, later Countess of Derby, to people little known outside their domestic circle such as Anne Farquhar, Marianne Nantes and Miss Lucy Nicholas with her pet dog (cats 40, 70, 35).

The onset of the nineteenth century brought notable changes to the art. Newcomers, led by Andrew Robertson, expressed their dissatisfaction with the methods of Cosway and his followers, which they regarded simply as a branch of drawing. They declared their intention of rivalling the force of oils when painting on their ivory support. At the same time, Robertson and his followers preferred the larger rectangular format to the customary oval. This signalled a change in the purpose of the miniature portrait. Instead of being a jewelled adjunct to the costume or a private focus for personal feeling, it tended to become a small cabinet picture to be hung on the wall or exhibited on the desk.

Queen Victoria maintained her enthusiasm for miniatures till the end of her life. Sir William Ross, who possessed a happy facility in large-scale composition and a benign insight into character, was her favourite painter in this medium. The example of his work here, a well-known portrait of his father in old age (c1842, cat. 109), is on a relatively small scale and clearly pervaded by real personal feeling. Ross's stature as the leading miniaturist of the mid-Victorian era was affirmed by an exhibition arranged by the Society of Arts in the year of his death, 1860. As well as being a retrospect of his career this was almost a requiem for the art he practised, for it came at a time when the miniature was losing its place to the photograph as the favoured form of small-scale portraiture.

The generous gift made to Kenwood by Marie Draper, augmented by the judicious additions made by the present curators of the house, gives a survey of the course of miniature painting from the early years of the eighteenth century. Examples by the leading masters, Meyer, Crosse, Cosway and Smart, are seen beside the work of many accomplished contemporaries. In its variety and diversity this collection provides a brilliant and intimate parallel to the imposing full-length portraits which are the glory of the Kenwood collection. In doing so, it gives further evidence of the high place which fine portraiture holds for British patrons of art.

**Graham Reynolds**

# The Art and Business of Portrait Miniatures in England

This chapter outlines the circumstances in which miniatures were commissioned, created and used during the period represented by the collection: broadly speaking, from the mid-seventeenth until the mid-nineteenth century.

The specialist requirements of painting miniatures meant that the majority of artists who practised the art concentrated on this discipline, along with the complementary use of drawing. Because of this separation from the mainstream of painting, only a limited amount of first-hand evidence survives which describes miniature painters at work. A handful of early treatises and the chance survival of artists' fee books and letters cannot compete with the wealth of information provided by illustrious portrait painters, such as Sir Joshua Reynolds, who were often encouraged to discourse on their work.[1] We are left mostly with glimpses of an artistic world separate from that of full-scale painting, with its own practitioners, working methods and sets of values.

By the mid-seventeenth century a long-established system of formal apprenticeship, sometimes bolstered with fee-paying lessons, was in place. Limning was very much a craft skill and students were required to apply themselves for seven or more years under a master, before setting up on their own. For a time this meant that strong links could be found across the styles of generations of miniaturists: the great Isaac Oliver taught his son Peter; John Hoskins studied with Peter Oliver; in turn Hoskins brought up his nephews Alexander and Samuel Oliver; and the latter appears to been been observed at work by Thomas Flatman. Each of these leading miniaturists, who span the seventeenth century, had a direct influence on his own circle of followers. There were also many families of miniaturists in the period covered who learned their trade at home, such as the Lens family in the early eighteenth century and the Scottish Robertsons, a century later.

A successful artist could afford to have studio assistants, who not only studied with their masters, but also prepared, finished and copied their works. The story of the young and impoverished Andrew Plimer, who joined Richard Cosway as a servant and was promoted to assistant on the basis of his great artistic ability, is well known. Although the use of apprentices began to disappear in the mid-eighteenth century, this close master-pupil relationship continued longer among the enamellists and goldsmiths who painted miniatures. The exacting skills of this branch of the art demanded years of practical training which often meant that styles changed rather slowly across generations of enamellists. Clear links can be seen between the works of Charles Boit, his pupil C.F. Zincke and finally Jeremiah Meyer, who was obliged to pay some £400 for Zincke's lessons.[2] In spite of the strong tradition in enamelling, Meyer did manage to attract wide patronage when enamels began to go out of fashion, roughly from the 1750s, by adapting successfully to miniatures in watercolour. He was, however, an exception, and few managed to juggle these two very different media.

In the latter half of the eighteenth century the system of formal studio learning began to break down. As with other classes of artists, talented young draughtsmen (women miniaturists had to learn in the home) were attracted to the new drawing academies. The first of these were private life- and sculpture-copying classes, centred in London on St Martin's Lane (re-founded in 1735). Drawing skills honed here could be turned rapidly into early acclaim and even profit with the introduction of prizes, first established at the newly founded Society of Arts. It was here that Cosway and Smart launched their careers in their early teens, when they both won junior prizes. Others might pay for formal lessons with a well-known artist or attend the Royal Academy Schools. The prodigy artist, Andrew Robertson, had to find a benefactor to pay the 1½ guineas for twelve lessons, from Alexander Nasmyth, in 1792.[3] A short while afterwards he had the confidence to bribe his way into the home of Henry Raeburn to look at his collection, and ended up being given a room in which to copy paintings, so impressed was the great man.

Once established, most miniature painters earned too modest a living to work other than from a well-lit room in their own lodgings. This studio space could be small, as no backdrops were required (these could be added after sittings) and only a few yards' distance from the sitter was necessary. Diffuse, north light was preferred, but not, surprisingly, a particularly strong light. In 1800, Archibald

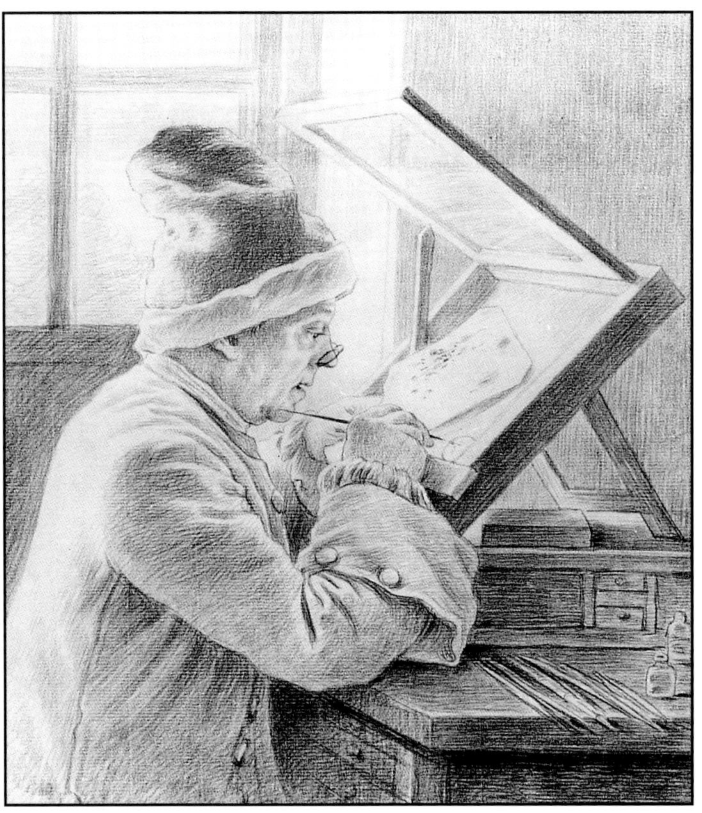

*Figure 1:* C.F. Zincke working in his later years, from his home in Lambeth. *Black and red chalk drawing by William Hoare, 1752. Note the easel box with its glazed dust protector (British Museum)*

Robertson, the elder brother of Andrew, instructed his brother: 'All your work should be done in rather a dim than a sharp light ... you can make it more mellow.'[4] Apart from good quality of light, the studio and equipment had to be kept scrupulously clean to avoid dust and dirt on the tacky paint surface. Necessary precautions can be seen in a rare image of the enamellist Zincke at work, by William Hoare (fig. 1). Even in Nicholas Hilliard's day (c1547–1619) limners were aware of the problems of pollution from coal fires affecting the vulnerable surfaces of their miniatures.

As with all portrait painters, the more aspiring miniaturists lived somewhere convenient for their patrons and sitters. In London, for example, this meant addresses near to the court at Whitehall in the seventeenth century, or in the City, where they could attract wealthy merchants, clergy and lawyers. The structure of the city before the Industrial Revolution allowed artists to rent lodgings within

yards of the largest private palaces. Samuel Cooper, for example, lived in Henrietta Street, Covent Garden, from 1642. A century and a half later another leading miniaturist, Samuel Shelley, worked in that same street, along with other artists. A few men attained enormous social status as well as financial gain and pushed themselves into public attention by establishing their own salons and picture galleries. Cosway provides the most notorious case of such social climbing in miniature. After lodging in the Strand, he moved to Berkeley Street on the edge of the West End. He then found a great apartment in Schomberg House on Pall Mall, next to the Court of St James's, where the Prince of Wales would visit. When health and patronage failed him, he ended his days modestly in the Edgware Road.

The materials and techniques of the miniaturist in watercolour changed very little between the seventeenth and late eighteenth centuries, save for the introduction of ivory as an alternative to vellum as a support, in 1707.

From the Elizabethan period, vellum, stuck on to smoothed pasteboard, was preferred as a base. This had to be carefully prepared to avoid blemishes. When ivory began to be used as a support from the 1700s it too needed meticulous preparation. The thin layers were hand cut (until about 1840), leaving the artist to rub them smooth first. Then oils in the ivory were blotted and dried out so that the water-based paint would apply evenly, and finally the surface was given a key by gentle abrasion. As J.V. Murrell's researches have pointed out, limners preferred a very restricted range of colours to ensure the purity and stability of their paint surface. Over thirty pigments, together with two whites and several carbon-based blacks, were used from the Elizabethan period. However, even in the nineteenth century, when many new colours were invented, Robertson was recommended to use only nine. Pigments could be bought from an apothecary or, later, an artist's colourman, and prepared in the studio. They were mixed with water or a mixture of water and gum arabic (Acacia tree gum) if more body was wanted. Sometimes white lead was used for opaque touches or colours, such as when painting the lace on a dress. Squirrel hair brushes could be bought ready-made from a very early date, although some artists made their own. These were

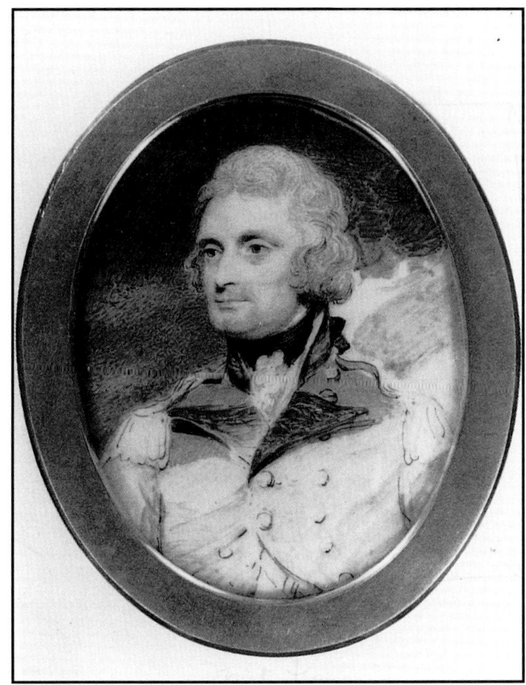

*Figure 2: Henry Edridge Unfinished miniature of* Lt. General Sir Henry Oakes *(Holburne Museum, Bath). This work is at mid-stage, probably from the second sitting. The practice of rapidly laying down the image and making alterations on ivory can be seen*

not very tiny, but had a fine point, and indeed larger brushes were used to lay on washes.

The main alternative medium was fired enamel, which was introduced into England from Sweden and France in the 1680s. The technique of firing enamel was slow, painstaking and prone to irreparable faults during firing. All the colours were based on solid silica materials (obtained from glass) with metal oxide pigments. These were applied to a white ground, fired on to copper, and each colour needed to be fired separately, leaving ample opportunities for blemishes and cracks. Most practitioners who worked in this medium specialised in it, and often came from a background as goldsmiths or jewellers, who shared the techniques and equipment. The benefits of such a slow process, when it was applied with skill, were brilliant and permanent colours. In contrast, watercolour was prone to fading, mould and cracking of the ivory. Its eventual dominance resulted from the speed and creative possibilities that it offered (fig. 2).

By the eighteenth century most miniaturists worked at a table using small, purpose-made drawing slopes with drawers for their palettes and brushes. The enamellist Zincke can be seen working at one of these in Hoare's drawing (fig. 1). Shells were first used as pots and palettes, later to be replaced by purpose-made ones of ceramic, enamel and ivory.

However talented a young miniaturist might be, he could not make a living from his chosen art without the very regular custom of a large clientele. Whom he could attract depended largely on social status and connections rather than ability or advertising. This meant that a man of fairly average talent such as Samuel Finney (cat. 18) could gain aristocratic and even royal patronage, probably because of his original profession as a London lawyer. In the seventeenth century, particularly, there were some gentlemen limners who relied on their circle of acquaintances for patronage, as with Thomas Flatman. An alternative route was found by the limner Richard Gibson, court dwarf in Charles I's time, who became a servant to the Earl of Pembroke and so gained access to the Earl's élite circle of friends. In the early nineteenth century, Andrew Robertson again provides an intriguing view of the intimate social world of the portrait painter, where business was mixed with pleasure. At a dinner with the fashionable portraitist Martin Archer Shee he recalled: 'Showed pictures to Duke of Kent, very likely will sit – Duchess of Gordon and Georgina. You may think I really do mean London as my residence ... if my new style takes, my fortune is made ...' . From 1759 onwards, the main alternative way of finding patrons was to exhibit at the new artists' societies and the Royal Academy. At the annual Academy exhibition, miniatures had a prominent position over the fireplace, in the best light, and by the 1800s some 200 odd were shown each year (fig. 3).

In the first few months of the year 1779 Richard Crosse's fee book recorded receipts from some fifty sitters, averaging about ten a month. Most of the names are now anonymous members of the gentry and merchant classes. A few names may be connected with other artists and there are a handful of aristocrats, including the Duke of Gloucester, two captains and one general. This gives a typical glimpse of a busy painter's patronage. As prices were fairly fixed, according to an artist's fame, he could not

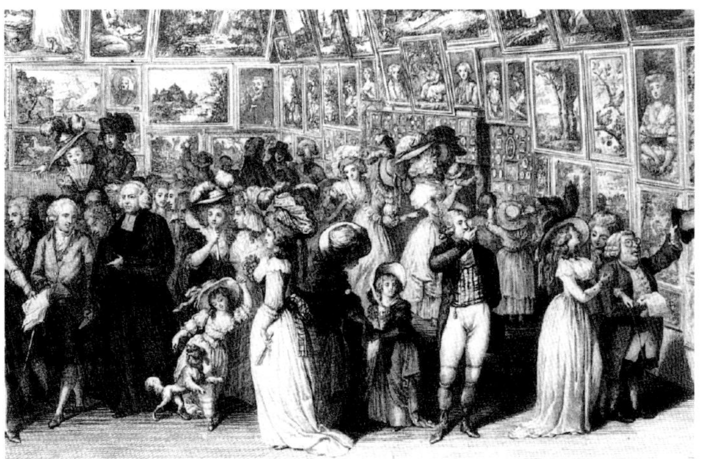

*Figure 3: Engraving after J. H. Ramberg (1763–1840) of the* Royal Academy Exhibition of 1787; *detail showing the display of miniatures (Royal Academy of Arts, London)*

afford to be too choosy in his sitters and an almost daily flow was needed to pay the bills.

The other important source of business was making copies. These could be reproductions of an artist's original miniature, made for members of the sitter's circle, or copies of other artists' (usually full-sized) portraits. Old masters were also copied, especially in enamel at the end of the eighteenth century. Sir Henry Bone made a good living almost exclusively from this trade. In 1800 he charged the King some £157 for a pair of 12-inch high enamels after Beechey, at a time when a full-length oil might cost just £100.[5]

Sittings were normally arranged in the artist's studio at home. In spite of enormous developments in style, the usual practice of three sittings did not change from the sixteenth to nineteenth century. There were of course exceptions: Mrs Pepys sat nine times to Samuel Cooper in 1668 and even then the likeness was not satisfactory. Typically, the first sitting was taken up putting in the outline and form using a neutral mid-tone. This might take from two to four hours. The second might be longer still and was spent working up the whole figure and background in colour. In the final sitting the whole picture would be refined and given the desired finish. Besides the sittings, time was spent before and between times preparing the ground and improving the miniature. Descriptions of sittings in any period are rare, but Archibald Robertson does discuss the question 'Of Attitude', that is, pose and expression. He advises

that it should be animated, except for older people, and that dress should be 'the same as the person who sits', by which he seems to imply that dress could be added after a sitting.[6]

Prices for miniatures were usually fairly consistent in the eighteenth century, according to the artist's reputation and the size of the work. Engleheart charged only 3 guineas in 1775, but could charge 20 guineas a decade later. Cosway could demand (but not always receive promptly) 30 guineas for a 3-inch portrait of George, Prince of Wales, in 1795. Royal appointment as a miniaturist could be lucrative or prove to be a royal disappointment. Bernard Lens III received a salary of £200 from George I but retained the same post at no salary from George II (George Vertue's notebook III, p. 50).

Once it was finished and the account settled, a miniature had a unique role in the home, regardless of whether the sitter was a tradesman or a connoisseur. As private and often very personal images, miniatures were accorded a special status beyond any artistic value. They were a commonplace token of love or affection and as such were given and exchanged for sentimental reasons. In Jane Austen's *Sense and Sensibility*, written in 1811, the capricious Lucy Steele reveals her secret attachment to the heroine Eleanor Dashwood's own beau, by showing her a miniature of him: 'Then taking a small miniature out of her pocket, she added, "To prevent the possibility of a mistake, be so good as to look at the face. It does not do him justice, to be sure, but yet I think you cannot be deceived as to the person it was drew for. I have had it above these three years."' (chap. XXII.) Lucy proclaims that she will have one painted to give in return. When the engagement is broken, her letters are burned and the miniature sent back! This type of smaller miniature could be secreted away, available only for the eyes of the intended. Often they would be exchanged formally before a betrothed couple had even met. Philippe Mercier's painting of *The Letter Writer* (fig. 4) shows a private drama taking place, with a young woman lost in thought, her lover's letters and a miniature beside her. This is propped against a strong box, no doubt to keep it and the letters out of harm's way.

Alternatively, smaller miniatures could be worn openly, around the neck, wrist or finger as an item of jewellery, in order publicly to profess an allegiance to another. Zoffany and Lawrence both painted Queen

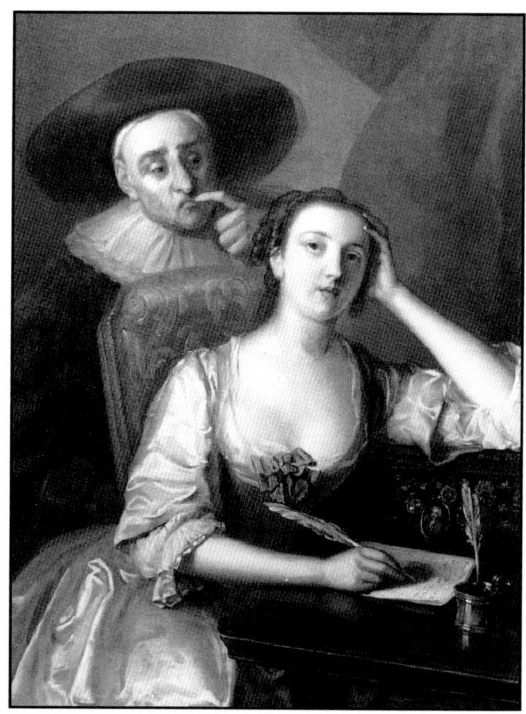

*Figure 4: Philippe Mercier (?1789–1760),* The Letter Writer, *c1738. The miniature is the type painted by Lens or Rosalba Carriera. (English Heritage – Marble Hill House)*

Charlotte, years apart, wearing the same pearl bracelet containing a portrait of the King. The second type of miniature, known as cabinet miniatures, also fulfilled a more public, yet still rather intimate role. These were larger, often rectangular in format, and hung in wooden or gilded frames on a wall of a closet or cabinet. A rare glimpse of miniatures hung in this manner can be found in George Vertue's self-portrait with his new wife (fig. 5). Such rooms were usually only privy to family and close friends. When picture cabinets fell out of fashion, miniatures found their way into the parlour or study. Although modest in size, they performed a parallel role to the great portraits of long-dead ancestors hung in the hall and gallery, except that they were more likely to record living persons. J.T. Smith, the biographer and acquaintance of Joseph Nollekens (1737–1823), recalled seeing three miniatures over the chimneypiece in the old sculptor's studio, which were given by Henry Edridge and John Smart. One of the latter's portraits was of Mrs Nollekens.[7]

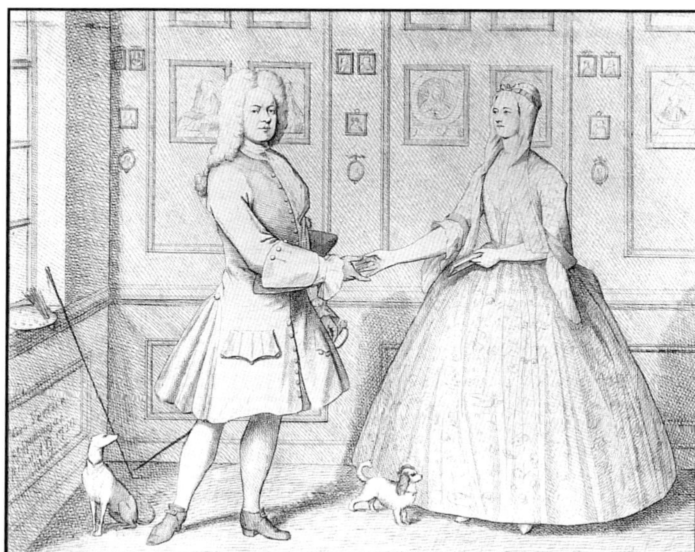

*Figure 5: George Vertue (1684–1756),* Self-portrait with his wife, on the occasion of their marriage, *1720. Miniatures and prints hang formally in this small room or closet. Vertue painted a few miniatures himself (British Museum)*

The specialised world of the miniaturist set many of these artists apart from their contemporaries and sometimes engendered professional jealousies. Part-art and part-craft, their products enjoyed enormous popularity, and at times status, far greater than their limitations would seem to justify. However, this particular chapter in the history of art and commerce came to an abrupt end around the 1850s, when a new technology – photography – coincided with a dearth of new talent in the field. Miniatures soon became the province of the wealthy connoisseur, rather than the commonplace image of educated citizens.

## Sebastian Edwards

**Notes**

1 For a summary of early treatises see Murrell, 1983, part II.

2 See Foskett, 1987, p. 374.

3 E. Robertson, *The Letters and Papers of Andrew Robertson,* London, 1895, p. 5.

4 Ibid., p. 32.

5 R.Walker, *Miniatures in the Collection of H.M. The Queen,* Cambridge, 1984, p. 273.

6 Robertson, op.cit., p. 33.

7 See J.T. Smith, *Nollekens and his Times,* London, 1949 edn., p. 181.

# Portraiture at Kenwood: The Broader Picture

In her portrait by Romney (fig. 6), Mrs Crouch, famous beauty, actress, and opera singer, strikes a pose beneath an overhanging rock. She turns away from the boat presumably carrying her husband, Lieutenant Crouch of the Navy, with an expression of sensibility. To her bosom she clutches a miniature portrait of her husband. It hangs round her neck – next to her heart – like a chain of office. The rock symbolises the character of her fidelity, while the miniature identifies the object of it. The musical score in her hand hints at her profession, the gesture has the operatic quality of higher feeling, her gaze suggests abstracted thoughts of the loved one. The picture, commissioned by Mr Crouch, is a token of love in itself, a testimony to his faith and pride in his wife, a tribute to her beauty and to her genius. The miniature's role is clearly crucial, since, to Mr Crouch, it is his representative. It stands in for him in his absence; it reminds his wife of his face; in private, it will comfort her in her desolation; in public, it will remind others that she is accounted for, that, in effect, he is set like a jewel in her heart, just as his image is set like a jewel in its gold frame and hung round her neck.

But Mr Crouch knew his wife too well. His commission to Romney may in fact have been an expensive form of wishful thinking, the prominence of the miniature a forlorn exhortation to fidelity. It failed. No sooner was he out of sight than out of mind, and Mrs Crouch was involved in an enduring affair with the Irish tenor, Michael Kelly. In Romney's painting, the emotional arena in which the miniature played its part could not have been more clearly defined.

As a portrait that you can toy with, that you can hold in your hand, that you can hide, or display to a chosen confidante, the miniature has a psychological value and impact very different from the full-scale portrait. The modern wallet photograph can fulfil some of the functions of the miniature, and can be precious for the sake of the image it records. But it cannot be precious in itself. Like a jewel, or a private religious icon, the miniature has tangible values – the gold, the jewels set round it, the skill of the artist. Like a religious reliquary, it can often contain a hidden treasure – usually the hair of the sitter, sometimes elaborately plaited. Invoked like some private saint, a miniature can be gazed at, even talked to, with a heightened sense of communication with the absent loved one.

Miniatures imply love, or at least devotion. Most are of family members, or love objects. Exceptions are some kinds of royal miniatures, where the relevant emotion is still a special form of devotion, made up of loyalty, national pride and admiration. The Kenwood collection contains two examples of princesses, by Bernard Lens (*Princess Mary*, cat. 6, and *Princess Louisa*, cat. 7, 1739). They are more formal, more 'image-conscious', and larger than usual. This form of miniature reached its peak with the many images of George IV by Richard Cosway, where the vanity (and person) of the subject was flattered by a glamorous representation of the 'first gentleman of Europe'. Such images had quasi-ambassadorial functions. They could be used as rewards, like medals, or as diplomatic gifts, symbolising the good favour of a powerful giver.

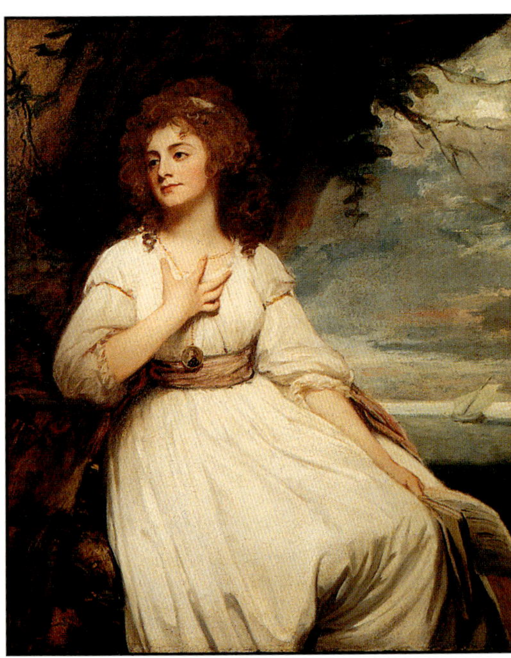

*Figure 6: George Romney (1734–1802),* Mrs Crouch, *1787 (English Heritage, the Iveagh Bequest, Kenwood)*

Another full-size painting at Kenwood features a (rather large) miniature portrait. The painting was bought from Sir Henry Raeburn's granddaughters under the title *Mrs Johnstone as 'Contemplation'*, by Raeburn (fig. 7). Whoever the sitter is, and whether or not the attribution to Raeburn can now be accepted, the message is clear enough. She wears a black veil, a sign of mourning; and she contemplates a miniature portrait in her hand, almost certainly the object of her mourning – in Mrs Johnstone's case it is probably of her husband, who died in 1787. The special intimacy of the miniature portrait is here at its clearest.

A related example from the Victorian era is seen in the painting of *Hard Times* by Thomas Reynolds Lamont (fig. 8). Here, the story is even more clearly etched, and the role of the miniature even more clearly defined. A young widow in black, with a small child to support, passes her most valued possession to a pawn-broker. It is the miniature of her dead husband. The power of the image derives very forcibly from the special qualities of the miniature. The woman's poverty is demanding a sacrifice, not just of a valuable bauble, but of her memories, her dreams, the last special link with her dead husband. The Victorians liked a moral, especially one that reminded them of the ephemeral nature of worldly happiness.

An object of so much potential power and value could not fail to develop special characteristics. The eyes are the mirror of the soul, it is said. Miniatures, therefore, as intimate objects of contemplation, tend to focus on the eyes, even on occasion showing a single eye only (cat. 96). In Andrew Plimer's case, he sometimes appears to take this idiosyncrasy to extremes, and all his huge-eyed beauties begin to look alike. Cosway, that emperor of the miniature portrait, could on occasion be guilty of the same thing.

In Plimer's lovely image of *Elizabeth Farren* (cat. 49) the fashionable sensibility is at work. In the first place, Miss Farren was a Beauty, and a Star of the Comic Stage, so there is more than a hint of those postcards of Gladys Cooper and her ilk that were so popular in the Edwardian era, or the 'Glamour Pics' of Hollywood goddesses that succeeded them.  But other images confirm that the miniature has been co-opted into the language of sensibility. It has become fashionable to pine

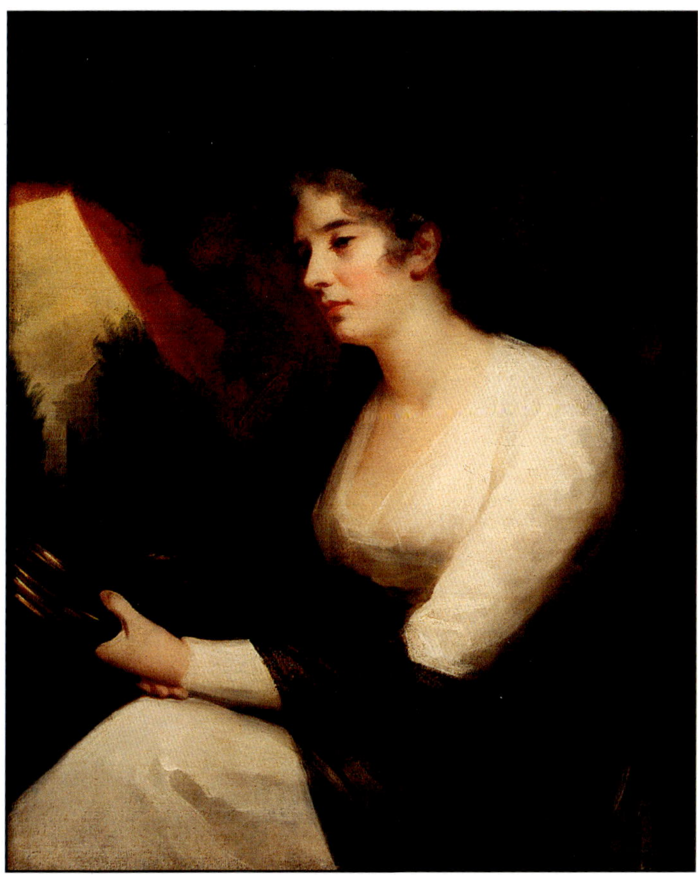

*Figure 7: Henry Raeburn (1756–1823),* Mrs Johnstone as 'Contemplation', *c1791 (English Heritage, the Iveagh Bequest, Kenwood)*

picturesquely over a miniature, and some of the directness and characterful individuality of earlier examples is sacrificed in favour of a more romantic, and often extremely beautiful, vision (compare, for instance, Gervase Spencer's *Unknown Woman* of 1754, cat. 19, with George Engleheart's exquisite *Unknown Woman* of c1805, cat. 55).

This aesthetic development was shared with the full-scale society portrait, though taking a different form. At Kenwood, we need only look at the development between Gainsborough's *Countess Howe* and his later *Lady Brisco*, where the former's graceful but solid beauty has given way to the airy, wraithe-like romanticism of the latter. Or again, Reynolds can be seen developing from his *Kitty Fisher*, a portrait with Old Master undertones, to his 'Grand Manner' portraits, where aristocratic

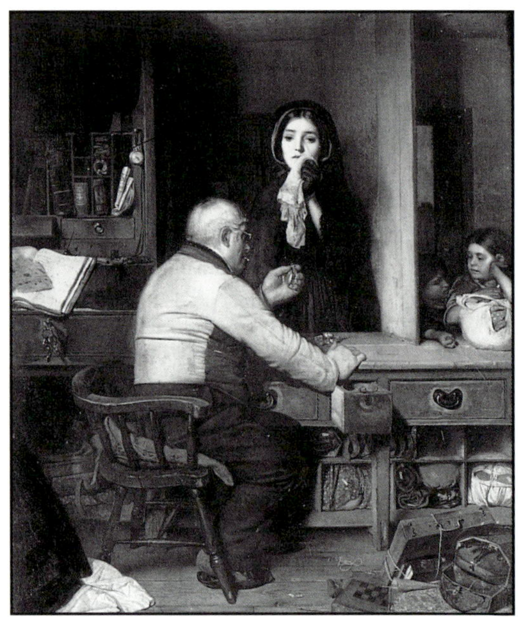

*Figure 8: Thomas Reynolds Lamont (1826–98),* Hard Times *(courtesy of Sotheby's)*

sitters are deprived of their contemporary costumes and draped *al'antica*, and presented as goddesses (*Mrs Musters as Hebe*, fig. 9), muses (*Lady Louisa Manners*) or heroines from Shakespeare (*Mrs Tollemache as Miranda*). The limited scale of the miniature could not allow much scope for this kind of fancy, which was, after all, an attempt led by Reynolds to marry the prestige and scale of history painting to the less highly regarded genre of portraiture. However, whatever fashionable drapery, and unnaturally enlarged eyes, could do, was done.

The kind of full-size portraiture that relates most strongly in style and manner to miniatures is represented at Kenwood by such works as *Mrs Musters* (again) by Romney (fig. 10). This is straightforward (though very beautiful) stuff, a simple head and shoulders against a blue sky. Miniaturists very often place their sitters against a formulaic sky backdrop. Costume, amongst the women sitters, is often a reflection of everyday dress and is at any rate never allowed to compete with the rendering of the face, although in the nature of things fashion decreed that the dress be both flattering and up-to-date.

Portraits of men are conspicuous by their absence from Lord Iveagh's collection of British portraits. Gainsborough's portraits of William Pitt the Younger and the Prince of Wales (now thought to show an unknown servant of the prince) made their way in because of Lord Iveagh's desire to reflect a vision of the eighteenth century, and such 'stars' played a vital role in that vision. The miniatures triumphantly redress that balance, and indeed some of the male portraits are of exceptional quality, by any standards. The rendering of unknown gentlemen such as that by George Chinnery (cat. 95) testifies to the power of miniaturists in capturing character, perhaps almost *because* the characters are unknown. Stripped of the trappings of power and status that lay behind so many of the formal portraits of the type of Gainsborough's William Pitt, the miniaturist's brief, which depended so much on the capturing of likeness and individuality, resulted in some

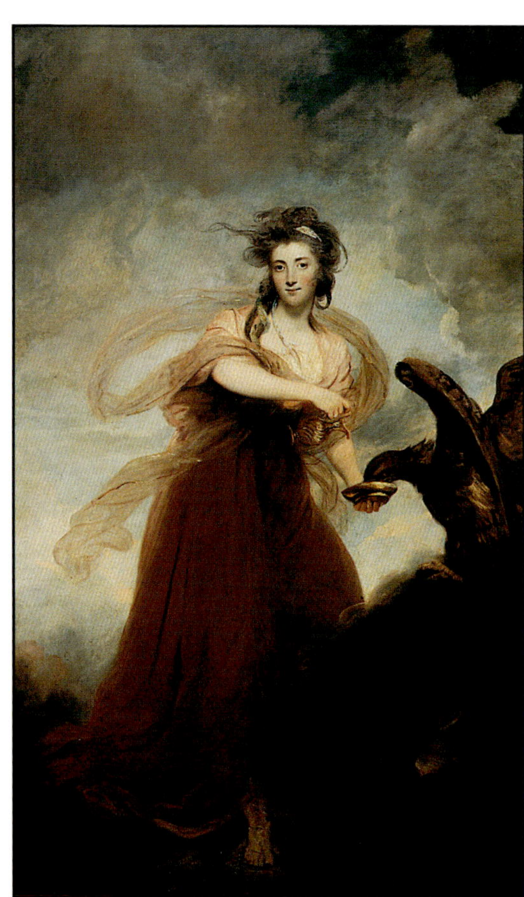

*Figure 9: Joshua Reynolds (1723–92),* Mrs Musters as Hebe, *1782 (English Heritage, the Iveagh Bequest)*

memorable images. One feels one knows these men. Many of them wear uniform, not surprisingly – the miniature, as for Mrs Crouch, found a natural market in those families separated by their menfolk's departure on the King's service.

The genre of child portraiture also provides an interesting comparison between the Iveagh Bequest and the miniatures' collection. This was another of the spheres in which Reynolds and Gainsborough excelled, and Reynolds in particular breathed new life into the genre. This was achieved largely, one assumes, through the simple fact of his liking children. His images, such as his *Philip Yorke*, or *The Angerstein Children*, or the allegorical *Infant Academy*, seem to this day to be unrivalled in their capturing of the essence of childhood. It is heartening to see, thanks to Reynolds, that there was a time when the future exquisite dandy, George (Beau) Brummell, was a young tearaway (*The Brummell Children*, fig. 11) like any other little boy. The miniatures tend to offer a far more formal view of childhood. While always charming, these little people (see cats 8, 11, 23) are posed like the adults. Perhaps, in an era of high child mortality, it was more important for the miniature to record the fact of the child, rather than his or her childishness. The influence of Reynolds was nevertheless felt here also, most charmingly in Richard Crosse's *Lucy Nicholas* (cat. 35).

Although the miniaturist rarely attempted the fantastic marriage of portraiture with history painting that was the particular achievement of Reynolds, there were occasions when the miniaturist was commissioned to produce a tiny copy of such a painting. In those cases, the existence of the miniature (very often in several versions) indicates another important function. Kenwood's miniature portrait of *Lord Mansfield* by Henry Bone after Reynolds (cat. 66) is a good example. The sitter was very famous, the most distinguished judge of the eighteenth century. His portrait by Reynolds was the imprimatur of that fame; it became a quasi-official 'image', like the campaign portrait of a modern presidential candidate. This particular image was circulated in countless forms, from crude prints to prestigious mezzotints, and there were many miniature versions of it. These were no doubt special

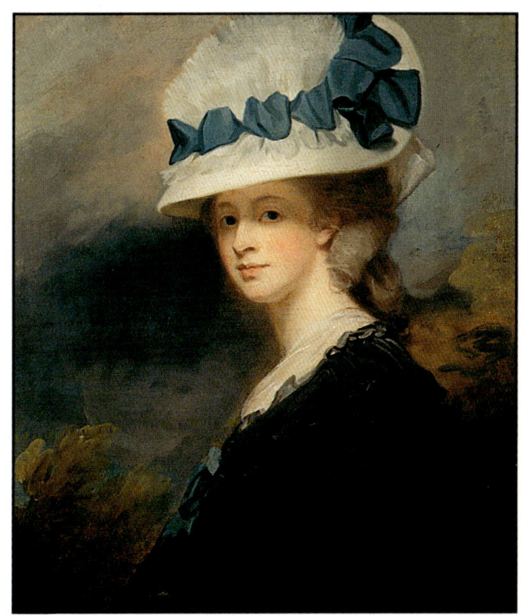

*Figure 10: George Romney (1734–1802),* Mrs Musters, *1779–80 (English Heritage, the Iveagh Bequest)*

possessions for those who revered the great judge, and may often have been gifts from him. They were at the luxury end of a huge multiple image market, precious tangible reminders of the fame and glory of the sitter.

Reynolds, the great master of experimental media, may have been responsible indirectly for another type of miniature. The regrettable tendency of his portraits to fade and die well before their subjects had given up the ghost was notorious, even in his lifetime. The technique of miniature painting was far more reliable. A miniature copy of a Reynolds could therefore record the colours for which he was renowned, before they faded. The art of Reynolds, as president of the Royal Academy and the leading portraitist of his generation, was an object for serious study, particularly for his colouristic and compositional skills. Many young students spent time copying his most famous works, often in very small scale if not precisely in miniature, and these works, like Henry Bone's *Lord Mansfield*, often give us a clearer idea of the glories of Reynolds' palette than the surviving originals.

The development of miniature painting, in conclusion, is a parallel development to that of full-scale portraiture. It takes on board some, though

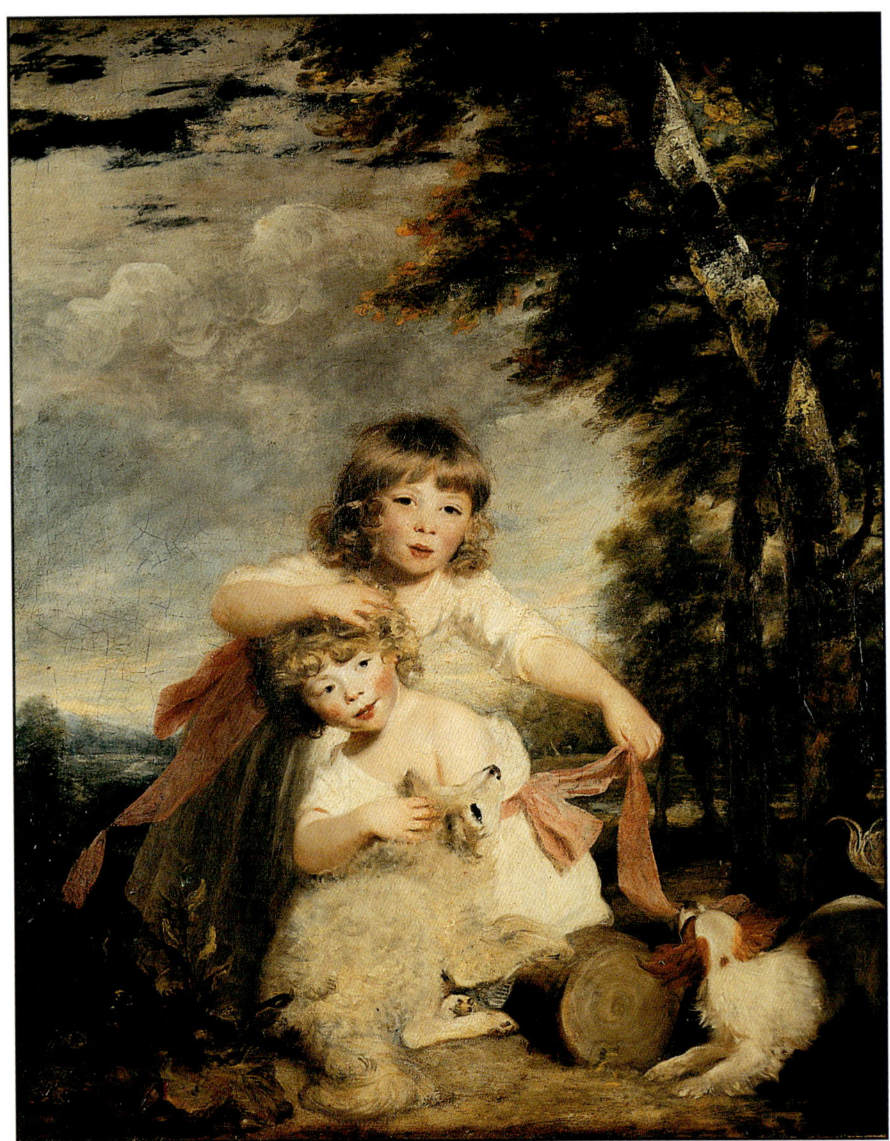

*Figure 11: Joshua Reynolds (1723–92),* The Brummel Children*, 1781–2 (English Heritage, the Iveagh Bequest)*

not all, of the important concerns of the full-scale artists, and can very often produce images that are extremely reminiscent of, and clearly influenced by, those artists' work. Andrew Robertson (see cat. 106) deliberately set out to rival full-scale portraiture. However, the miniature's special qualities, its intimacy, its size, its preciousness, the personal and private significance it could bear, meant that the two traditions remained parallel and separate. Kenwood is the perfect setting in which to experience the shock, and delight, of the shift from the grandeur of that parade of famous beauties and aristocrats by Reynolds, Romney and Gainsborough, to the lucid and intense world of the miniaturist. Something of the value of the miniature to its original owner always clings to it, and this catalogue of small faces often provides a shock of recognition, as if these are our own loved ones, recalled with the force of memory.

**Ian A C Dejardin**

# Fashion in Miniature

The intimate and contemplative nature of miniatures — to recall the features of absent loved ones, as a remembrance of times past, even as a *memento mori* — is reflected in their use as the most personal form of jewellery, visible testimony to the ties of family and friends. This is most obviously the case with women, whose portraits often depict them wearing miniatures, usually on a chain round the neck. In Angelica Kauffman's portrait of *Lady Elizabeth Foster* of 1786 (fig. 12) the eye is drawn to the jewelled oval miniature that she wears, the 'beloved medallion' of her friend Georgiana, Duchess of Devonshire.[1] Men, also, commissioned miniatures of family members (often small copies of large-scale portraits), particularly when far from home either in war or long-distance travel. Those making the long voyage to India, for example, carried miniatures with them: the miniaturist William Wood's ledgers record a portrait of 'old Mrs Petrie' in 1791 'in a shawl & black lac'd Hood....for her son William going to Madras'.[2]

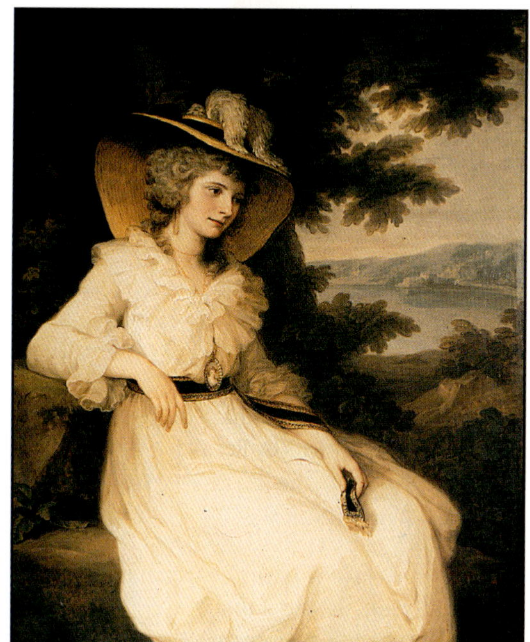

*Figure 12: Angelica Kauffman (1741–1807),* Lady Elizabeth Foster, *1786, Ickworth (National Trust Photographic Library/J. Whitaker)*

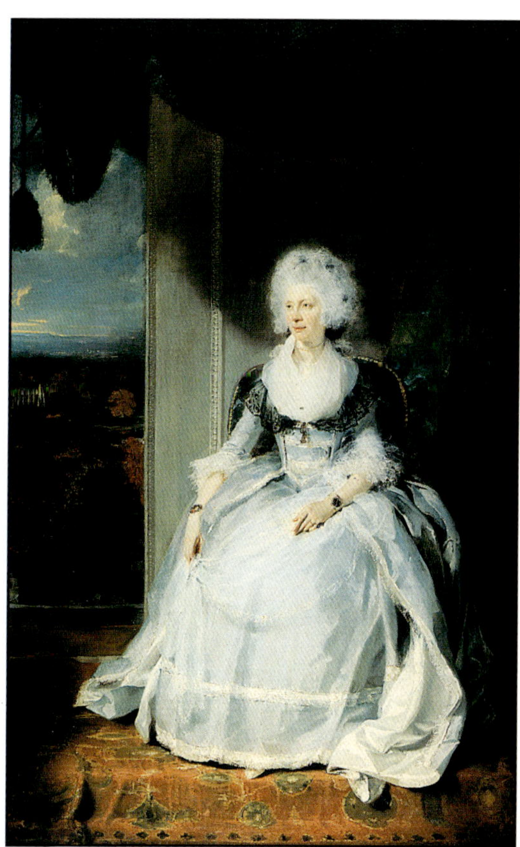

*Figure 13: Thomas Lawrence (1760–1830),* Queen Charlotte, *1791 (reproduced courtesy of the Trustees, the National Gallery, London)*

From the second half of the eighteenth century, the growing trend towards romantic sensibility is evident in the use of the miniature as a devotional relic: Wood's ledgers make frequent reference to the mildew on miniatures caused by them being 'breathed upon'. Miniatures were appropriate mourning tokens which often incorporated locks of the deceased's hair skilfully plaited at the back. Such memorial jewellery provided a tangible record for posterity, either in everyday bereavements within families, or in such exceptional circumstances as the Terror (1793–4) during the French Revolution when many prisoners about to be guillotined had their portraits painted in miniature as a token of memory for friends and relatives.[3]

Not all miniatures had such a melancholy context: many were celebratory, recording personal achievements and important events such as marriage. Women were sometimes painted wearing a miniature of their fiancé or husband either as a pendant to a necklace or in the form of a bracelet. Lawrence's portrait of *Queen Charlotte* of 1789 (fig. 13) shows her stranded pearl bracelets, given by George III in 1761 to his new bride, which incorporate his portrait and royal cipher; both are set round with brilliant-cut diamonds — the hardest precious stone, equated with fidelity and loyalty and thus especially suitable for tokens of love. On the little finger of her left hand is a ring with a medallion portrait of the King; at her wedding ceremony the Queen wore a ring with a miniature of George III by Jeremiah Meyer on the little finger of her right hand.

Miniatures could also be worn as brooches, or hanging from the waist as part of a chatelaine. When men wore miniatures (a custom seen less in England than in the rest of Europe, where such items were hung on a chain round the neck, or fastened with a ribbon bow on the breast), the usual practice was to carry them at the waist along with seals and a watch. In the 1789s there was a fashion for men (and sometimes women) to wear two watches, one real and the other a *fausse-montre*, often made to match, which could contain a miniature.

In terms of dress, how far do the images in miniatures correspond to those in large-scale painted portraits? Allowing for the fact that a miniature is obviously more restricted in body area than a full-size portrait, some correlations can be observed. In art generally, male sitters can be depicted as men of fashion (tending in England towards less formal modes), and in occupational and official costume. So, miniatures depict a considerable number of men in clothes of status. These include military and naval officers in uniform, particularly during the period of the Napoleonic wars in Europe which encouraged an increasingly complex system of sartorial regulation. Also on display is the image of *William Murray, 1st Earl of Mansfield* (cat. 64) in his scarlet and miniver robes of office, basically medieval in style as is the Collar of SS which he

wears — a gold chain formed by the letter S together with Garter knots, and in the middle a rose with a portcullis on either side.[4] Knightly orders were another visible sign of high rank, and the miniatures show examples of the Garter (the sash and star worn by *George III*, cat. 33, in a ring), and the Golden Fleece (in Boit's portrait of *James FitzJames, Duke of Berwick* (cat. 4, c1710), honoured for his services to the Spanish monarchy).

Women did not, of course, have the option of official costume in their own right, and in all forms of portraiture one can see other possibilities such as the taste for generalised drapery and for fancy dress. In the latter category there are miniatures of women in 'oriental' costume, a popular fad throughout the eighteenth century[5]; an *Unknown Woman* (cat. 37) of the mid-1770s by Ozias Humphry is depicted in vaguely 'Turkish' style, a white dress with gold fringe on the shoulder, and in her hair a white and gold striped scarf. Similar costume can be seen in the work of Sir Joshua Reynolds in this decade, the idea being to make portraits more 'timeless', less prone to date through the vagaries of fashion. Another fashionable artist who preferred to paint women in flowing draperies was Francis Cotes, and he clearly inspired his younger brother Samuel whose *Frances Dickson* (cat. 24) of 1769 is dressed in lilac drapery and with a blue ribbon in the hair. This type of costume was called 'fancied dress'; it followed the general line of fashion but omitted distracting details, preferring the uniformity of plain silks, floating scarves and pearls in the hair.[6] An example of this kind of fantasy dress can be seen in the fine miniature by Smart of *Anne Farquhar*, 1770 (cat. 40).

For the majority of sitters whose interest lay in being shown in contemporary styles, it was important for the miniature artist to have a keen sense of fashion, and skill in the depiction of fabrics and jewellery; they had to be prepared to alter their portraits when clients demanded to be kept up-to-date in dress and hairstyle. Artists had to study the fashions for an upmarket clientele, and one miniaturist, Bernard Lens III, was the author of a series of fashion illustrations entitled *The Exact Dress of the Head* (1725–6, fig. 14).

Lens' miniature of *Princess Louisa* of 1739 (cat. 7) shows the sitter in a simplified version of court dress: and the artist has taken care with the lace 'sleevelets' and the costly white and gold silk damask of the gown. Other examples of virtuoso skills in the painting of textiles on such a small scale might include the blue velvet coat of Cosway's *Unknown Man*, c1790 (cat. 38), and the stylish costume of Robertson's *Unknown Woman* of 1816 (cat. 106) which consists of a sprigged white muslin dress bound round at the waist with yellow satin ribbon and set off by a black net stole.

Another reflection of mainstream art is the way in which women preferred to be painted in less formal styles of dress, which, like the 'fancied dress' drew more attention to the face. 'The Face is the chief Seat of Beauty' stated the author of a treatise on cosmetics, *Abdeker or The Art of preserving Beauty* (1754), and the ideal complexion was pale, with 'rather more of the lily than of the rose', as the novelist Henry Fielding described Sophia Western in *Tom Jones* (1749). Cosmetics (sometimes with harmful ingredients) were certainly used to produce the smooth glazed look which was admired,[7] along with an oval face, large eyes and small, gracefully pouting lips.[8] Not surprisingly, miniatures of young women tend towards a conventional form of beauty, a uniform 'prettiness' which can lack character. In contrast, portraits of older women, such as Spencer's *Unknown Woman*, 1754 (cat. 19), show greater freedom in depicting personality; this middle-class sitter in her brown dress, lace-edged kerchief and mob-cap tying under the chin has a face which can only be described as 'homely'.

The appearance of the fashionable woman changed considerably during the second half of the eighteenth century, from the coloured silks and simple hairstyles of the 1760s, through the white cottons and extravagant powdered coiffures of the 1780s, to the understated neo-classical look of 1800. Sullivan's *Unknown Woman* of 1761 (cat. 16) wears a pink silk dress with pink and white ribbon on the bodice front; the same kind of ribbon ties her necklace of pearls, and completing this outfit so typical of the restrained rococo style in England is a delicate hair

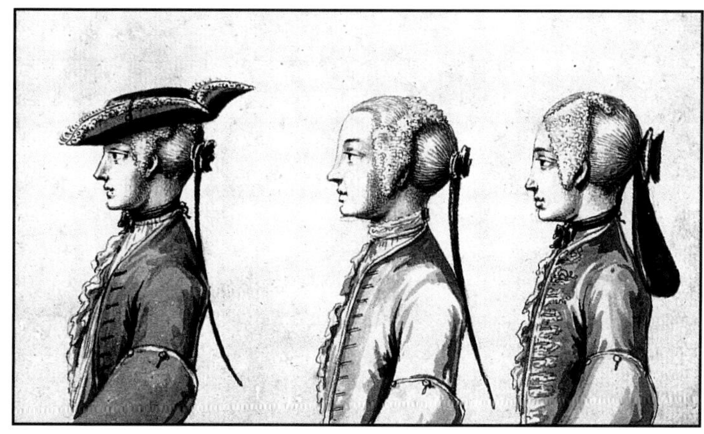

*Figure 14: Bernard Lens III (1682–1740), illustrations to* The Exact Dress of the Head, *1725–6; drawing, ink with stipple and grey wash (Victoria and Albert Museum)*

ornament of pink silk flowers. Convention dictated that women should wear some form of head covering or decoration both indoors and out. These could include a range of informal frilled caps for day wear, and on more formal occasions flowers, feathers and jewelled ornaments. The 1780s saw the introduction of large hats swathed with ribbons and feathers, which in terms of miniaturists can best be seen in the work of Cosway.[9] An example of the smaller hats of the early 1790s is worn by Daniel's *Mrs Margaret Roper* (cat. 75) whose modest middle-class taste is evident in her white silk hat tied with ribbons over her indoors cap.

Such complete head covering is rare, for women on the whole wished to show off their hair, and artists their skills in the depiction of the elaborate styles of the late eighteenth century. In the 1780s clouds of powdered bouffant hair were in vogue, a perfect match for the hazy muslin gowns which slipped on over the head and tied at the waist with a sash; examples of this style of dress (called a *chemise* from the French name for the basic female undergarment or shift) can be seen in the Kauffman portrait of *Lady Elizabeth Foster* (fig. 12) and in Cosway's *Unknown Woman* c1790 (cat. 39).

The finest muslin came from Bengal, which inspired the Lancashire cotton industry to produce imitations; it could be plain, patterned (Hayter's *Unknown Woman*, 1803, cat. 91, wears spotted muslin) or embroidered (see

# THE CATALOGUE

The introductions to each artist are in large part based on the two encyclopaedic works on miniatures by Daphne Foskett, her *Dictionary of British Miniature Painters* and *Collecting Miniatures* (1987 editions). These in turn have incorporated the seminal works of G.C. Williamson and Basil Long on British miniaturists.

The artists in the catalogue are arranged to give, as far as possible, a sense of the chronological development of the art of miniature painting over the period covered. The exception is catalogue 111, acquired in November 1996, too late to be included in its proper place. Where an artist is represented by more than one miniature, they have been placed together, so as to allow comparison between different periods of an individual artist's work.

Individual entries list, in order, the media with inscriptions; size (height is given before width); provenance; and references to literature and exhibitions, only given where a specific work or subject is mentioned. Provenance details include, where known, previous owner(s); auctioneer, date of sale and lot number; purchaser; date of acquisition by English Heritage/Kenwood and Kenwood accession number.

## Dutch School, seventeenth century

### 1 Unknown Woman

Oil on copper; silver frame with diamond decoration
Oval, 6.2 x 5.0 cm

Charles Woollett and Son, Wigmore St; Marie Draper, 1971; given to Kenwood, 1988  (88029167)

This is the earliest miniature in the present collection and the only one painted in oil on copper, a medium with a long history in the Netherlands. The sitter's appearance, characterised by short frizzed hair with a fringe and large lace and gauze collar of squarish cut, dates the image to the 1630s.

In contrast to English works on vellum of the period, this miniaturist makes no attempt to hide his brushwork, which ranges from fine lines in the hair, to impasto on the lace and glaze for the collar. There is scratching-in on her bodice too. The cerulean blue background is, however, reminiscent of early English miniature styles. It has been suggested that this may be a copy of a larger picture. The frame may be slightly later in date.

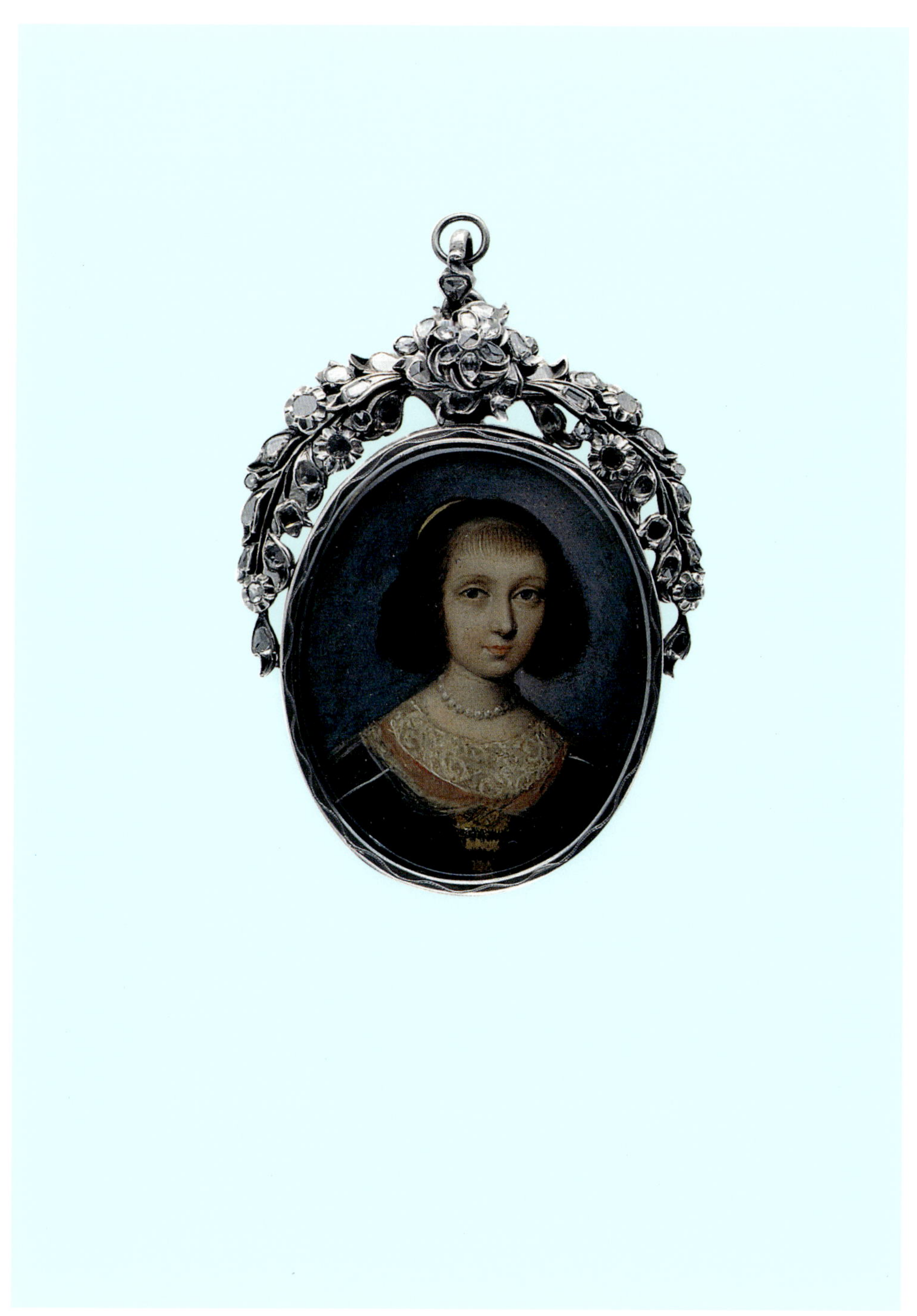

# Franciszek Smiadecki  (mid-seventeenth century)

A number of oil miniatures signed *F.S* have been attributed to Franciszek Smiadecki. He is believed to have learned his craft in Sweden, possibly with Alexander Cooper who was working there during the Commonwealth. He is not known to have worked in England, but some of his sitters were English. His style is reminiscent of that of the Coopers but his persistence in using oil paint as well as gum colour has meant that not all of his works can be fully appreciated today. Those on vellum, with a sky background, show quality rivalling the best British limners. The heads are strongly modelled and show plenty of character.

### 2  Unknown Man

Oil on vellum; silver locket frame
Oval, 6.4 x 5.4 cm

Limner Antiques, London; Marie Draper, 1973; given to Kenwood, 1988  (88029881)

This work is attributed to Smiadecki but is somewhat coarser than usual in the features and not so finely finished in the hair and dress. The sitter is a gentleman of the Restoration period, painted about 1670. His hair is long and he has a starched lace cravat which is tied in a prominent bow.

The face is well painted in smooth, broad strokes, using warm-coloured pinks and reds with glazes to create strong contours. This contrasts with the cravat, which is rapidly put on with thick white paint. No doubt the olive-coloured background has darkened with time.

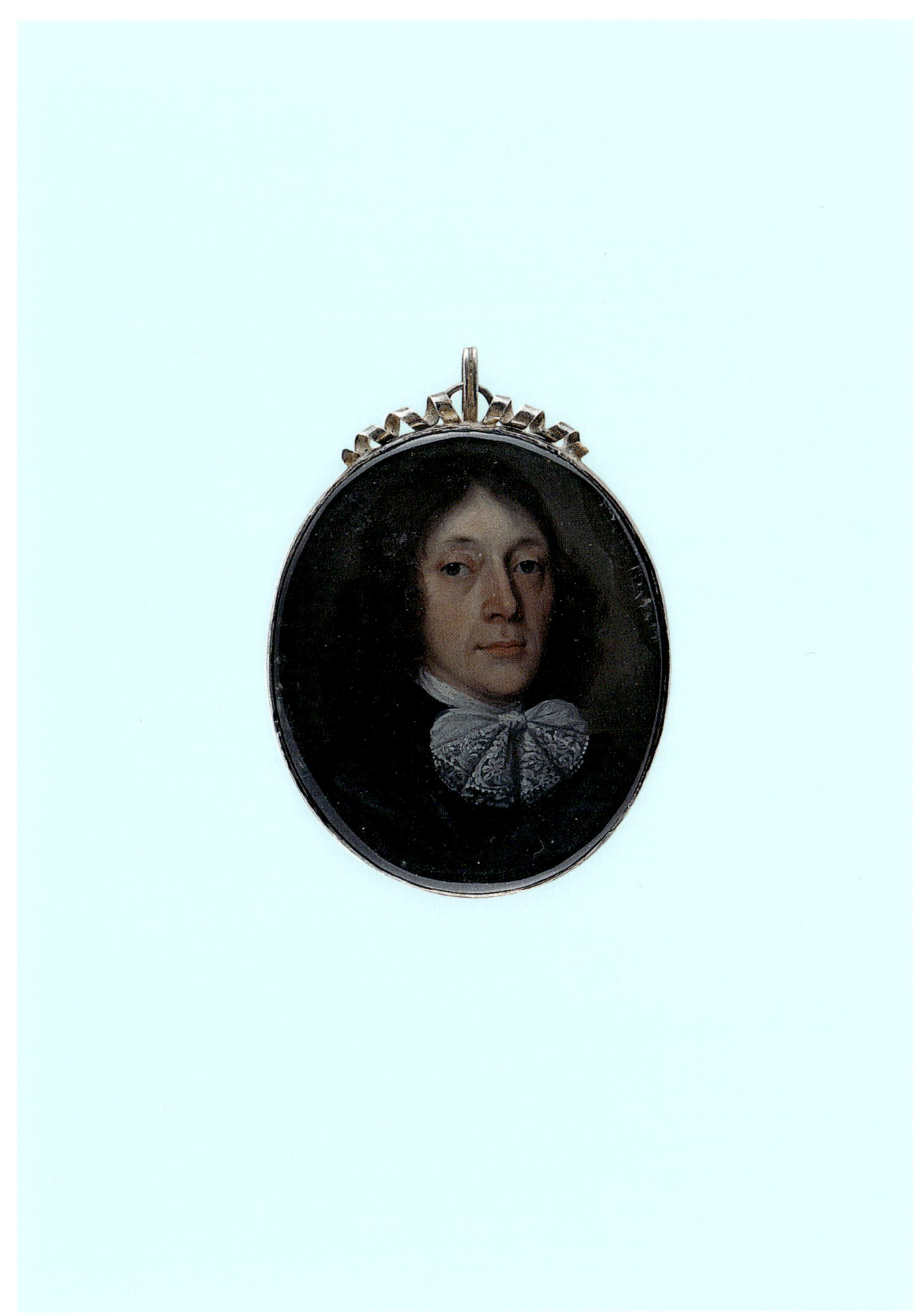

# Matthew Snelling (1621–78)

Snelling was a gentleman limner from Norfolk, who is known to have produced miniatures between the 1640s and 1670s. Early works included copies of royal portraits, probably for a member of the court. Because of a reversal in family fortunes, it appears that Snelling had to support himself as an artist and depended on a circle of aristocrats and gentlemen scientists for patronage. His early career may have been influenced by the group of Anglo-Netherlandish draughtsmen, of which the Oliver family were foremost. The influence of Samuel Cooper's bold manner can also be seen in his work, but without his mastery of technique and colour. The artist and chemist Charles Beale (senior) seems to have known Snelling well.

Snelling's mature works have a graphic quality, and use strong colours. They sometimes appear rather coarse, but this manner was to become fashionable during the Restoration period, although Snelling never gained the pre-eminence of, say, Samuel Cooper.

### 3  Unknown Woman

Watercolour and gouache on card; gilt metal locket frame
Oval,  7.4 x 5.6 cm

Bonham's, 21 Nov. 1995 (10); purchased by the Draper estate; given to Kenwood, 1995  (88029844)

Judging by the lady's hairstyle and dress, this portrait was made about 1660, or a few years earlier. The background with castle in the landscape can be compared with a dated Snelling miniature of a gentleman of 1663 (Victoria and Albert Museum), although that example is more finely painted. The sitter's style of dress, with tight bodice and jewelled clasps, returned to popularity with the Restoration of the monarchy in 1660, but her hair is more loosely dressed than it might have been in Charles I's reign.

Snelling's manner of painting is rather disconcerting compared to the suave late works of John Hoskins or the younger Samuel Cooper. The use of strong colours — blues and reds — in the flesh, and the rapid execution of the background are not subtle, but this bold image is not untypical of the second rank of portraiture of the time. One interesting feature is the use of gold powder in the paint to add lustre to the dress, a technique developed by Cooper.

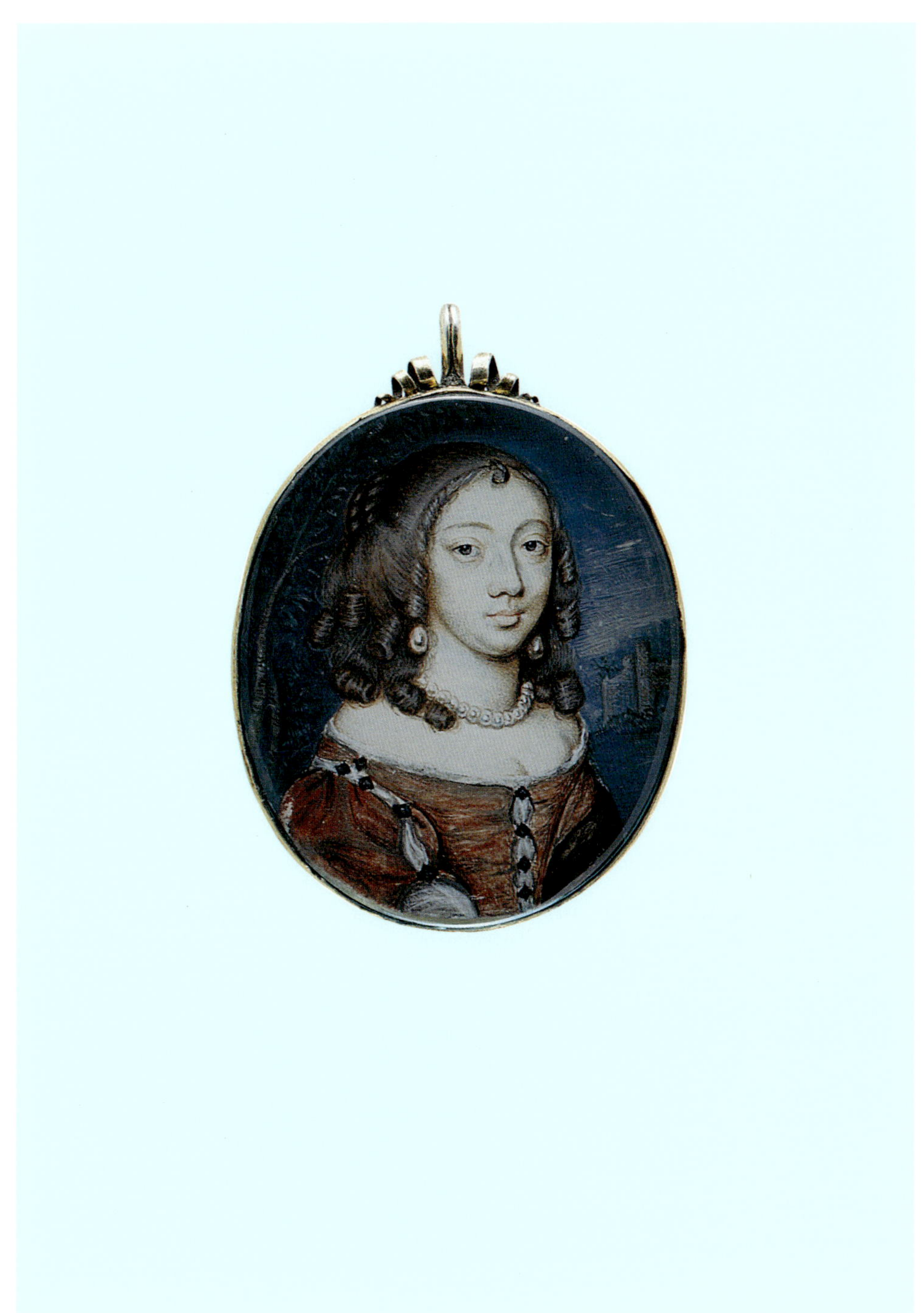

# Charles Boit (1662–1727)

Boit was a goldsmith and enamellist from Stockholm, credited with re-introducing the art of enamelling to this country with such success that the native art of painting miniatures in watercolour suffered a serious decline for several decades. He may have trained under rivals of the great French enamel painter, Jean Petitot, who had worked for Charles I of England. Boit came to England in 1687, and worked alongside fellow Swedes Michael Dahl and Hans Hysing .

He was technically very proficient and soon became Court Enameller to William III. This led to travels in Holland and to the courts of Germany and Austria between 1699 and 1703. On his return he secured a commission to produce an enamel of unprecedented size – some 2 feet high – celebrating the Duke of Marlborough's victory at Blenheim. Boit took advantage of interest in this technical feat and managed to string out his unsuccessful attempts for ten years, gaining £2,000 payment from the treasury. In 1714, however, repayment was sought and the artist fled to France where he remained, leaving no great enamel but a flourishing school of enamellists, led by C.F. Zincke (cat. 9).

### 4  James FitzJames, Duke of Berwick (1670–1734)

Enamel; gold locket frame, inscribed *JAMES FITZ JAMES/ DUKE OF BERWICK*. Signed on the verso *C Boit*
Oval, 3.1 x 2.6 cm

Christie's 18 Dec. 1990 (30); purchased by the Draper estate; given to Kenwood, 1991 (88029859)

This is the only known version of this portrait of the Duke of Berwick, who was a natural son of James II and Arabella Churchill. He was born and brought up in France and came to England in 1685 on his father's accession. After the Glorious Revolution of 1688 he joined the Stuart court-in-exile at St Germain, where Louis XIV even proposed that he succeed to the throne after William III. Berwick was a very distinguished soldier under both his father and Louis, and he died in battle leading the French army of the Rhine.

The enamel was probably painted between 1715 and 1720 for an English visitor to France. The Duke wears deliberately antiquated military dress, consisting of armour with an ermine-lined stole, and has the Order of the Golden Fleece.

Boit's refined stipple technique is shown to good effect in this finely detailed, small enamel. The naturalness and brilliance of colour he achieved in this difficult medium is clearly demonstrated.

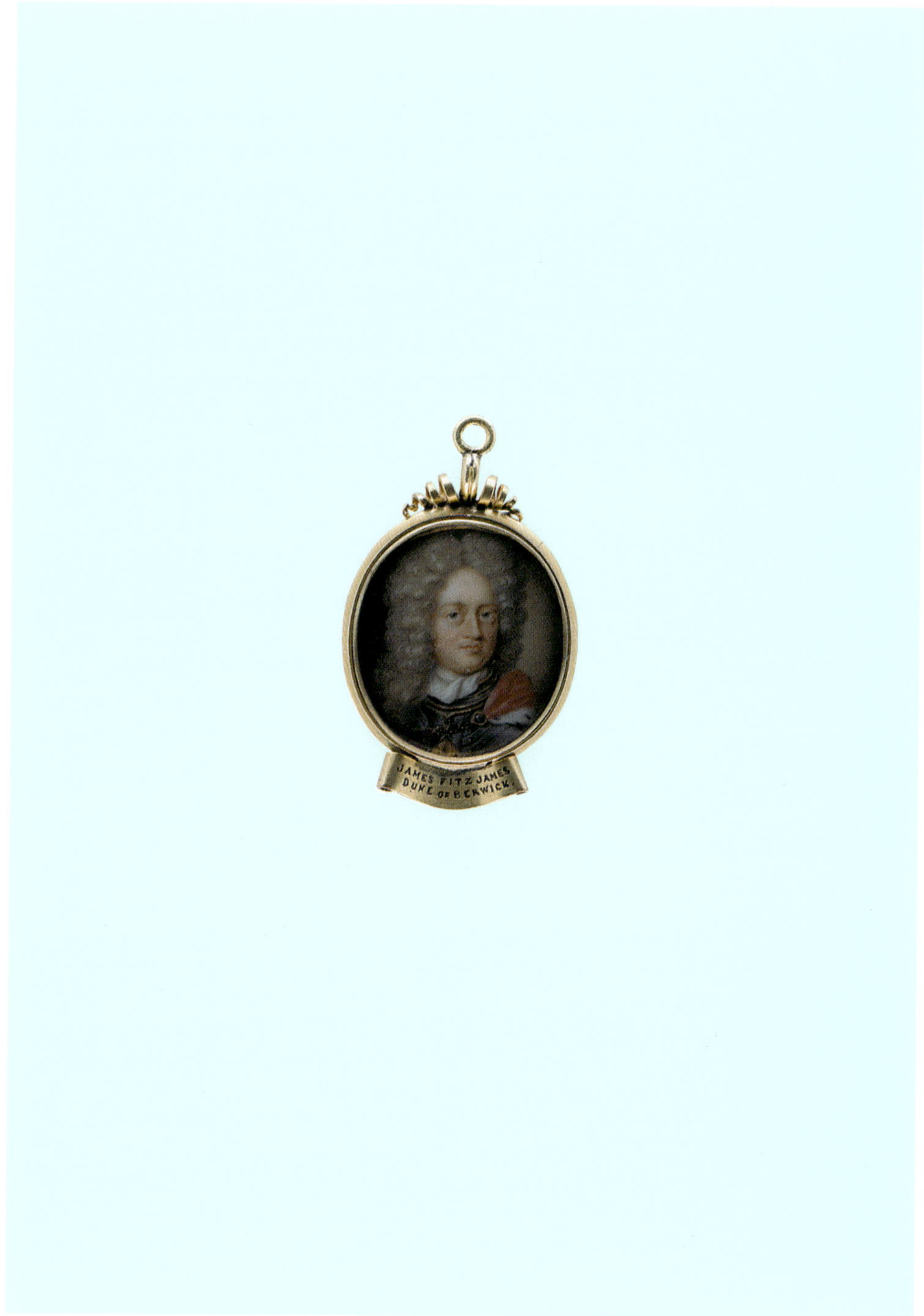


JAMES FITZ JAMES
DUKE OF BERWICK.

# Christian Richter  (1678–1732)

Richter, like Boit before him, was a Swedish artist who came to England in 1702, where he continued in a continental manner of miniature painting. He had studied as a goldsmith and engraver but worked mostly making copies on vellum of oil portraits. This specialism was attributed to a severe facial disfigurement that George Vertue described as 'no agreeable prospect for fine ladies to see'. His copies, which include portraits by his compatriot Michael Dahl as well as earlier works by Samuel Cooper and Van Dyck, are not slavish. They reveal a talent for reinterpreting portraits in miniature. Richter's technique was quite different from most English miniaturists: he used fine stippling on the face, with blue and sometimes brown to model the carmine (flesh colour) ground. This was combined with broader treatment of the hair and clothing.

### 5  William, Duke of Gloucester (1689–1700)

after an unidentified artist
Watercolour and gum on vellum; later silver-gilt locket frame.
Signed on backing card with monogram and date, 1706
Oval, 6.6 x 4.2 cm

Hans Freiherr von Reitzes; Greta Heckett, Pittsburgh; Sotheby's 11 July 1977 (152); Sotheby's 6 Jan. 1996 (17); purchased by the Draper estate; given to Kenwood, 1996  (88029844)

William was the longest-lived of Queen Anne and Prince George of Denmark's several children, none of whom survived beyond childhood. As future heir to the throne, he was made Duke of Gloucester by the childless King William III and appointed commander of his Dutch regiment of foot guards in his ninth year. Richter's miniature was made before his arrival in England and after William's death and is presumably copied from an oil portrait, although it does not correspond to any known portraits. William was painted in oil on several occasions by Kneller, including a portrait with his mother, and also by two lesser English painters, Edmund Lilly and William Claret.

Even as a copy this is a lively portrait of the young duke, very much in the tradition of Kneller and Dahl. The bright blue drapery is attractively painted with white highlights, against a warm grey background. Richter's technique, employing stipple on the face and neat vertical hatching for the clothing, is very individual.

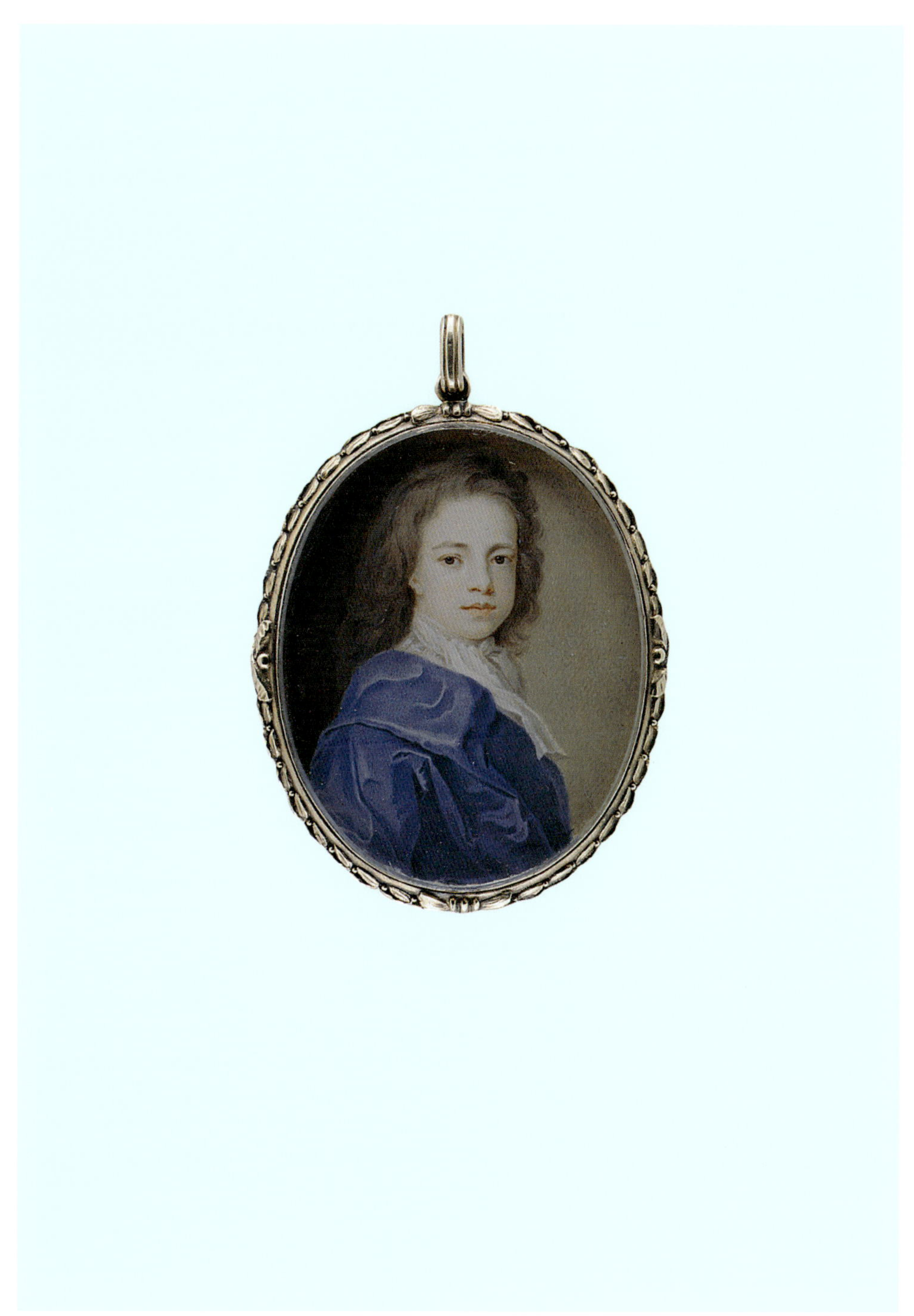

# Bernard Lens III (1682–1740)

Lens was directly descended from two generations of artists of the same name, all of whom worked in London. He studied at the informal academy at Great Queen Street and became the most eminent member of his family, reaching the distinction of being Miniature Painter to both George I and II. He taught drawing, as his father had before him, to members of the royal family and aristocracy (including Princesses Mary and Louisa, who are represented in this collection) and at Eton College.

Lens' portraits follow the style made popular by Sir Godfrey Kneller, but he can be regarded as an innovator himself for being the first British miniaturist to make the transition from vellum to ivory as a support. Although primarily he used opaque gouache (or body colour), he did realise the potential of translucent ivory in his sitters' hands and faces, which are usually painted in pale watercolour wash. Lens was also at the end of a tradition for making miniature copies of religious and history subject paintings. His sons Andrew Benjamin and Peter Paul were also miniaturists.

### 6 Princess Mary (1723–72)
Watercolour on ivory; gilt metal frame. Signed lower left *BL / 1739*
Oval, 7.8 x 6.5 cm

'Wentworth heirlooms'; Christie's 11 Nov. 1994 (12); purchased by the Draper estate; given to Kenwood, 1994  (88029818)

Lit.: Walker, 1992, pp. 6–7; G. C.Williamson, *Catalogue of the Duke of Cumberland's Collection*, 1914 (private press), pp. 3–5

Lens painted the fourth daughter of George II at the very end of his life. A contemporary version of this miniature, although only showing the sitter bust-length, is in the Duke of Cumberland's collection at Calenberg, Germany. John Faber produced a mezzotint after a drawing by Edward Pond, claiming to be drawn from life: this is remarkably close in the sitter's dress but the face differs greatly, suggesting that Lens may also have attended the sitting.

The sixteen-year-old princess has her hair loosely curled in ringlets with strands of pearls and a jewel with two contrasting feathers. Her simple blue robe is trimmed with lace and a jewelled band on the sleeve. Like her sister (cat. 7) she is wearing an ermine stole and a corsage made of an apple or orange with leaves and blossom.

Mary married Frederic, Prince of Hesse-Cassel, the year after this portrait was made. She remained in Germany after her separation in 1754 from the Prince, who was a man of bad morals – and had become a Roman Catholic. When she fled her home with the French invasion, she was left penniless and had to be voted an annuity by the English Parliament.

This miniature, and its pair, show Lens making good use of the luminous quality of thinly applied watercolour on ivory for the youthful sitter's skin. However, typically, he relies on opaque gouache to capture the detail of her dress and jewellery with great care.

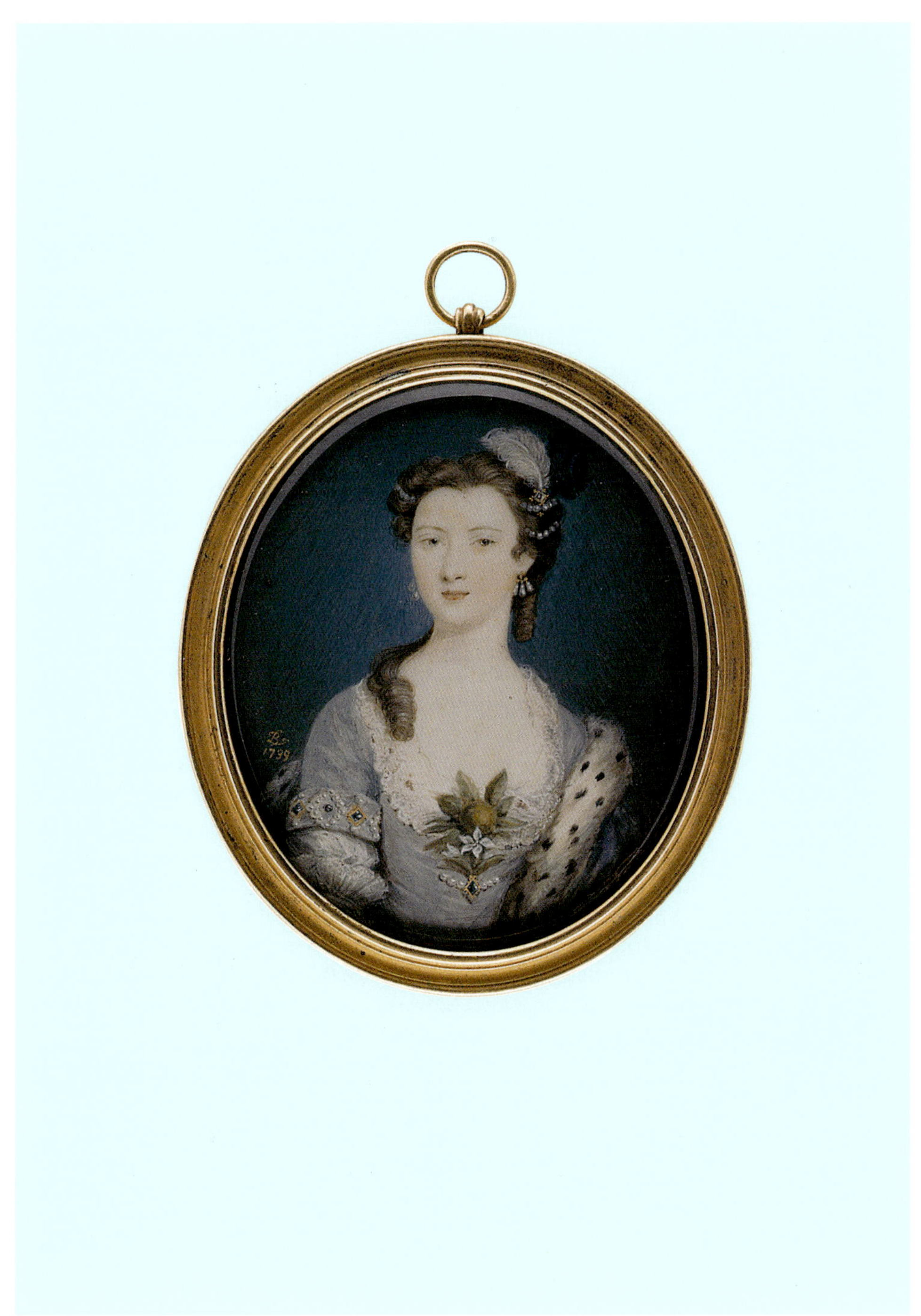

# Bernard Lens III

## 7  Princess Louisa (1724–51)

Watercolour on ivory; gilt metal frame. Signed lower left *BL/ 1739*
Oval, 7.9 x 6.5 cm

'Wentworth heirlooms'; Christie's 11 Nov. 1994 (13); purchased by
the Draper estate; given to Kenwood, 1994  (88029817)

Lit.: Walker, 1992, pp. 6–7

The youngest daughter of George II was painted as a pair with her
sister (cat. 6) and there is a reduced version with a royal
provenance in the collection at Windsor. Although almost identical
in her dress, the face of Princess Louisa in this miniature is less
well-rounded, but more flattering. Again there exists a closely
related print by Faber after Pond that is supposedly from the life.

   She is wearing more formal dress than her sister, consisting of
gold brocaded gown with lace trimmings and pearls in her hair and
on her bodice. Lens has based this on court dress of the day.

   Princess Louisa married the Crown Prince of Denmark in 1743
and brought up her sister Mary's children in Denmark after the
latter's marriage had broken down. Both sisters appear together as
children in a sketch for a conversation piece in the Royal
Collection, painted by Hogarth in 1733.

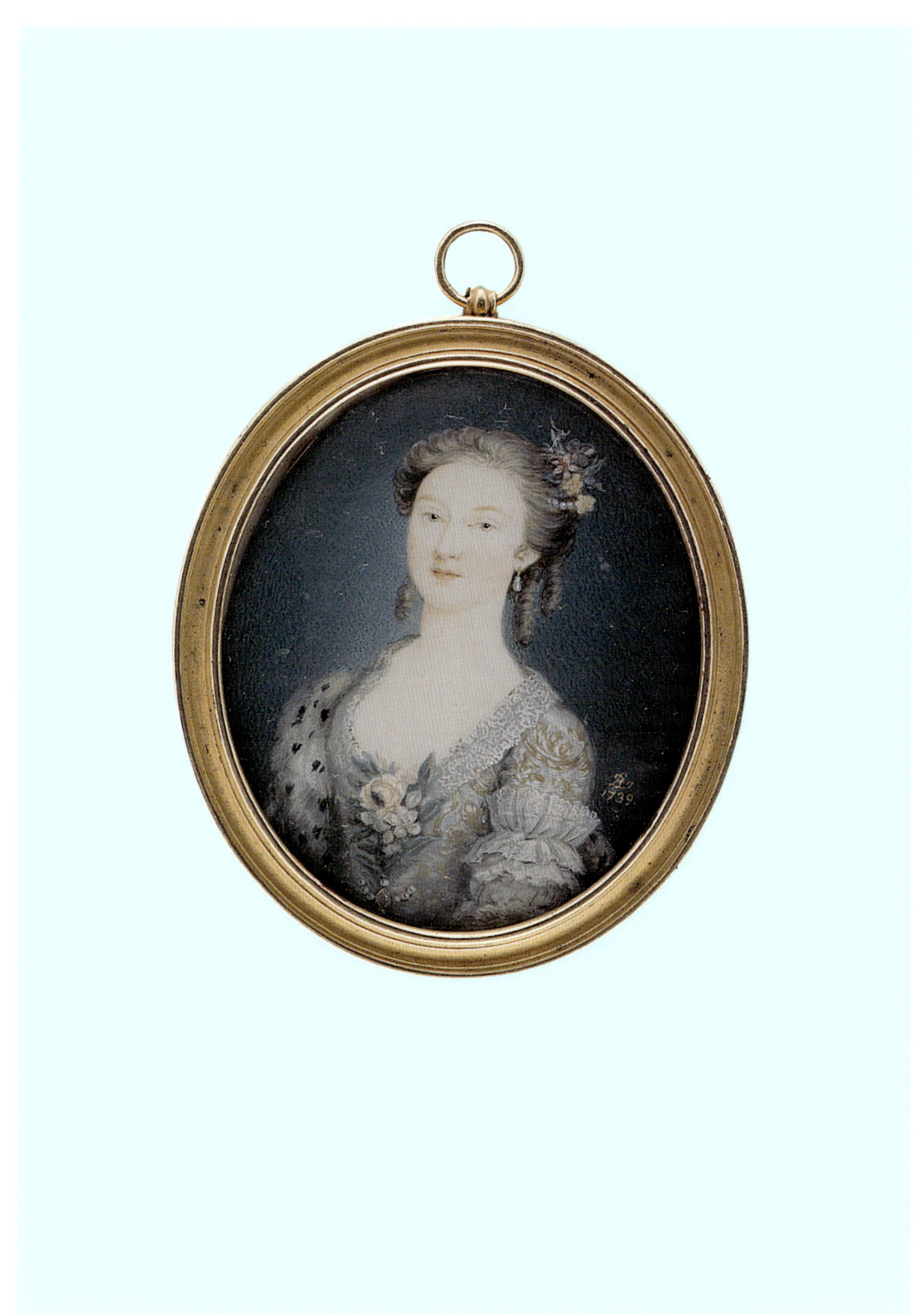

# English School, eighteenth century

### 8  Master Baines
Watercolour on ivory; gold locket frame
Oval, 3.2 x 2.5 cm

Descended in sitter's family; gift to Marie Draper; given to
Kenwood, 1988  (88029166)

A good example of the almost primitive quality of some of the lesser
artists in the middle of the eighteenth century, this charming image
might even be by a member of the sitter's family. The subject's
muslin dress with red sash is nicely set off by the grey green
background.

   This miniature is very neatly painted, using a typical stipple and
hatched technique of the period which follows the pattern set by
Lens. However, the drawing is somewhat naive and the figure quite
flattened in perspective.

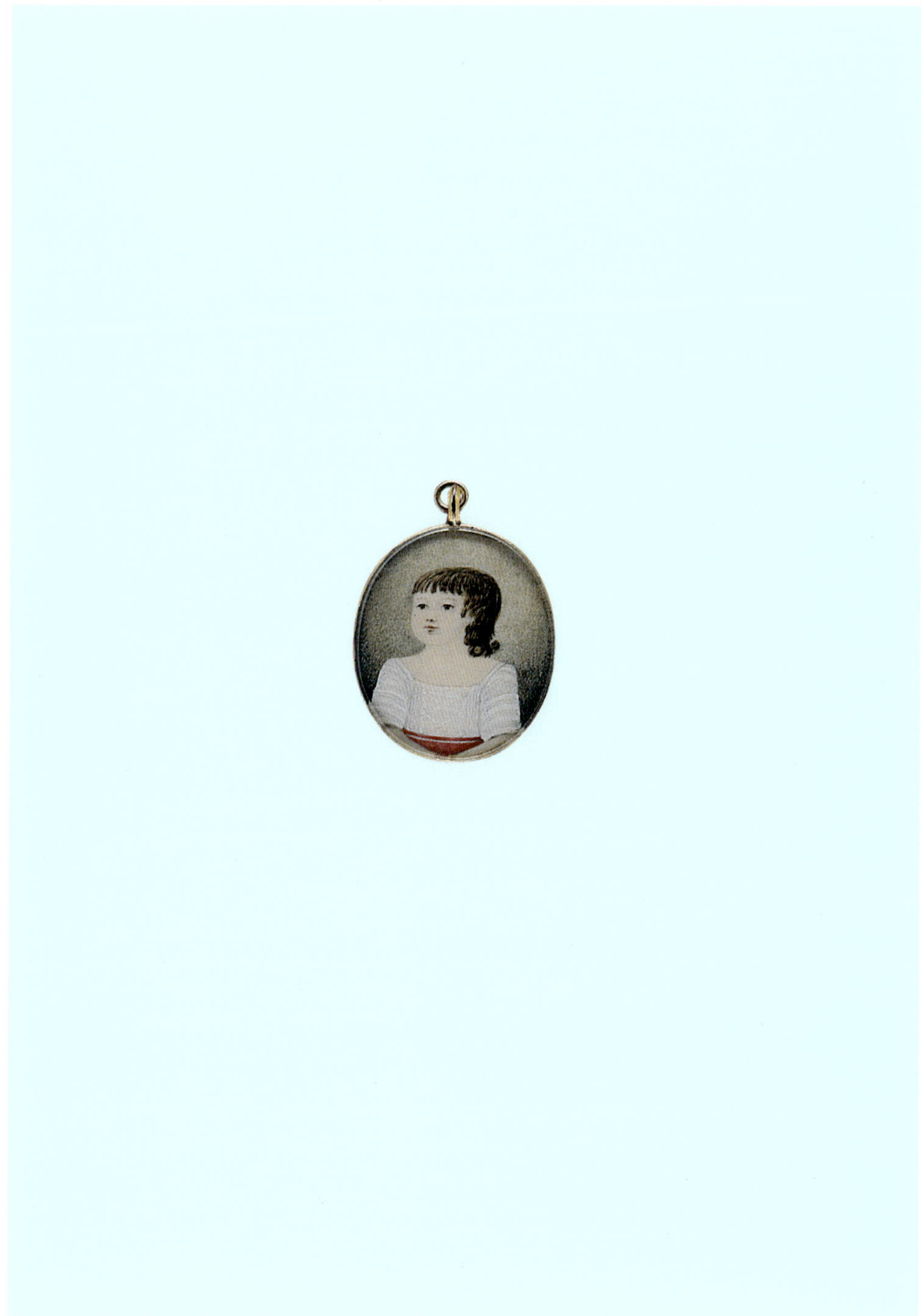

# Christian Friedrich Zincke (1683/4–1767)

Zincke trained in Dresden as a goldsmith and came to London to assist
Charles Boit, probably in 1706. When Boit fled the country in debt in 1714,
Zincke was left running his workshop. He worked in a manner similar to his
master, but his enamels have a more blended finish and cooler colours. This
facility gave him the pick of sitters at Court and he produced enamels at a
prodigious rate. Two important patrons were the Duke of Portland and the
Earl of Oxford. George II made him his Painter in Enamel in 1732. Zincke's
eyesight began to fail from the end of the 1720s, and within ten years he was
producing relatively few works. His studio is believed to have included
André Rouquet as well as Jeremiah Meyer, who paid a large sum for
instruction in enamelling. Many of Zincke's lesser quality works must show
the hand of his assistants. William Hoare drew Zincke at work at his later
home in Lambeth (fig. 1).

### 9  Lord William Beauclerk (1698–1732/3)
Enamel; gold locket frame, engraved *Lord William Beauclerk*
Oval, 3.9 x 3.1 cm

Christie's 10 Sept. 1990 (29); purchased by the Draper estate; given
to Kenwood, 1990  (88029853)

Lord Beauclerk was the second son of the 1st Duke of St Albans, a
leading soldier under William III. His paternal grandparents were
no less than Charles II and Nell Gwynne. He was a captain of the
Royal Horse Guards, Member of Parliament for Chichester and vice-
chamberlain of Queen Caroline's household, an influential position
at the Court of George II. He was buried in Westminster Abbey.
Beauclerk's red coat, with silver lace and military stock, are
probably his military uniform, which was not very fixed at the date
of this work in the 1720s. The full-bottomed wig remained
fashionable throughout these years.

   This work is painted with quite a pronounced stipple for Zincke,
especially in the face. His treatment of the eyelashes, using minute
flecks of paint, is notable. The way the red velvet coat is simulated,
using the fairly intractable medium of enamel, is especially
successful.

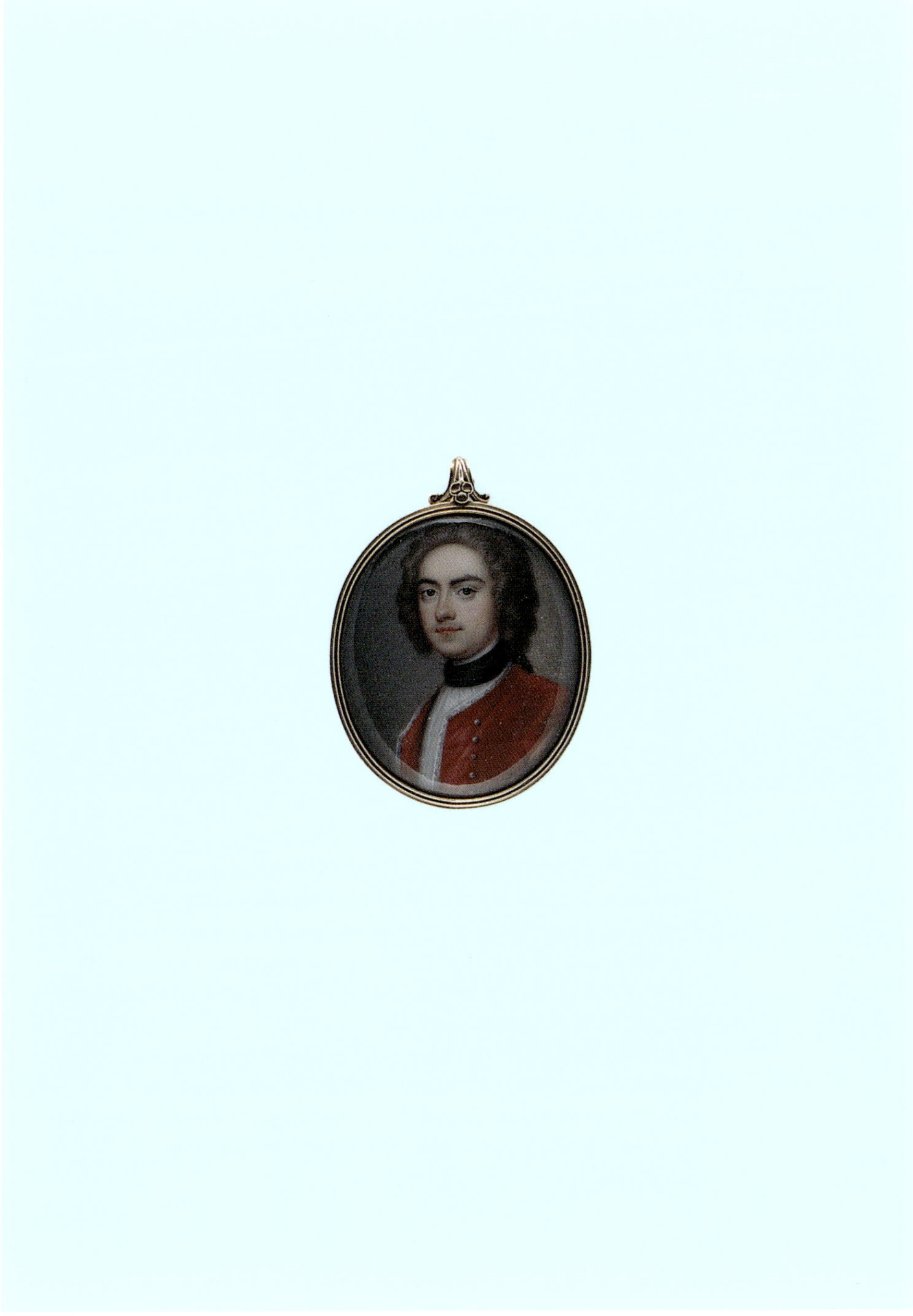

# English School, eighteenth century

### 11 Unknown young girl

Watercolour on ivory; gold bracelet frame (adapted)
Oval, 3.2 x 2.4 cm

Limner Antiques, London; Marie Draper, 1972; given to Kenwood,
1988  (88029172)

This little girl wears a white dress and bonnet that is almost a
parody of a woman's dress of the 1730s and 40s, with its blue bow
trimming. She wears a coral necklace, which was then believed to
ward off evil spirits and give protection (cf cat. 23).

The drawing is more plausible than the young boy of similar date
in the collection (cat. 8), and could be the early work of an artist
destined to paint more sophisticated works.

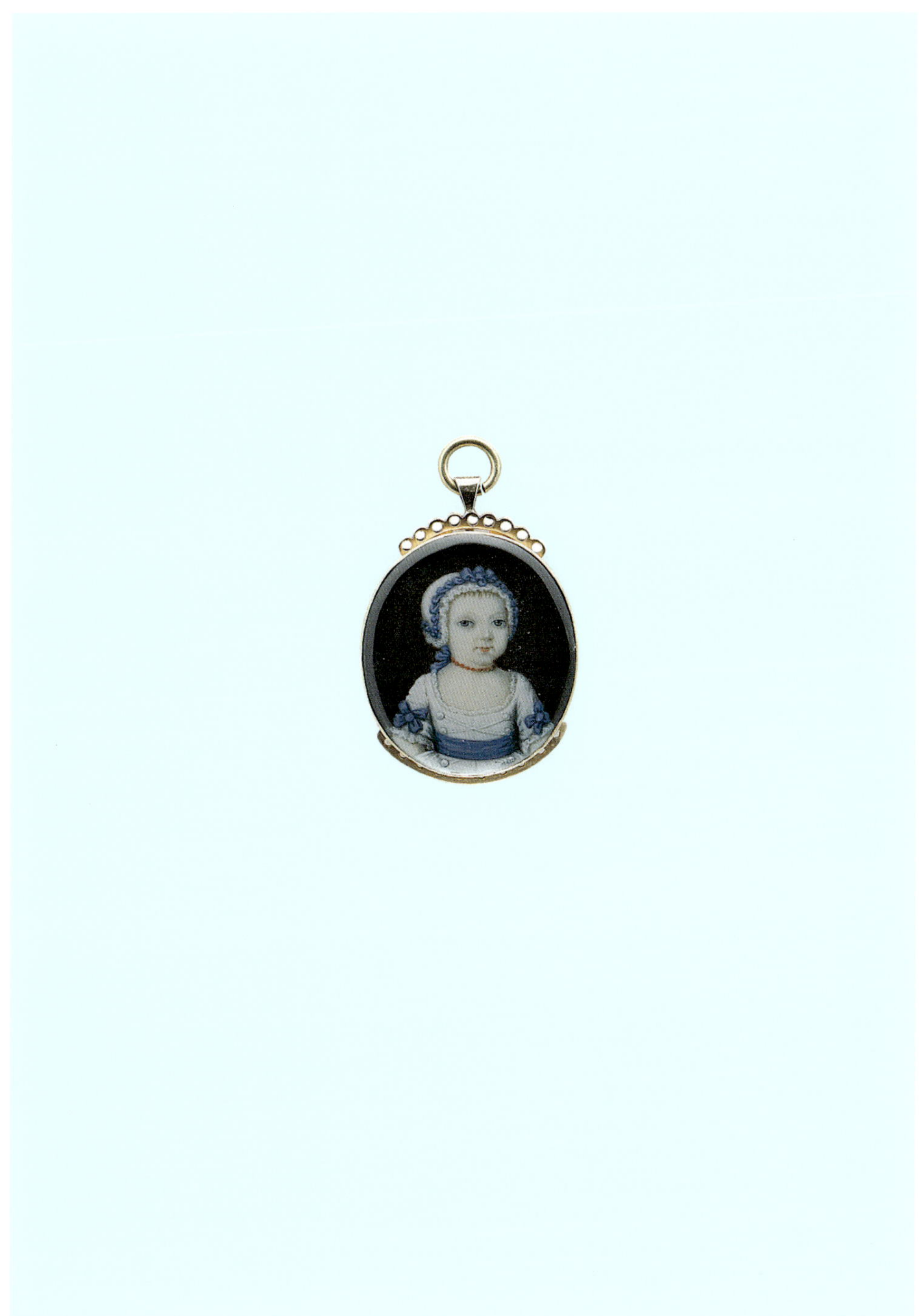

# Nathaniel Hone RA (1718–84)

Born in Dublin, Hone came to England, where he settled in London as a portrait painter.  His early works are modest but he became one of the leading miniaturists of the mid-eighteenth century. He worked in Covent Garden and Soho, painting full-sized oils as well as watercolours and enamels, as he aspired to become one of the leading portrait painters.  To this end he became an early member of the Society of Artists and founder member of the Royal Academy (1769). His celebrated submission of 1775, *The Conjuror*, was rejected for being a satire on the working methods of Reynolds, which he saw as plagiarism. This forced him to establish his own exhibitions in St Martin's Lane.  His oils share much of the polish of his enamel miniatures.

Hone's miniatures are generally small in size, neatly painted with opaque colours and employing impasto to create details of dress. The latest miniatures known by him date from around 1770. Two of his sons, John Camillus and Horace, also worked as miniaturists.

### 12 and 13  Two Young Women
Watercolour on ivory; adapted gold bracelet frames. Both signed right side *NH / 1756*
Oval, (12) 3.2 x 2.8 cm; (13) 3.1 x 2.6 cm

Limner Antiques, London; purchased by the Draper estate, 1991; given to Kenwood, 1991  (88029871/2)

These two young women must have been close relatives, probably sisters. Each wears Hone's interpretation of a simple coloured silk gown with lace trimming and has her hair closely tied back. The girl in pink has a jewel with three pearl pendants, perhaps indicating that she is the more senior of the two.

Hone's early watercolour technique and style, seen here, are still very dependent on the previous generation of artists. Faces are still thinly stippled and the remainder built up of parallel hatching or quick strokes over coloured ground. His choice of a light blue background is more unusual and hints at his knowledge of continental portraiture.

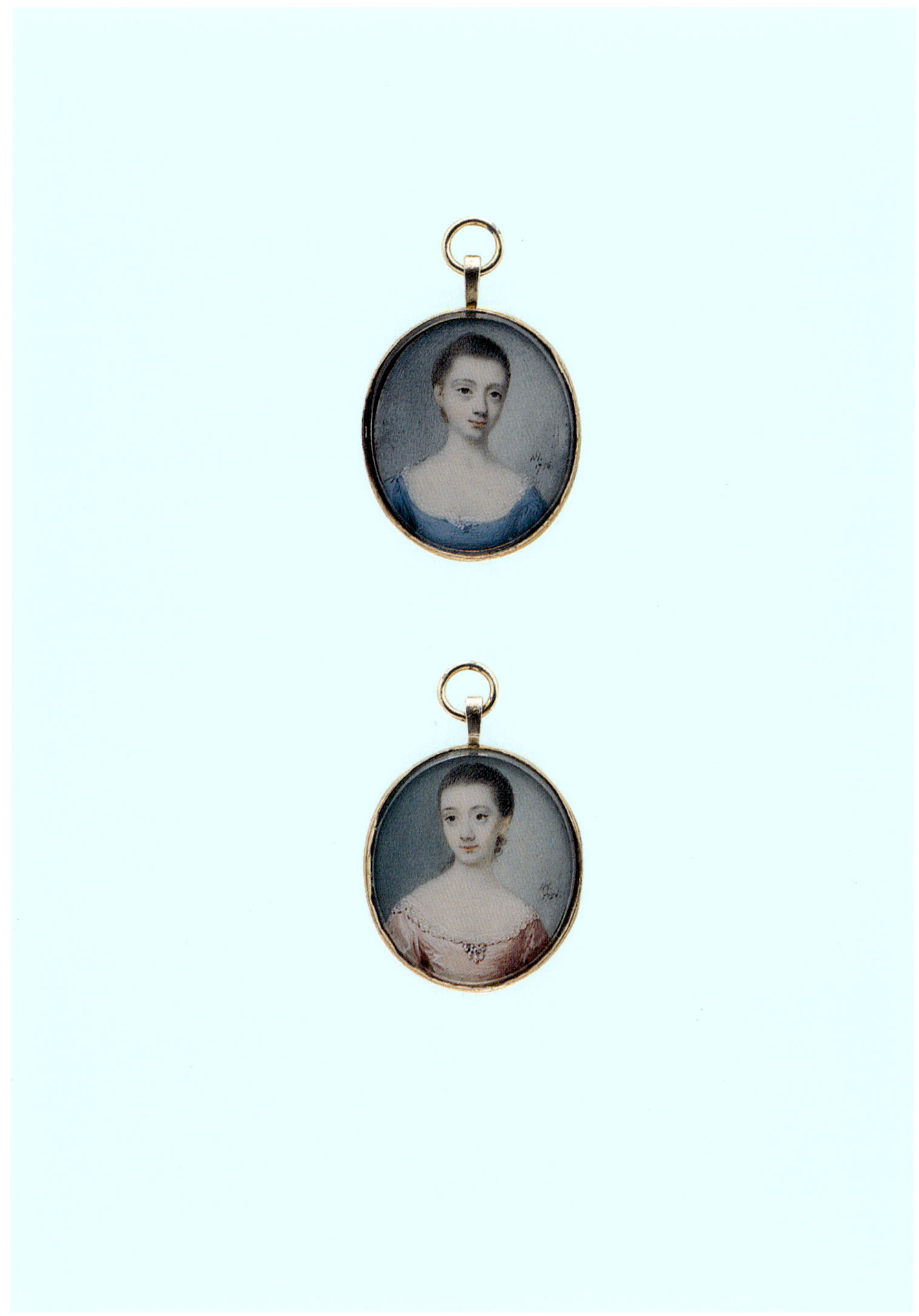

# Nathaniel Hone RA

### 14  Unknown Woman

Enamel; gilt metal locket frame. Signed middle right *NH 1764*
Oval, 3.0 x 2.6 cm

Limner Antiques, London; Marie Draper, c1974; given to Kenwood,
1988  (88029174)

The sitter here wears her hair in a slightly looser fashion, falling at
the back. Her white dress is complemented by a bright blue stole
attached with pearls: this makes the most of the enamel colour's
intensity.

Hone achieved a high degree of finish in his enamels, even on a
small scale such as this. The sitter's face is convincingly modelled
by using fine stipple shading in grey over a pinkish skin colour.
Again his choice of a fairly light-coloured background sets off the
figure rather well. This miniature bears his usual monogram, a
capital *N* and *H* conjoined.

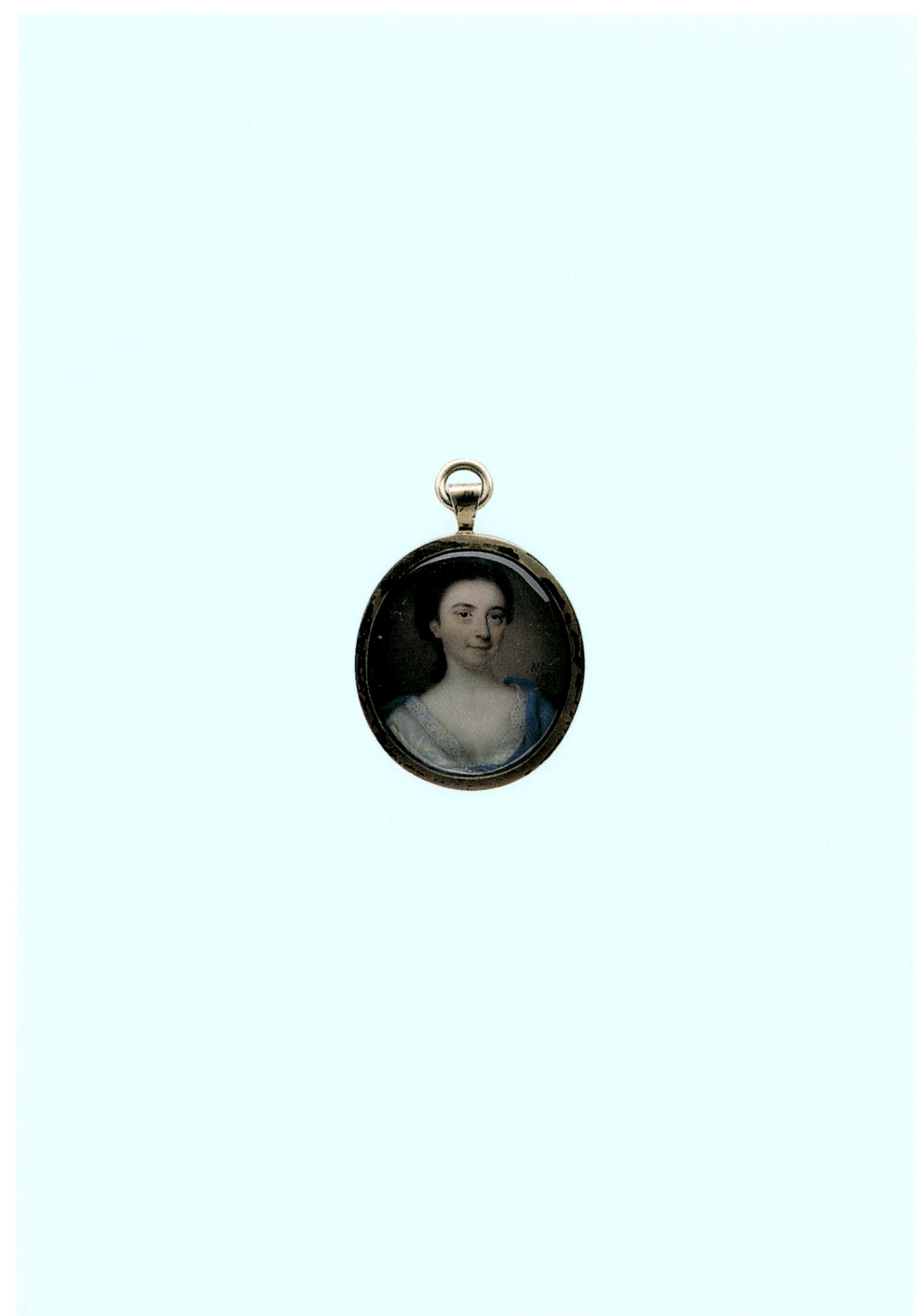

# Luke Sullivan  (1705–71)

An Irishman, who came to England at an early age, Sullivan trained with an
engraver and produced prints after Hogarth and others before turning to
miniatures around 1750. He also painted landscapes and topographical scenes
in watercolour. His portraits of women are well above average and display a
very harmonious use of colour that suggests he was familiar with French
painting of the mid-century. Sullivan enjoyed the good life, spending much of
his time drinking and frequenting brothels around Piccadilly.

His miniatures are finely painted in watercolour, although the heads of the
women he painted can be rather alike. However, they show off his use of
bright, complementary colours in the dress and backgrounds, in a manner
only rivalled by Ramsay's full-scale portraits.

### 15  Unknown Man

Watercolour on ivory; gold locket frame (adapted) with hair verso.
Signed lower left *LS/ 17 [?65]*
Oval, 3.9 x 3.3 cm

R.L. Bayne-Powell; Sotheby's 11 Oct. 1994 (44); purchased by the
Draper estate; given to Kenwood, 1994  (88029827)

The date on this miniature is very indistinct, but the bag wig and
collarless coat of the sitter would suggest a date around 1760–5. He
has his black solitaire ties (for the wig's bag) tucked in his coat,
with a lace jabot protruding.

The treatment of the face here is very soft, and unfortunately the
flesh tints (probably a lake) have faded. This gives the work a
slightly ghostly effect. However, the detail around the eyes and
nose is extremely well drawn, as are the curls of the wig.

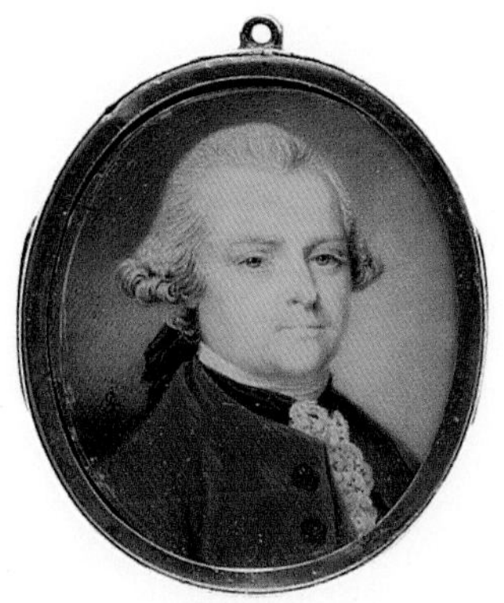

# Luke Sullivan



## 16  Unknown Woman
Watercolour on ivory; gold locket frame with blue glass foil back.
Signed lower left *LS / 1767*
Oval, 4.0 x 3.3 cm

Limner Antiques, London; Marie Draper, 1980; given to Kenwood,
1988  (88029168)

This charming portrait shows a woman fashionably attired, her hair
dressed with pink and white flowers that match her silk robe with
its two-coloured bow and white lace trimming. She wears large and
prominent pearls which add a greater note of luxury to her dress.

Sullivan's neat painting of the face and dress, achieved with fine
stipple and hatches fused together, allows him to concentrate on
the incidental details of the portrait and to use carefully applied
colour. The bright pink of the silk is brilliantly contrasted against
the bluish, gradated background that seems to push the figure
forward in space.

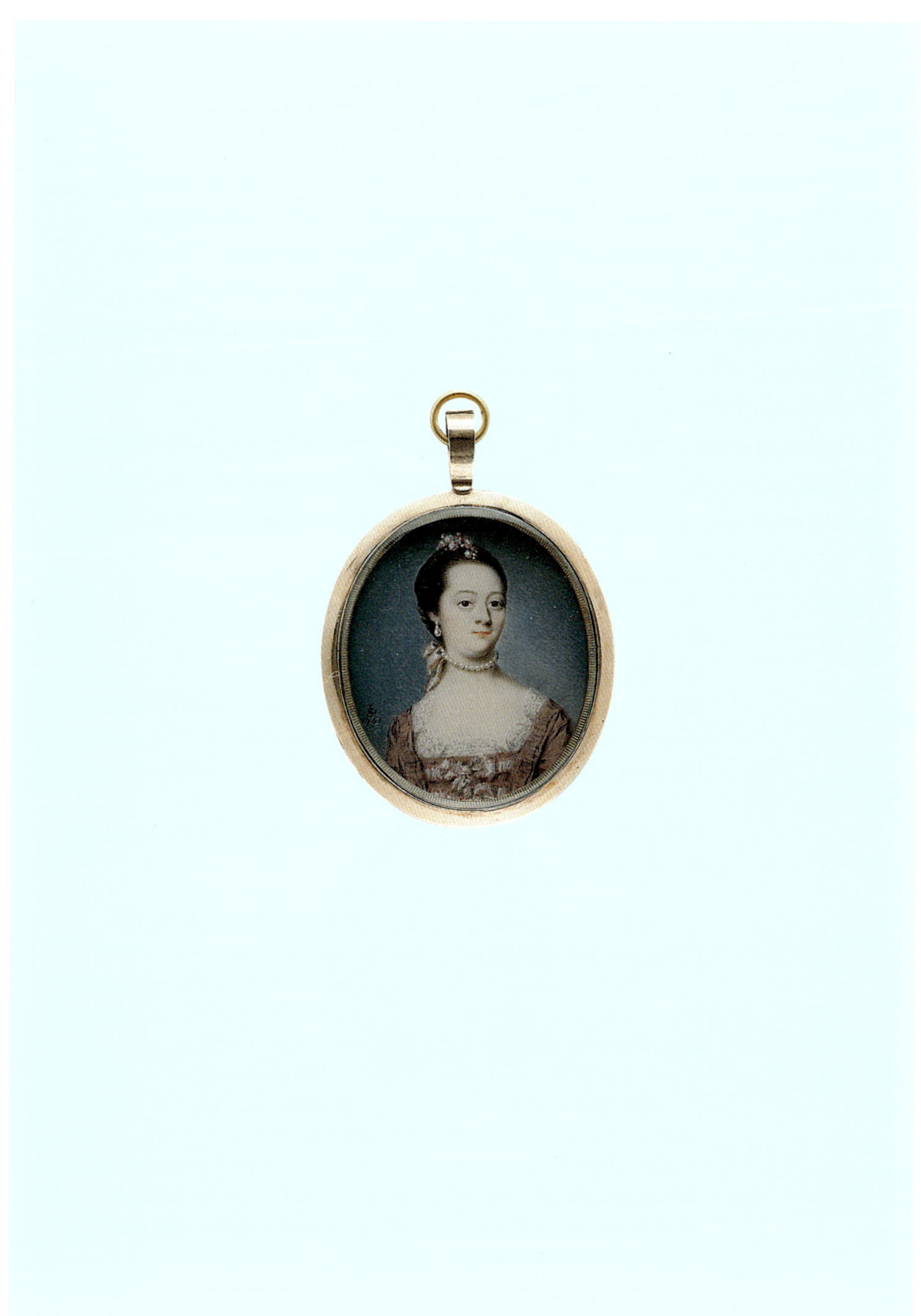

## Samuel Finney  (1718–98)

Finney came from Wilmslow, Cheshire, and studied to be a lawyer in London.
He abandoned this career to become a portrait painter, working in oil and
enamel as well as painting miniatures on ivory and paper. His work was
exhibited at the Free Society and Society of Artists, where he was a fellow.
Although rather old-fashioned in his technique, he attracted notable patrons
in Bath and Bristol as well as London. He was said to have copied the painting
of the future Queen Charlotte for George III, that led to the King's final
choice of bride. This may well account for his becoming Enamel and
Miniature Painter to Queen Charlotte in 1763. He retired to Cheshire in 1769,
returning to his original vocation, for he became a JP.

Finney collected works by other portrait artists, including those of earlier
generations. These were probably used for study purposes, to improve his
own drawing.

### 18  Unknown Officer

Watercolour on ivory; modern gilt metal locket frame. Signed lower
right with initial *F*
Oval, 4.0 x 3.1 cm

?The Gell family, Hopton; by descent to Lt-Col Chandos-Pole;
Christie's, Newnham Hall 11 July 1994 (290); purchased by the
Draper estate; given to Kenwood, 1994  (88029824)

This officer wears the uniform of about 1760 of one of several
regiments of foot distinguished by green facings with silver lace.
The portrait was made before several items of military uniform were
regularised later in the 1760s, such as the wearing of white or buff
waistcoats. This officer still has a rather fancy matching waistcoat,
with a great deal of silver lace. One interesting feature is his
shoulder cord, a precursor of the epaulette.

Finney's style has been likened to that of Bernard Lens (see cats
6,7) with its reliance on stippling, especially in the background. The
use of opaque white highlights on the face and hair are a less
common characteristic in helping to identify this artist, who did not
often sign his work.

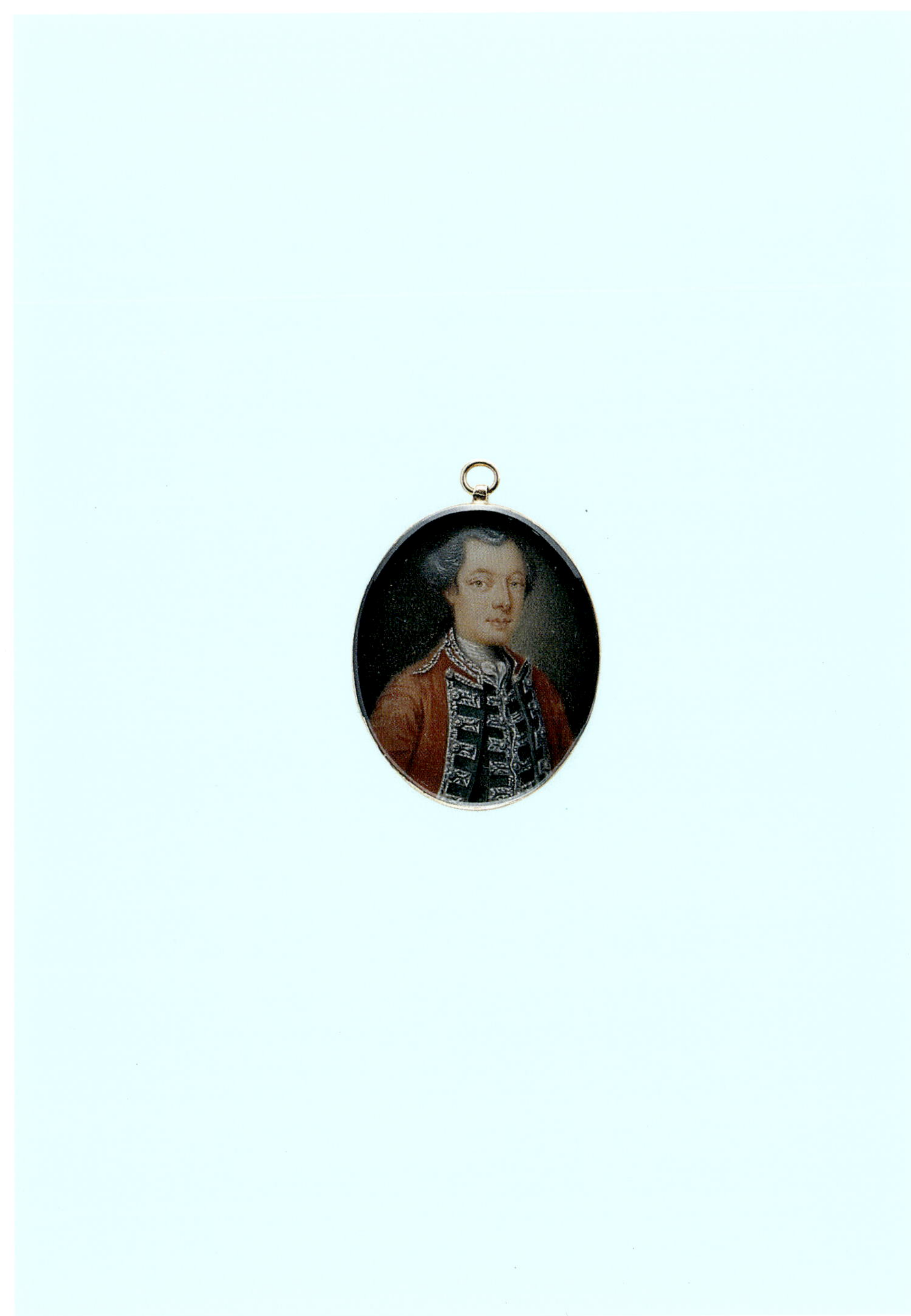

# Gervase Spencer (fl c1740–63)

Details of Spencer's early life are vague, but the artist and diarist George Vertue suggests that he was perhaps the servant of Dr Wall, a physician and connoisseur  who was involved with the Worcester porcelain manufactory. Spencer was equally able in enamel as in watercolour and must have studied the former with a master, who has not been firmly identified.

His works can be painted with much skill and sensitivity and he was unusual in being able to adapt his style from the hard, bright images of the 1740s (and earlier) to the softer, more restrained works of the 1760s. This transition was made easier thanks to his ability with watercolour as well as enamel. Most of Spencer's works are on a small scale, precisely finished and often signed with initials. As well as miniature painting, he produced drawings and etchings and taught the art of enamelling.

### 19  Unknown Woman

Enamel; gold locket frame. Signed on left of obverse, S  and on verso, *G S Pinxt / DD.. Aetat 59  1754*
Oval, 4.4 x 3.4 cm

Christie's, Geneva 28 April 1976; Christie's 20 March 1990 (71); purchased by the Draper estate; given to Kenwood, 1990 (88029851)

This would appear to be a very life-like copy of an earlier portrait of c.1740-5, since the inscription gives the woman's age as fifty-nine at her death in 1754, and she appears rather younger in this portrait. Her dress consists of a lace mob cap and a lace-trimmed kerchief, held in place by the tie of her green robe. This could well date the miniature to the 1740s.

Spencer uses enamel with great skill in this work, with realistic colouring and a very smooth surface. His choice of greenish background against the green dress is particularly subtle for the period.

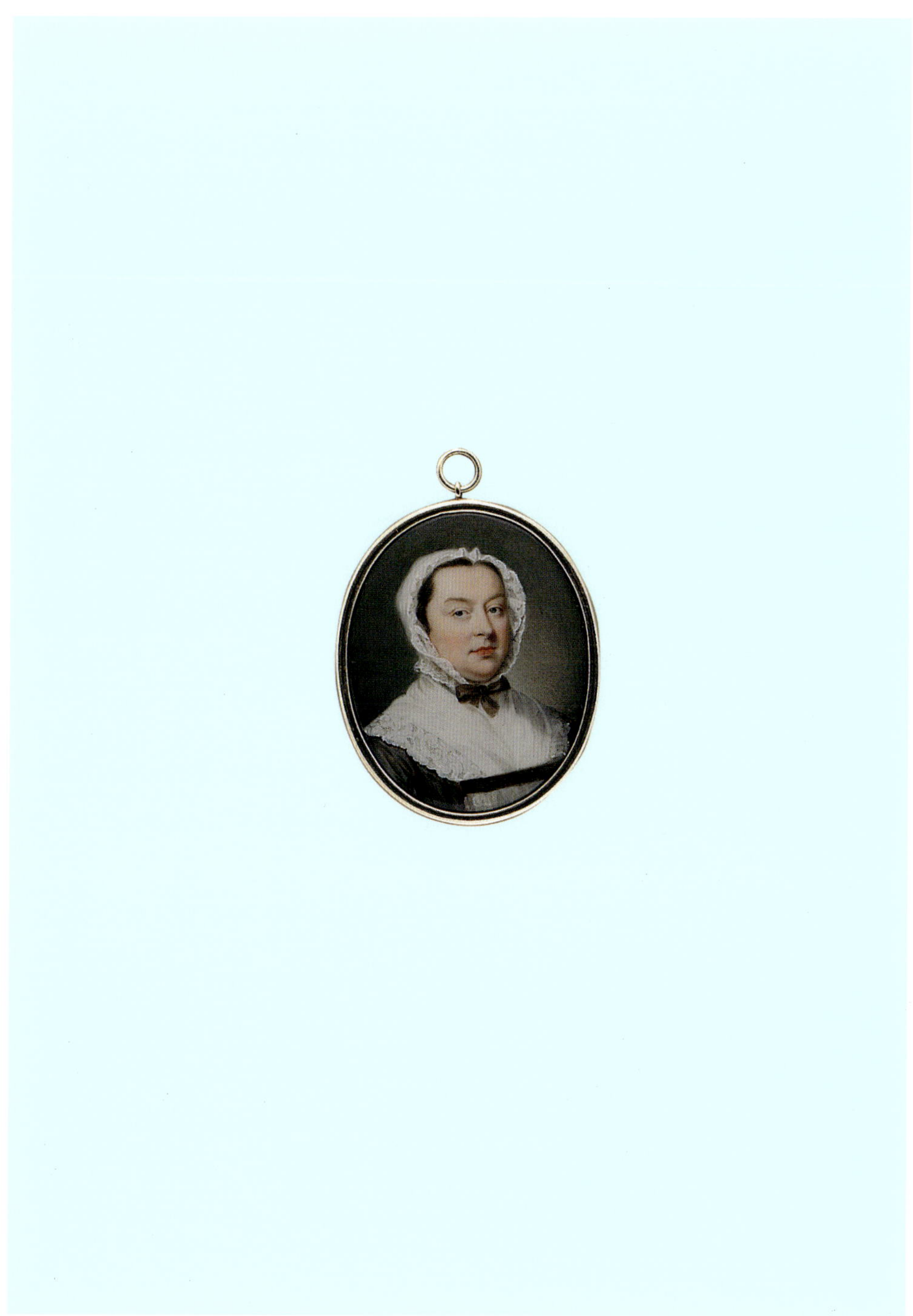

# Penelope Carwardine (c1730–1801)

Like other women artists of the period, Penelope Carwardine was compelled
to turn the gentlewoman's art of drawing into a means of earning a living
when her large family became dependent on her as the eldest daughter. She
came from Withington in Herefordshire and was working from around 1750
until marriage in about 1772 to a Mr Butler, the organist at (among other
places) Ranelagh pleasure grounds in Chelsea. As social mores of the day
dictated, she gave up her business on marriage.

Her work is fairly modest in scope and scale, although a rare surviving
sketch book of sitters allied, perhaps, to the fact of her acquaintance with the
younger artist Ozias Humphry (cat. 37) suggest that her talent was greater
than her miniatures might lead one to believe.

### 20  Alicia Maria, Countess of Egremont (1729–94)

Watercolour on ivory; gold locket frame with hair inset on verso,
engraved *Alicia Maria Css. Egremont 1757*
Oval, 3.4 x 2.6 cm

Christie's 27 Nov. 1991 (229); purchased by the Draper estate;
given to Kenwood, 1991 (88029877)

Alicia Maria Carpenter was the wife of Charles Wyndham, 2nd Earl
of Egremont, heir to the great house at Petworth in Sussex. He was
a politician and ambassador as well as an admirer of old master
paintings and antiquities. Alicia Maria was a noted beauty. She later
made a second marriage, to the Saxon ambassador, Count Brühl.

The Countess of Egremont's hair is combed back and pinned flat
in the manner of the 1750s with centre ornament of flowers. Her
gown is open to reveal an embroidered bodice in pink and green.
Unusually she wears a prominent crucifix.

This is a typical portrait by Carwardine and it shows how she
developed the rather solid looking manner begun by Bernard Lens,
making greater use of the ivory support with more translucent
colours. She still uses some stipple, particularly on the face.

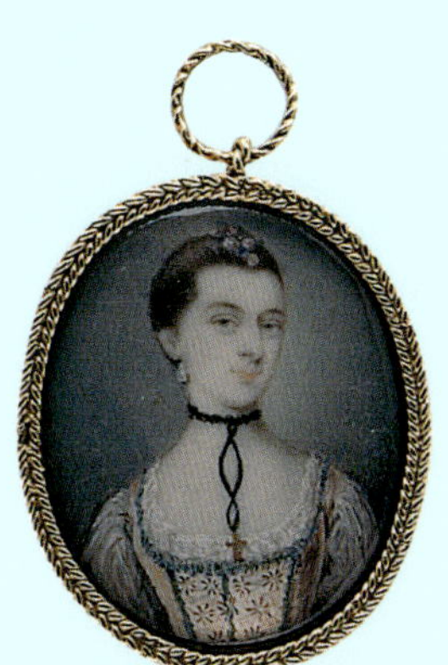

# William Hopkins Craft (c1730–1811)

There has been some uncertainty as to the identity of this enamel painter, who variously signed his work *W Craft and WH Craft*. He painted for Wedgwood from 1768 and had also worked in Paris. Apart from painting enamel portraits, mostly copies of originals, Craft also produced jewellery, enamel plaques and decorative clock faces. These show him to be a competent decorative artist, heavily influenced by neo-classicism. His preference for strong, often harsh colours in this field is unfortunately carried through to his portrait miniatures. He did paint some original works, including his self-portrait in the National Gallery of Ireland.

### 21  George Frederick Handel (1685–1759)
after Thomas Hudson (1701–79)
Enamel; gold ring setting
Oval, 2.46 x 1.6 cm (shown opposite at acual size (above) and twice actual size (below))

Broadwood family, by descent; Sotheby's, Geneva 21 Nov. 1991 (12); given to Kenwood by Dr John Pearce, 1991  (88029878)

Lit: J. Kerslake, *Eighteenth Century Portraits in the National Portrait Gallery*, 1977, pp. 123–5; Bayne-Powell, 1985, pp. 50–1

Handel was born in Saxony but made his reputation travelling through Europe and settled in England in 1712. Here he introduced Italian style opera to a voracious music world and effectively became court composer to George I and II. Hudson painted Handel in 1756 (National Portrait Gallery), blind and in old age, for his librettist Charles Jennens. In his reduced version, Craft has altered Handel's dress, by replacing his day gown with a pale purple coat.

Craft's copy of Hudson's sensitive portrait seems rather hard, although he may be forgiven somewhat as he rarely worked on such a small scale. There are other known versions by him, including a ring and box setting, both in the Fitzwilliam Museum, Cambridge. The former is very similar in size and detail. This output suggests there may have been some demand for souvenir images of Handel after his death: this enamel was probably made some time after 1759. The Kenwood version belonged to John Broadwood, founder of the keyboard instrument makers, whose father-in-law, Burkat Shudi, was a friend of Handel. The story is that the ring was a gift from Handel to Shudi.

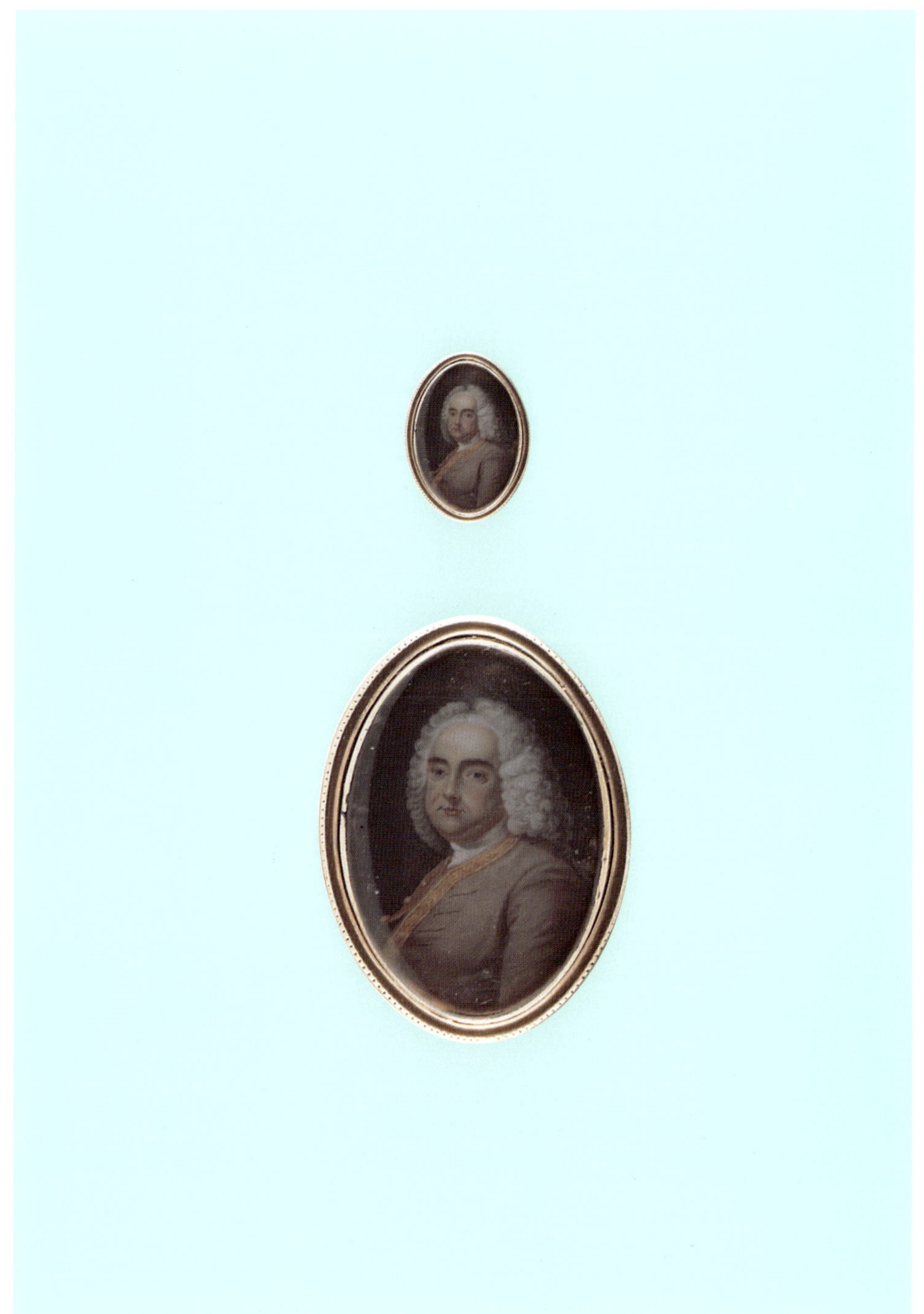

## Samuel Cotes (1734–1818)

Born in London of Irish descent, Samuel Cotes studied painting under his
better known elder brother, Francis, who painted portraits in pastel and oils.
Samuel exhibited miniatures and pastel portraits at the Society of Artists and
then the Royal Academy. He worked from Rathbone Place at the height of his
career and is also thought to have worked in Bath.

Like his brother, Cotes was a good observer of fashion even within this
limited format. Many of his miniatures are signed. Where a monogram is
used, there can be some confusion with Samuel Collins, although the latter
wrote more fluidly than Cotes.

### 22  Unknown Man

Watercolour on ivory; gold bracelet frame. Signed lower right
*SC/ 1759*
Oval, 3.2 x 2.6 cm

Limner Antiques, London; purchased by the Draper estate, 1991;
given to Kenwood, 1991  (88029874)

This plainly dressed gentleman of the mid-eighteenth century
shows the Englishman's preference for sober, largely unadorned
dress. He wears a bag wig, popular at this time, and a lace or
embroidered cravat, which together with the gold braid buttons are
the only signs of an interest in fashion.

This early work by Cotes has much in common with the 'modest
school' miniaturists of the period and reveals none of this artist's
later, elegant technique. It is quite broadly painted with fairly flat
areas of colour, hatching to the face and long brush strokes on the
body and background.

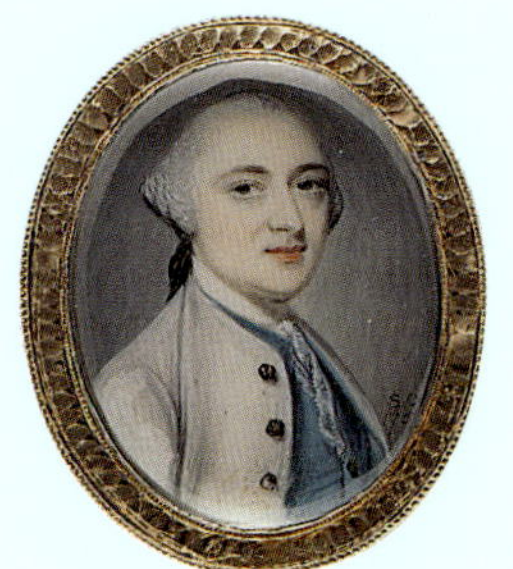

## Samuel Cotes

**24  ?Frances Dickson, 1769**
Watercolour on ivory; gold locket frame. Signed lower right
*S. Cotes / 1769*
Oval, 4.7 x 3.8 cm

Christie's 25 Nov. 1975 (37); Bonham's 30 Nov. 1994 (92);
purchased by the Draper estate; given to Kenwood, 1994
(88029837)

The sitter was identified when the miniature was sold in 1975. Her
hair is loosely piled up with a ribbon and falls in a tress round her
shoulders, a style which was to become rather exaggerated in the
following years. The dress is typical of the fanciful gowns preferred
by portrait painters of the neo-classical period.

   Cotes' suave technique and soft, fine brushwork captures the
texture of the sitter's hair well. His use of a lost profile reveals his
awareness of current developments in full-scale portraiture –
possibly through his brother's work. This gives a feeling of
sensitivity not possible with the limited poses and  skills of the
previous generation of miniaturists.

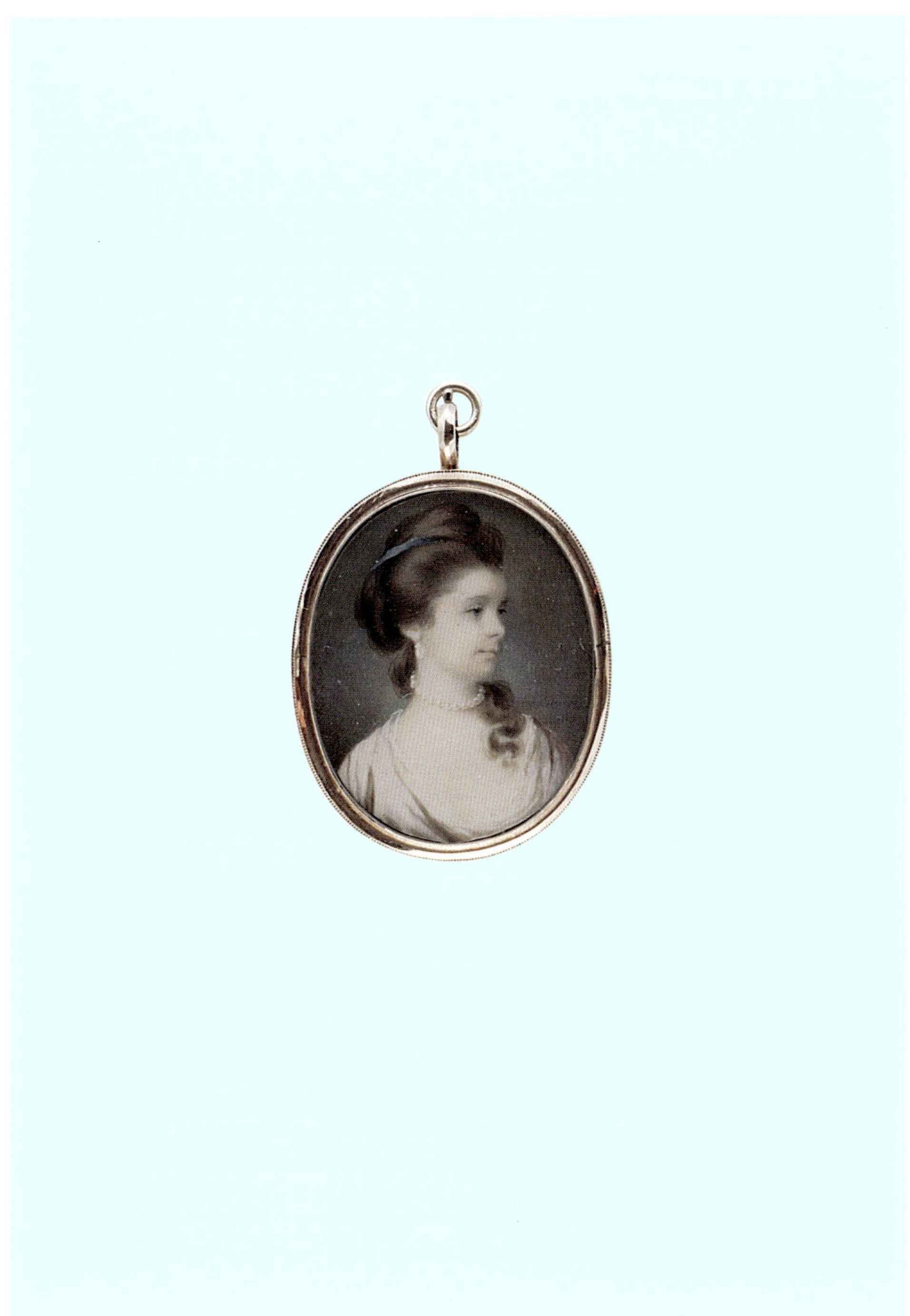

# Samuel Collins (?1735–68)

The son of a Bristol clergyman, Collins was intended to become a lawyer but abandoned that career to pursue his interest in art. He became one of many 'modest school' miniature painters based in Bath in the 1750s and 60s, until he was forced to move to Dublin to escape creditors. His works can be quite well painted and have often been confused with early works by Samuel Cotes (cats 22–24) whose style is not dissimilar and who signed with the same initials. Collins signed in full and with his initials; the latter are smoothly painted, unlike the short strokes of Samuel Cotes' monogram.

Perhaps Collins' greatest legacy was that he trained Ozias Humphry as a young artist in Bath. Humphry (cat 37) became one the best artists in pastel and pencil. Daphne Foskett (1987) relates that Joseph Nollekens remembered Collins as 'a very indifferent miniature painter and what was worse, a man of gay and expensive habits!'

### 25  Unknown Woman
Watercolour on ivory; gold bracelet frame (adapted)
Signed with initials on left side *S.C/ 1755*
Oval, 4.0 x 3.2 cm

Bonham's 21 March 1995 (38); purchased by the Draper estate; given to Kenwood, 1995  (88029841)

This middle-aged lady has the modest dress commensurate with the status of Collins as an artist. Her lace cap and under-gown trimming, together with her black jacket or gown, give a sense of propriety – perhaps she was a widow.

Collins' work carries on from the tradition of Spencer, with a mixture of fine stipple and line work around the face and careful hatching of the background. Only the dress is broadly painted. His observation of a prominent mole on the sitter's cheek may suggest some naivety on the artist's part. Alternatively, the sitter may have demanded that he not flatter her as he might a younger woman.

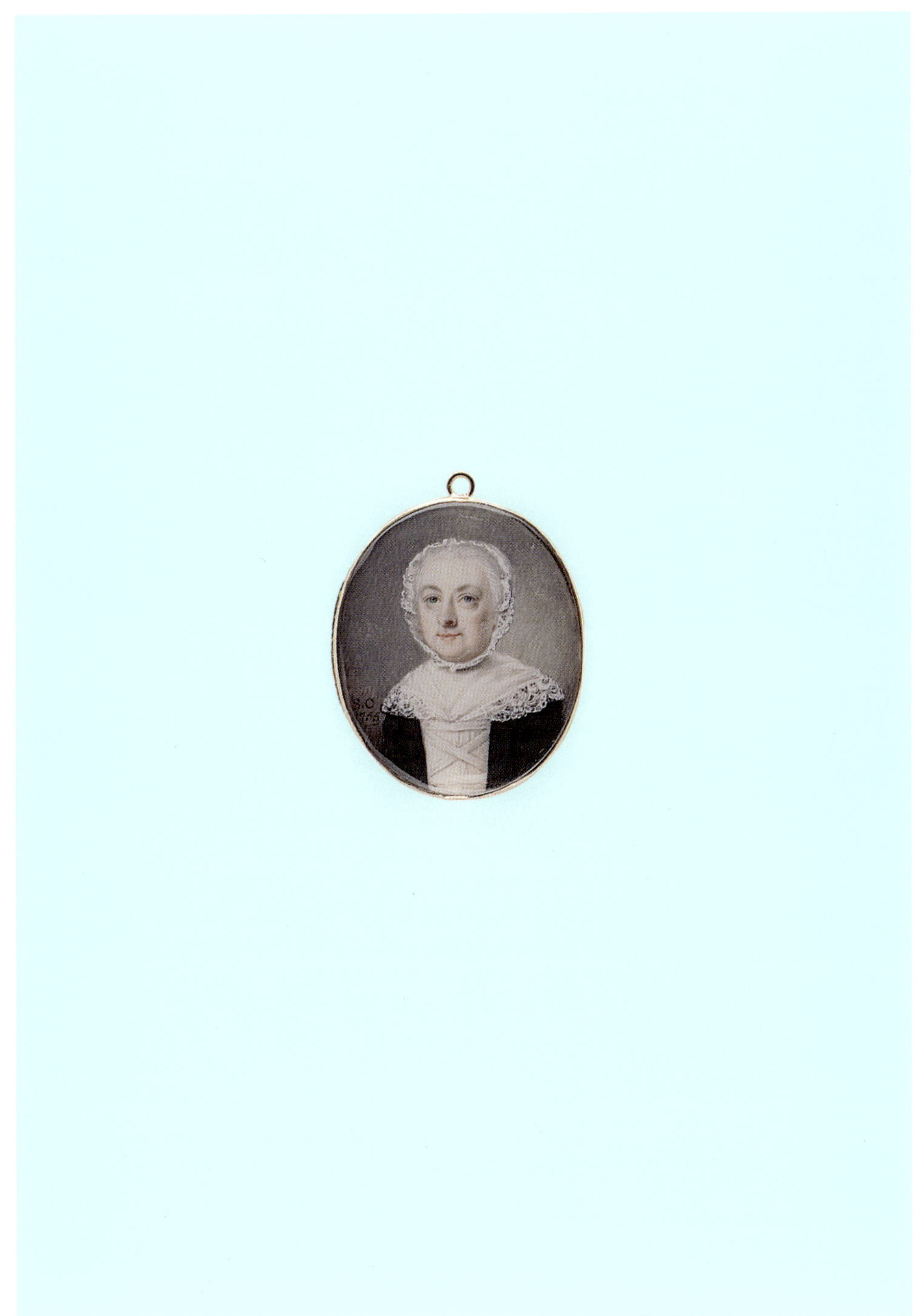

# Samuel Collins

### 26  Unknown Man

Watercolour on ivory; gilt metal and steel locket frame
Signed lower right *Collins/ 1764*
Oval, 3.8 x 3.2 cm

Brig. and Mrs G. Viner; Sotheby's 8 April 1993 (303); purchased by
the Draper estate; given to Kenwood, 1993  (88029805)

Lit.: Foskett, 1987, p. 251

In this later work Collins has matured and refined his technique,
and is working in a manner that appears to be influenced by the
early Reynolds. The sitter wears conventional clothing of the early
1760s: powdered wig, white shirt with ruffled front, and a maroon
coat with broad flat collar and lace-trimmed buttonholes.

Collins' representation of the face is far more convincing than in
the earlier work in this collection (cat. 25), and this is partly due to
a much subtler technique. He uses more variety of brush strokes,
from stipple to broad hatching, and a fairly cool range of colours,
the face being slightly green in its shading (although this may have
faded somewhat). The signature is typical of the artist.

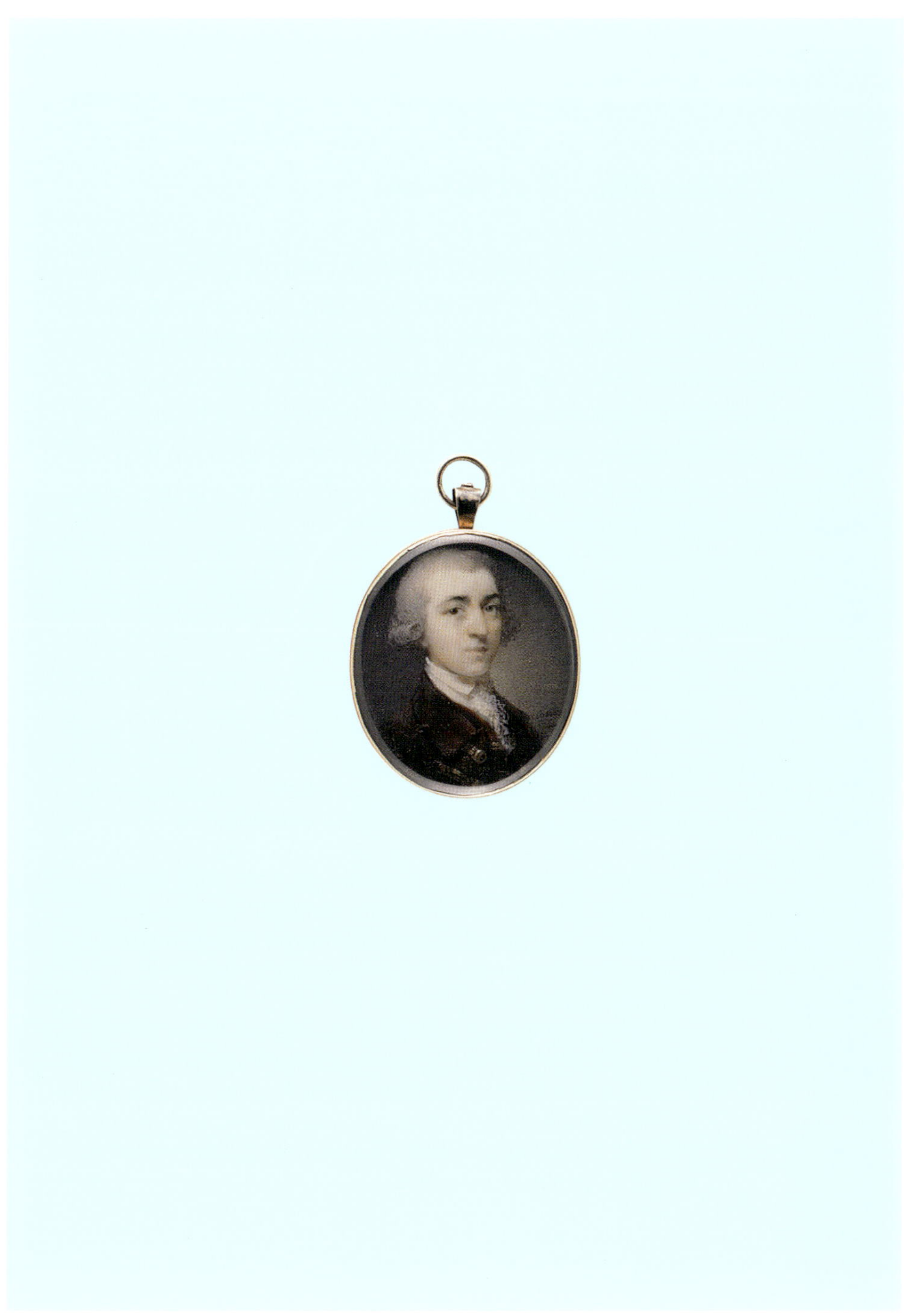

# Jeremiah Meyer RA (1735–89)

Meyer was born in Tübigen, Germany, and came to England at the age of
fourteen. Here he followed in the footsteps of a number of successful *émigré*
painters, studying at the St Martin's Lane Academy in London and with Zincke
(cat. 9) in the 1750s. He successfully assimilated the technical skills (in several
media) of the previous generation into the more naturalistic manner of
portraiture of the latter half of the century. Success, coupled with his German
origins, led to Meyer becoming Miniature Painter to Queen Charlotte and
Painter in Enamel to King George III in 1764, following naturalisation. He was
a frequent exhibitor at the Society of Artists between 1760 and 1767 and a
founder member of the more progressive Royal Academy in 1768.

Members of Meyer's family were painted by both Reynolds and his friend
Romney. He worked mostly from Covent Garden and died at Kew, where he
is buried next to Thomas Gainsborough.

### 28  Unknown Woman

Watercolour on ivory; gold locket frame
Oval, 5.5 x 4.5 cm

Christie's, 27 April 1983 (360); Marie Draper; given to Kenwood,
1988  (88029165)

This portrait of a middle-aged lady in dress of the early 1770s was
made when Meyer was at the height of his career. It shows his
characteristic technique, relying on hatched lines to build up the
sitter's face with finely delineated details, as in the strands of her
hair. The limited range of colours would once have  blended
harmoniously but typically for Meyer, his use of a fugitive red
colour in the flesh tones has left the sitter looking unnaturally pale.

The sitter was probably a lady of some rank and wealth, to judge
by the pearl strands in her fashionably tied-up hair. Her gown is
fairly plain, perhaps invented by the artist, who has only hinted at
the detail of its lace trimming with judicious use of opaque white
paint.

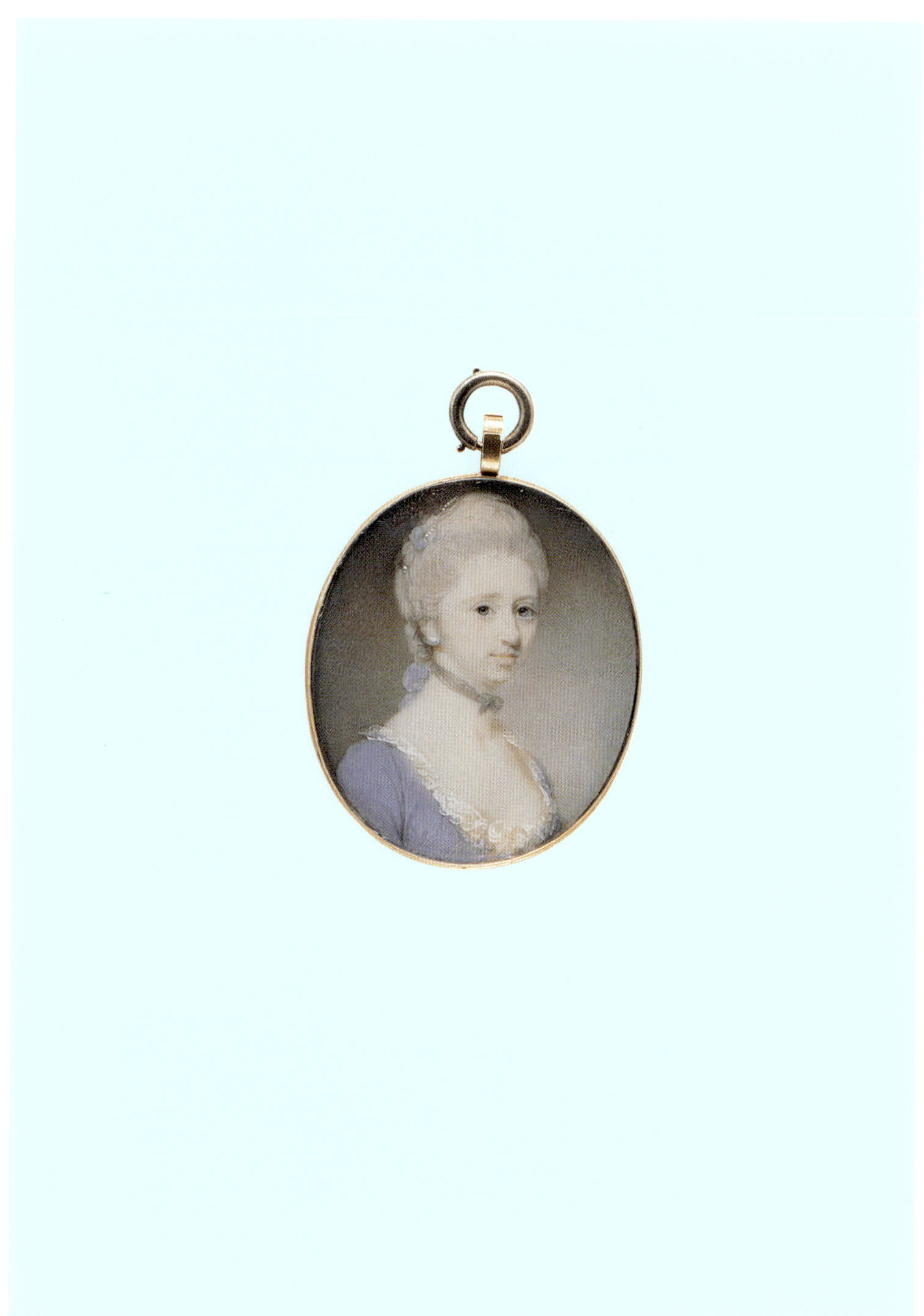

# Jeremiah Meyer RA

**29  A Vice Admiral**
Watercolour on ivory; gold locket frame with plaited hair verso
Oval, 4.4 x 3.5 cm

Bonham's, 2 March 1992 (124); purchased by the Draper estate;
given to Kenwood, 1992  (88029230)

The gentleman wears the undress uniform of a vice admiral, of a
date between c1774 and 1783. Several men would have been
eligible to wear this dress at the time of painting, at the end of the
1770s or early 80s. This type of coat was adopted without authority
and still has a strong resemblance to everyday dress.

   Meyer's great ability as a draughtsman is revealed in this
miniature that bears close inspection. He has made no attempt to
hide his linear technique, but has chosen his colours so carefully
that the delicate lines seem to blend together perfectly. There is a
real sense of character about this portrait. Meyer does not flatter
the sitter, but uses the sitter's direct gaze and recognisable uniform
to create a sense of dignity.

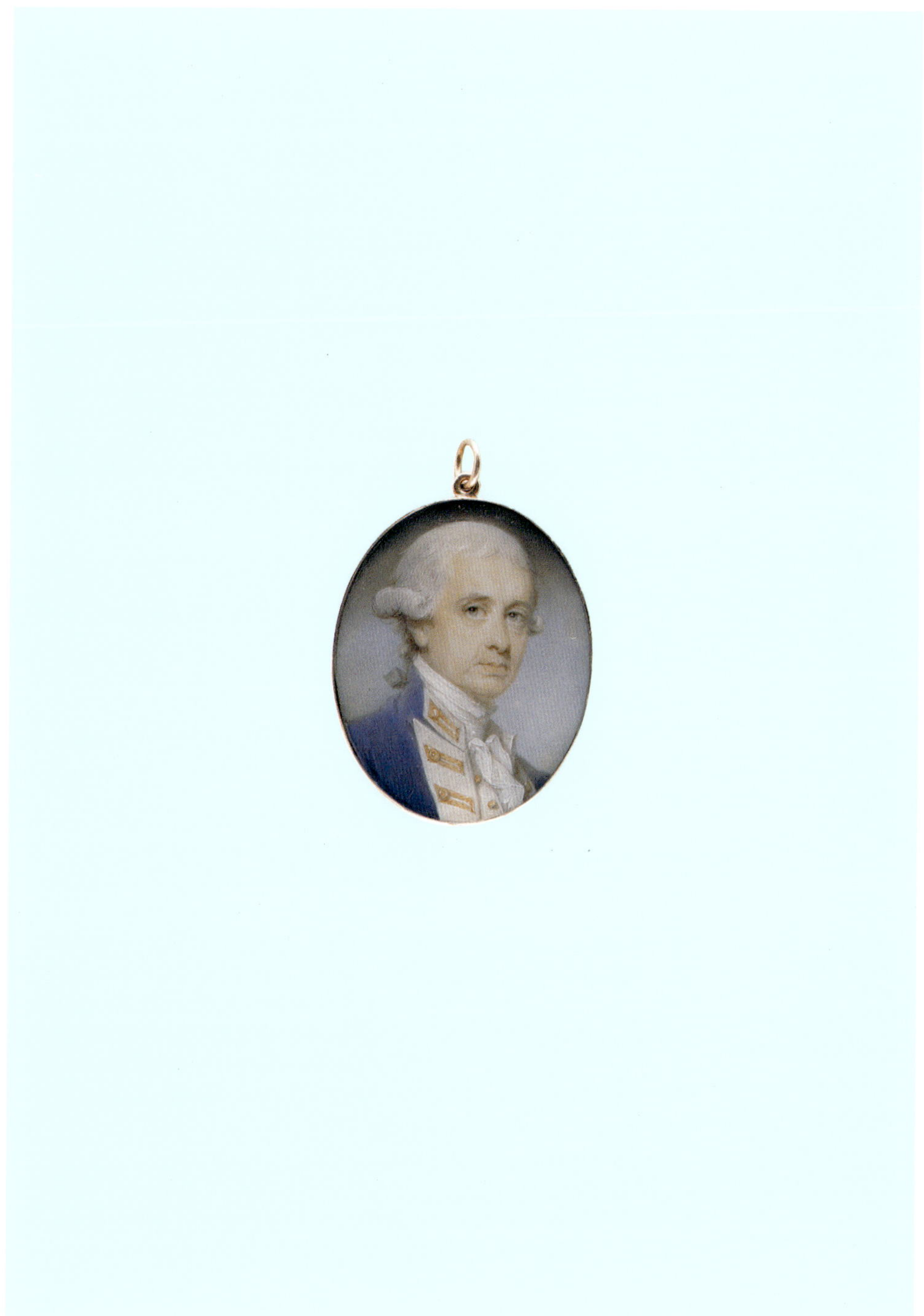

# James Scouler  (c1740–1812)

Scouler was the son of an Edinburgh turner and began his own career making
musical instruments. By the 1750s he was studying drawing in London and
won a prize at the Society of Arts. He exhibited at the Society, the Free
Society of Artists and the Royal Academy during the years 1761 to 1787. Most
of his life was spent in London, apart from a possible spell in India in the late
1780s, where his brother Robert was working.

Scouler's early works are generally small and painted in quite a broad
manner with plenty of gum as a medium. Occasionally these have been
confused with the early work of John Smart, who signed his works with the
same initials. Some later works are of a larger size, and are generally very well
painted in a precise, detailed manner with opaque colours.

### 30  Unknown Young Woman

Watercolour on ivory; gold locket frame. Inscribed by the artist on
the backing paper *This paper must not be taken off*
Oval, 4.2 x 3.5 cm

Limner Antiques, London; purchased by the Draper estate, 1991;
given to Kenwood, 1991  (88029864)

The attribution to Scouler is based on comparison to contemporary
signed works and the peculiar inscription, which only he is known
to have used. The sitter wears a simplified form of dress of about
1760. The colours of the silk are particularly striking against the
warm grey background, and reveal an awareness of general
developments in portraiture. The sitter's purple shawl is well
chosen to add emphasis to her slight figure.

Scouler has elongated the shape of the figure, with its
exaggerated oval face, to add perhaps a sense of sophistication to
his rather limited technique at this time. This combines light
stippling to shade the face with thick, broadly applied gum-based
paint on the body and background.

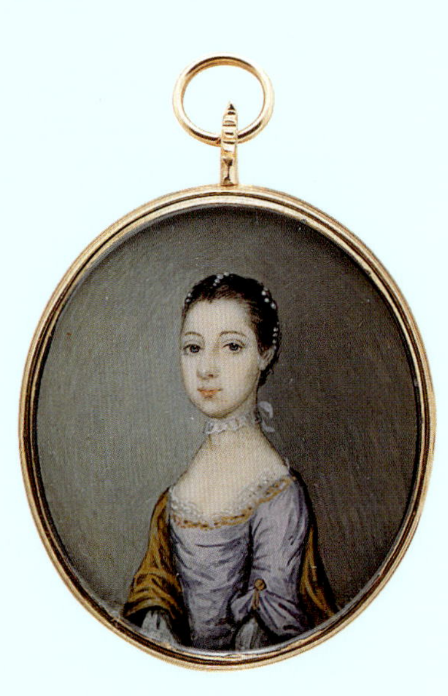

# James Scouler

### 31  Unknown Woman

Watercolour on ivory; gold *fausse-montre* frame with plaited hair
verso. Incised signature, left side *Scouler 1790*
Oval, 7.2 x 5.5 cm

Christie's 4 March 1992 (88); purchased by the Draper estate; given
to Kenwood, 1992  (88029232)

This lady, painted at the beginning of the 1790s, has her hair piled
up in a buffon with ringlets falling at the bottom — the start of the
reduction in size of coiffure during that decade. She wears a white
gown with a double-frilled collar and a tightly gathered blue outer
robe, suggesting that this is her morning dress.

At a time when most British miniature painters were aiming to
use transparent watercolour and ivory to create an image, Scouler
was concentrating on careful brushwork and the use of colour —
showing more in common with contemporary French miniaturists.
To this end, he still used stippling on the face and close hatching in
the background. However, the dress does employ bare ivory with
pencil-like line, an effect that contrasts the lightness of the white
dress material with the figure.

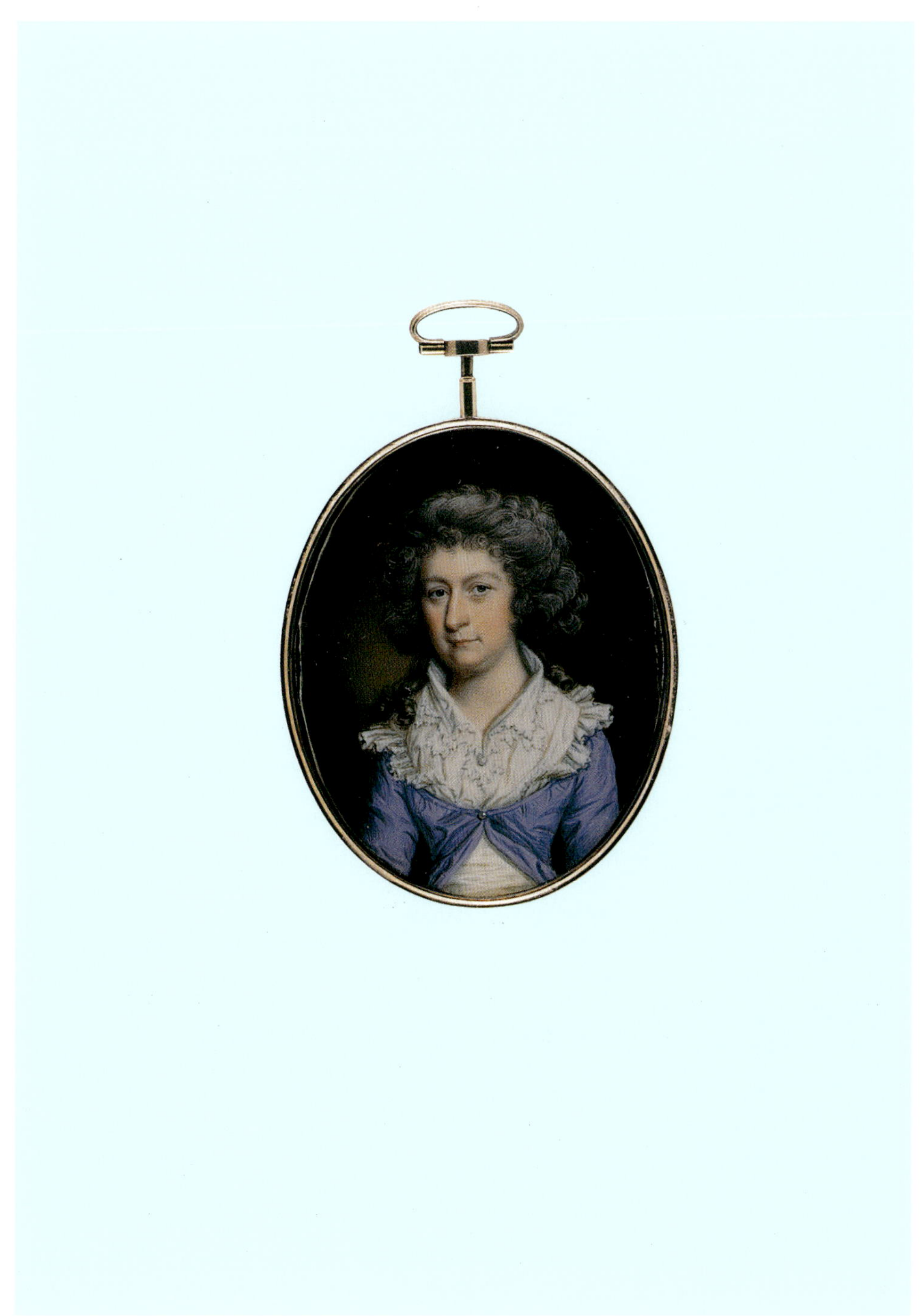

# Thomas Redmond  (c1745–85)

Redmond was born in Brecon, in Wales, and worked as a house painter in Bristol before moving to London, where he studied at the St Martin's Lane Academy. He exhibited at the principal artist societies between 1762 and 1783 from addresses in London and Wales. In 1769 he settled in Bath.

The works of this modest artist are typical of many miniaturists who made a living from an itinerant business, based in the provinces. They are conscientiously finished but sometimes have rather strangely proportioned faces. Redmond usually signed in full or with initials that sometimes appear as 'IR' or 'JR'.

### 32  Unknown Woman

Watercolour on ivory; gold bracelet frame. Signed left side, *IR 1762*
Oval, 3.7 x 3.0 cm

Sotheby's 20 Dec. 1994 (544); purchased by the Draper estate; given to Kenwood, 1994  (88029840)

This lady wears a warm pink dress with lace trimming. Her hair is worn up with a flower ornament as a form of head covering. Overall her dress suggests a woman of some standing.

Redmond paints here with soft, blended brush strokes which are very neat. Somehow, he does not succeed in making all the carefully painted parts of the face sit together well. The sitter's rather pinched mouth, in particular, gives her an unfortunate, smug look.

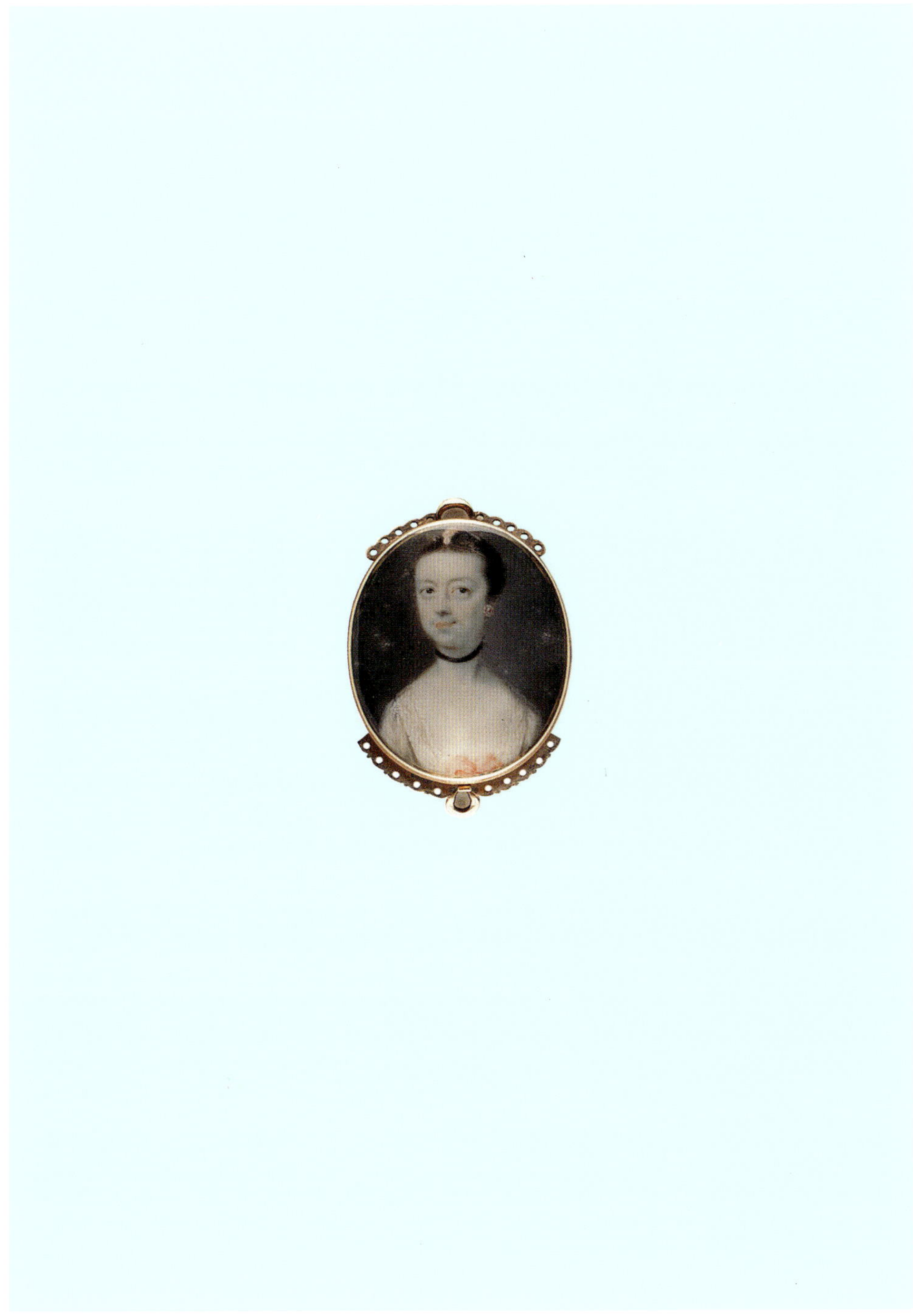

# English School, eighteenth or early nineteenth century

### 33  George III  (1738–1820)
Watercolour on ivory; set into a small gold ring
Oval, 1.3 x 1.0 cm (shown opposite at actual size (above) and twice actual size (below))

H. Knowles-Brown (Jewellers), Hampstead; Marie Draper, 1973; given to Kenwood, 1988  (88029176)

Profile images of George III, in either civilian or military dress, were a common form of popular image of the King, especially when his son George, Prince of Wales, was out of public favour for attacking his father. Allan Ramsay (1713–84) had painted a profile for the coinage, showing George in a bag wig and wearing his garter star, and this probably provided the prototype for subsequent images such as this presentation ring.

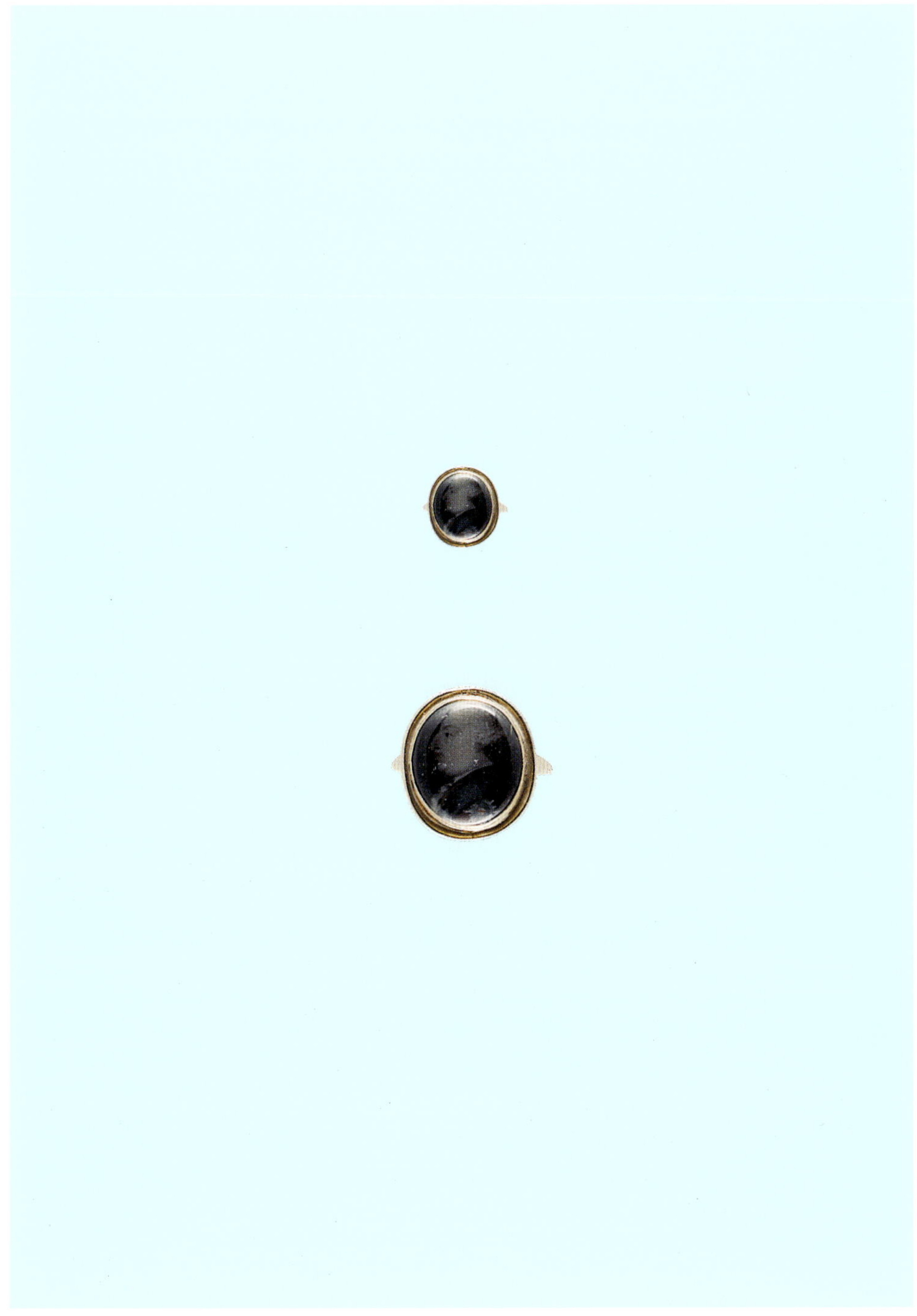

# Richard Crosse  (1742–1810)

Crosse came from a prosperous Devonshire family but had the misfortune to
be deaf and mute, a condition that caused him to lead a rather solitary life.
He started painting for pleasure, but embarked on a career as a painter after
winning a prize at the Society of Arts. His beautifully executed works and
prolific output made him a popular miniaturist and he was made joint Painter
in Enamel to George III in 1788. Crosse worked in various media from his
home in Henrietta Street, Covent Garden. Much can be understood of his
business from the extensive sitter books that have survived.

Although Crosse rarely signed his miniatures, they can easily be recognised
by his bluish shading (sometimes exacerbated by the fading of flesh colours),
and neatly drawn strands of hair. The eyes are also often emphasised by
being dark, with heavy eyebrows. He occasionally painted large miniatures
(for the period) such as his self-portrait (Victoria and Albert Museum).

### 34  An Army Officer
Watercolour on ivory; adapted gold bracelet frame
Oval, 3.5 x 2.8 cm

Limner Antiques, London; Marie Draper, 1970; given to Kenwood,
1988  (88029873)

The sitter probably wears the uniform of the 2nd Regiment of Foot,
also known as the Queen's Royal Regiment. At the date when this
was painted, in the mid-1770s, such uniforms still bore much
resemblance to gentlemen's attire apart from the trimmings, and
were still open to interpretation by officers.

This miniature shows Crosse's excellence as a draughtsman, as
he creates a very three-dimensional figure with his distinctive,
somewhat linear technique. The detail around the features of the
face and his treatment of the hair with a mass of neat lines are
unmistakable. Similarly, the angle of the eye lids and brows are
characteristics that he managed to use constantly without them
becoming a distracting mannerism. His colouring of the face is
rather grey, which tends to emphasise the portrait's graphic quality,
but the warm background colouring does bring out the form of the
figure.

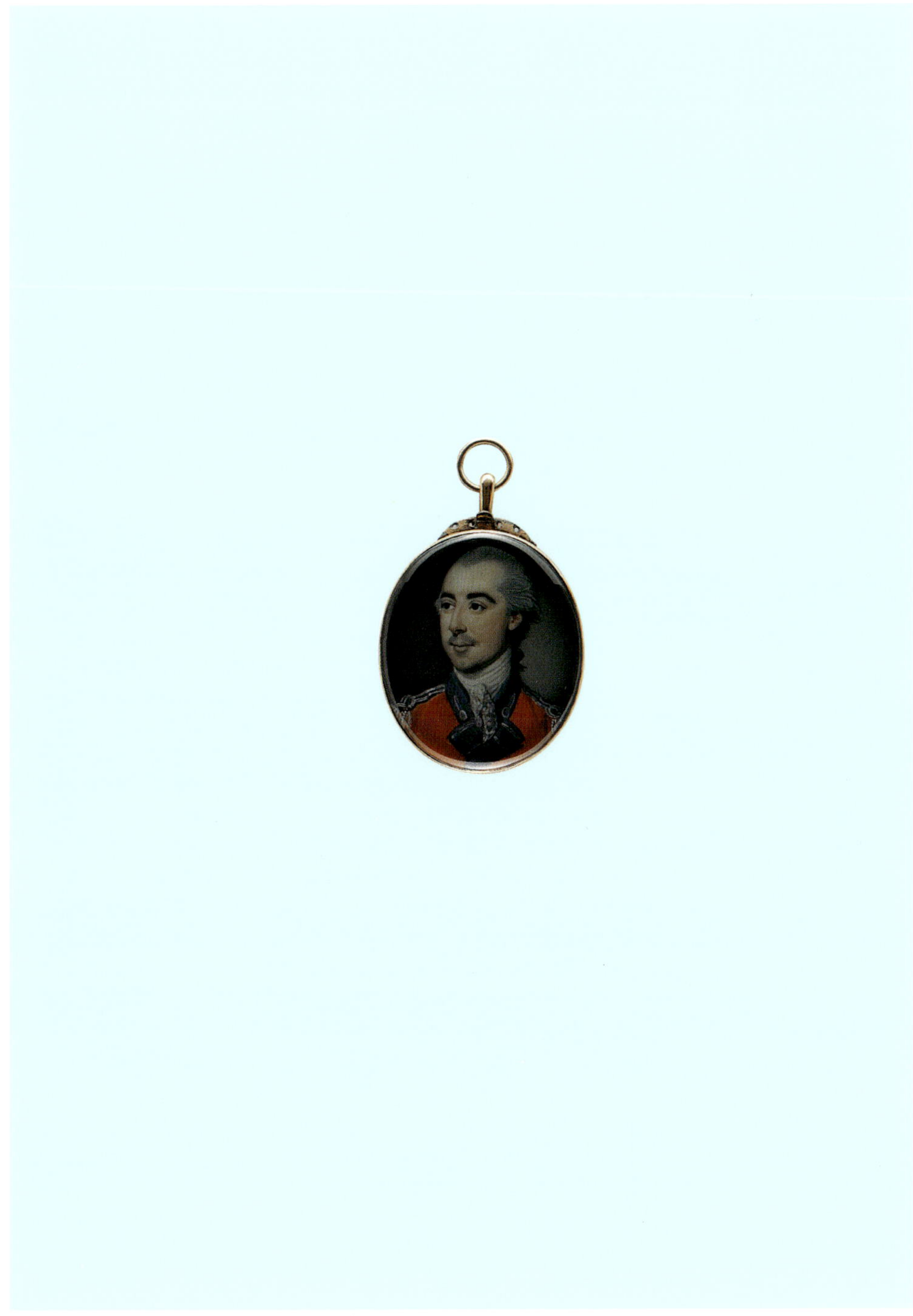

# Richard Crosse

**35  Lucy Nicholas**
Watercolour on ivory; gilt metal locket frame with blue glass and
hair verso (altered)
Oval, 3.3 x 2.8 cm

?The Gell family, Hopton; by descent to Lt-Col Chandos-Pole;
Christie's, Newnham Hall 11 July 1994 (294); purchased by the
Draper estate; given to Kenwood, 1994  (88029825)

Crosse painted children with particular charm, as in this portrait of
Miss Nicholas aged about five, holding her pet King Charles spaniel.
It would seem to have been painted around 1785–90. His choice of
colours, with a clear blue background and the girl's white dress
with blue sash, is pleasing. Although there is no record of this
commission in Crosse's remaining sitter books, he did receive £8 8s
for 'a copy of a picture' from a Mrs Nichlas (*sic*) in May 1779.

This artist's gift for characterisation is apparent even with such a
simple subject. There is a sense of light-heartedness in the way the
young girl's neatly painted hair, with its glossy sheen, mirrors the
dog's, which he has dashed off with a few brush strokes.

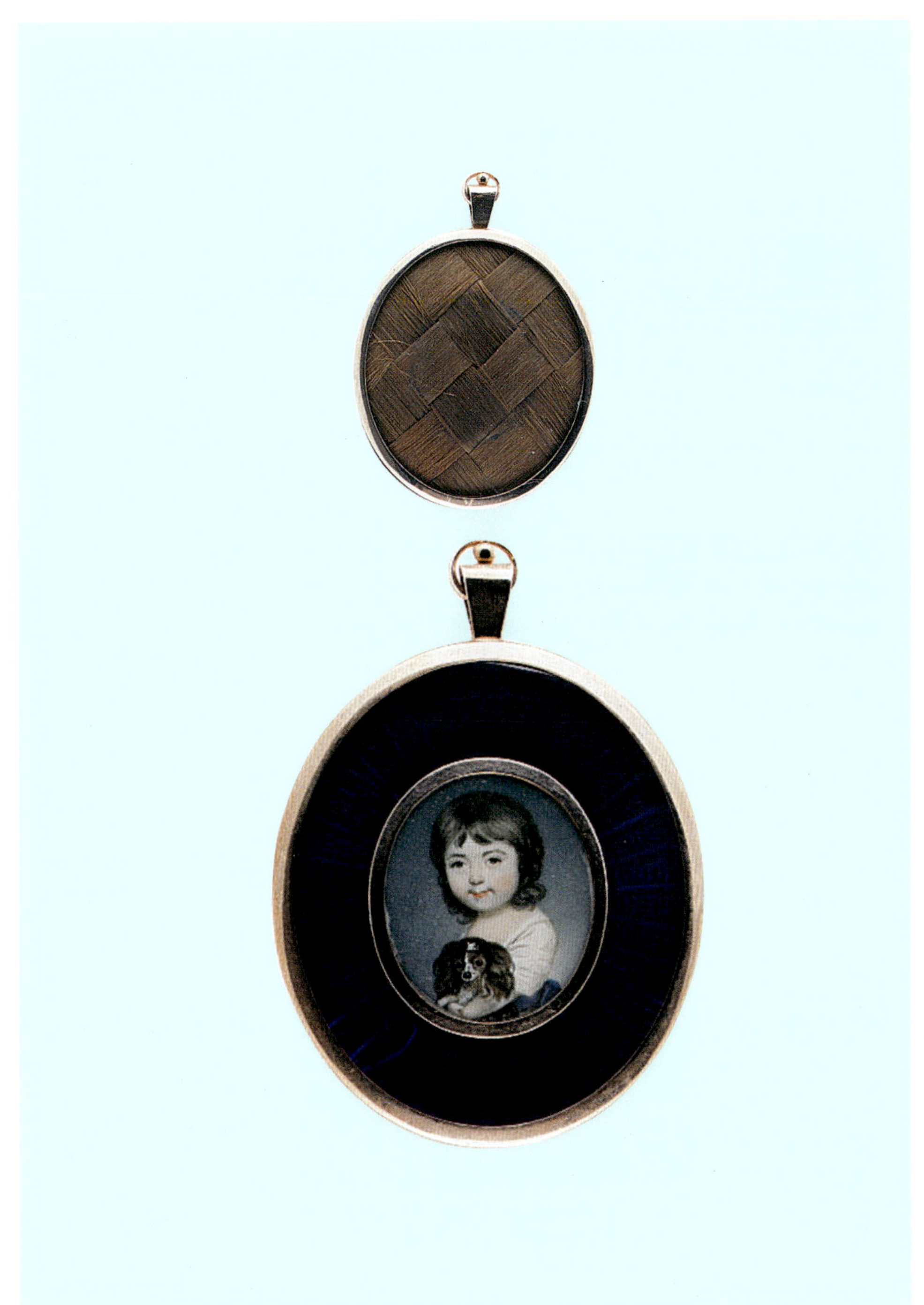

# Ozias Humphry RA  (1742–1810)

A fellow Devon artist with Cosway, who was born in the same year, Humphry was a talented draughtsman and painted miniatures that have a strong affinity with the work of his friend, Joshua Reynolds.

At thirteen he trained with William Shipley in London, but returned home and moved to Bath, where he was apprenticed to Samuel Collins (cats 25,26). When Collins fled creditors in 1762, Humphry took over his business. In Bath he lodged with the Linley family of musicians, friends of Gainsborough, who encouraged him to return to London (1764). There he built up a good reputation, exhibiting regularly and joining the Society of Artists. One celebrated miniature was bought by George III for the exorbitant sum of 100 guineas.

Between 1773 and 1777 Humphry travelled to Italy with George Romney and returned with the intention of concentrating on oils, but never did, perhaps because of worsening eyesight. His ambitions for greater financial reward then led him to India in 1785. This two-year trip was not a career success but did lead him to paint some interesting Indian sitters. He became a Royal Academician in 1791 and spent his last working decade drawing larger portraits on paper, until his eyesight failed completely.

## 36  Unknown Woman

Watercolour on ivory; later gold-coloured metal bracelet (adapted)
Oval, 3.8 x 3.0 cm

Limner Antiques, London; purchased by the Draper estate, 1991; given to Kenwood, 1991 (88029865)

This work has much in common with contemporary portraits by Reynolds. The lady is wearing somewhat informal dress of the mid-1770s, with its oriental influences. Her hair is covered with a gold woven, gauze scarf and her loose dress is also trimmed with gold embroidery.

Whilst Humphry's miniatures of men are full of character, those of women, as here, often appear somewhat detached and coolly painted. Allowing for some fading of the thinly applied flesh tones, the warm colours used here are an attempt to follow Reynolds' lead by alluding to the appearance of old master portraits. Humphry applies the minimum of soft brush strokes to create the face with some success and he uses a dark background to good effect.

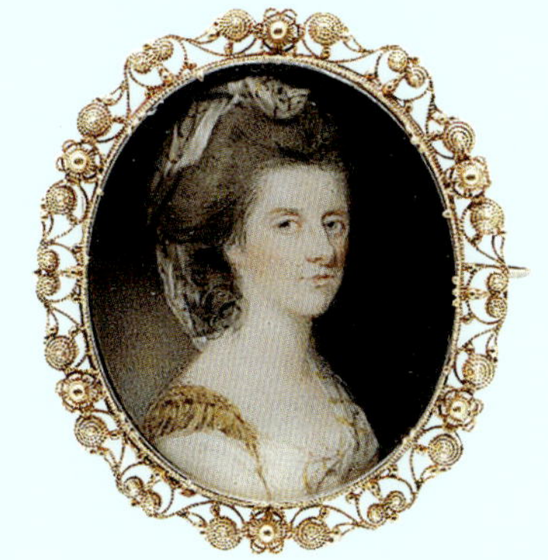

# John Donaldson  (1737–1801)

The son of an Edinburgh glove maker, John Donaldson was an itinerant painter and sometime poet and inventor. He was a good draughtsman and gained prizes in Edinburgh and London, where he became a fellow of the Society of Artists in 1764. As well as producing miniatures on ivory and enamel, he worked as a painter for the Worcester porcelain manufactory.

He was not successful in his scientific ventures, in spite of finding a method of preserving food on voyages. His aspirations as an artist must have been great for he published an essay on the *Elements of Beauty*. After partially losing his sight, he died in Islington. Donaldson's works on ivory are quite well drawn and his portraits of women are particularly decorative, with much emphasis on the detail of their dress and hair. The colouring of their faces can make them look rather made up, as he tends to use pink flesh tones with blue shading.

### 37  Lady Hobhouse (Charlotte Cam) (d 1791)
Watercolour on ivory; gold locket frame
Oval, 5.6 x 4.0 cm

Christie's 14 Oct. 1992 (36); purchased by the Draper estate; given to Kenwood, 1992  (88029800)

A good quality version of an original (formerly Bayne-Powell collection). Charlotte was the daughter of Samuel Cam M.P. of Chantry House, Bradford, Wiltshire. She married a barrister, Sir Benjamin Hobhouse in 1785. Her son, John, was a writer and close friend of Lord Byron.

Charlotte Cam's hair is elaborately dressed with curls and pearls in the looser style of the later 1780s. This makes her white gown and blue jacket seem almost modest.

This portrait has a little in common with the work of Andrew Plimer, with its emphasis on the eyes and nose using shadow and fine dark lines around the features. However, Donaldson is altogether harsher and more laboured in comparison. Nevertheless, the features and hair are finely painted with delicate stipple and hatching.

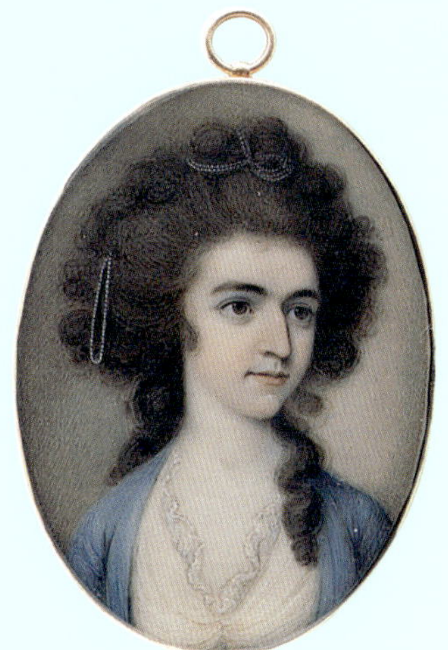

# Richard Cosway RA  (1742–1821)

Cosway was the most successful miniature painter of the late eighteenth century and equally one of the most notorious members of the London art world of his day. He was born in Okeford, Devon, into an educated middle-class family where there were paintings for him to copy. His precocious talent led him to London at the age of twelve where he trained with Thomas Hudson and then at William Shipley's drawing school. In 1754 he won first prize at the new Society of Arts in a class for under-fourteens, in which Smart (cats 40,41) was runner up.

He worked in pencil and oil as well as producing miniatures, the medium in which he found early success. Works of the 1760s and 70s are small scale, neatly drawn and well coloured but with little of the verve found in his later miniatures. During the 1770s Cosway gained a reputation as a publicity-seeking dandy, in spite of his small size and unusual looks. His social position improved further with marriage to Maria Hadfield, who had been brought up and trained as an artist in Florence and was a friend of Angelica Kauffman.

The early 1780s saw Cosway moving to Pall Mall and gaining the patronage of the Prince of Wales after painting his morganatic wife, Mrs Fitzherbert. Cosway's lodgings in Schomberg House became a magnet for society and something of an unusual art gallery as well. His works during these years led the field in both their free use of washes and informality of subject and execution. However, his career became dogged by his own behaviour, which attracted public mockery, as well as relations with Maria, who spent several long periods in Italy alone, after the birth of their daughter. In later years he lost favour with the Prince Regent as he became more eccentric. After a series of illnesses he sold off his art collection and moved to a more modest home.  When he died Maria moved to Lodi in Italy, where she had founded a convent and college which remains as a memorial and archive.

### 38  Unknown Man
Watercolour on ivory; gold locket frame with blue glass verso
Oval, 4.3 x 3.8 cm

Limner Antiques, London; Marie Draper, 1973; given to Kenwood, 1988  (88029178)

This modest-sized portrait of a gentleman was painted around 1790. To judge by his dress the sitter was not particularly distinguished and Cosway has done him justice without untoward effort. His hair is powdered and tied with a ribbon, soon to be outmoded, and he wears a loose cravat or shirt ruffle with a blue coat.

Cosway has neatly drawn the face, with his usual emphasis on the eyes. The light, hatched modelling and linear treatment of the hair in grey are more like a pencil drawing than watercolour. He has used his typical, cloudy sky background, which is built up of rapid transparent hatching. In contrast the sitter's coat has been floated on with a larger brush and the detail added when dry.

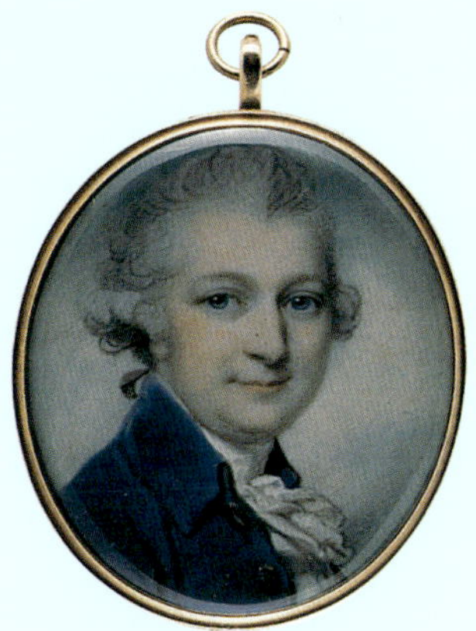

# Richard Cosway RA

### 39  Unknown Woman

Watercolour on ivory; modern gilt metal locket
Oval, 5.2 x 4.4 cm

Bonham's 2 March 1992 (124); purchased by the Draper estate;
given to Kenwood, 1992  (88029229)

This young lady wears an elaborate collar and neckerchief
arrangement of stiffened muslin that shows Cosway's economy of
means with his sitter's dress to great effect. Her shorter hair and
high-waisted dress, tied with a coloured sash, suggest a date of the
early 1790s. Cosway uses this dress to set off her loosely worn hair,
which he has painted with decorous, parallel brush strokes.

Cosway was at the height of his powers when this miniature was
painted and although not ambitious, it bears all the characteristics
of his work that made others imitate him so often. The face is
carefully worked with pale brown hatching over delicate washes.
The hair is very linear and more opaque. Most typically, the white
of her dress is sketched in, using grey brush strokes in a pencil-like
manner over largely unpainted ivory. This last effect was perhaps
Cosway's most important contribution to the technique of
miniatures.

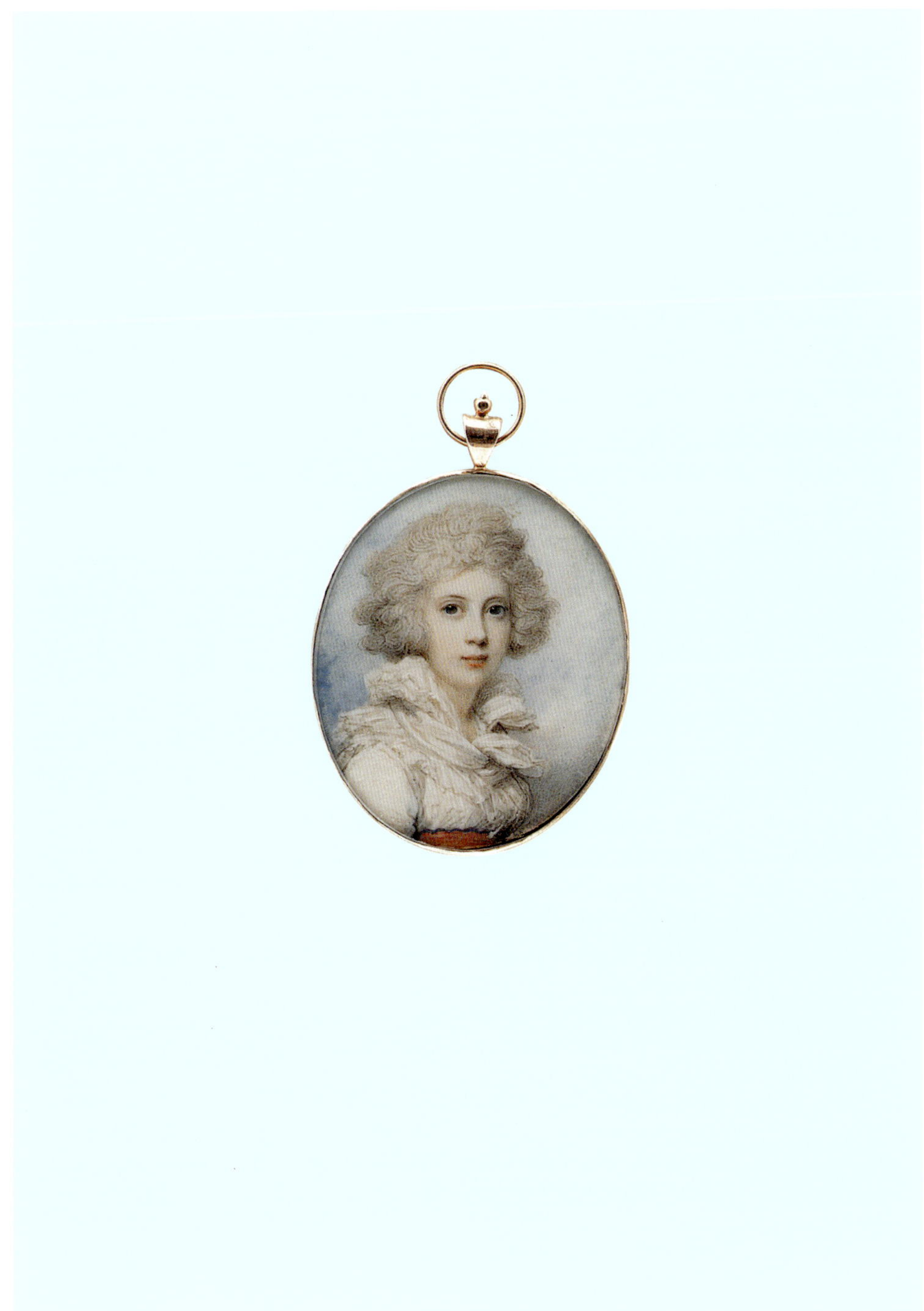

# John Smart (1742/3–1811)

Smart is one of the outstanding miniaturists of the later eighteenth century with an unmistakeable style of his own. Little is known about his early life until he came to the attention of the London art world at the first competition of the Society of Arts, when he came second to Richard Cosway in the class for under-fourteens. He then won several first prizes under the tutelage of William Shipley at his drawing academy in St Martin's Lane. Smart frequently exhibited at the Society of Artists (of which he was president in 1778) and Royal Academy, until 1783.

In spite of success in London he went to Madras in 1784 and remained in India for eleven years, where he painted officials of the East India Company and the Indian aristocracy. On his return to London be worked from Grafton Street and later Russell Place off fashionable Fitzroy Square. He married three times, but his son John, who was also a miniaturist, was born out of wedlock to Sarah Midgeley.

John, the father, was a brilliant draughtsman and skilled colourist. He often made pencil and watercolour preparatory sketches and occasionally worked in enamel. His works manage both to portray a convincing likeness and flatter most of his sitters at the same time. They are also enormously detailed, very three-dimensional looking and brilliantly coloured.

### 40  Anne Farquhar (d1793)
Watercolour on ivory; gold locket frame. Signed lower left *J.S. / 1770*; engraved *Anne Widow of Dr Harvie and Wife of Sir Walter Farquhar Died 1793. By John Smart*
Oval, 4.4 x 3.5 cm

Limner Antiques, London; Marie Draper, 1986; given to Kenwood, 1988 (88029880)

This portrait captures with great vividness the likeness of the young Anne Farquhar, who after the death of her first husband married another doctor, Sir Walter Farquhar (1738–1819). He was a Scottish army surgeon who became a physician to the Prince of Wales. Anne has her hair piled up in the fashion of the early 1770s, with a gauze and gold-thread scarf trailing down a tress of hair. She is wearing a light blue gown with pearl necklace, jewelled clasps and full, pinned-on sleeves, reflecting the interest in the dress of Van Dyck's era around the time of this portrait.

The miniature displays Smart's very fine technique, using bright, warm colours to model the face and carefully observed detail, particularly in the eyes and hair.

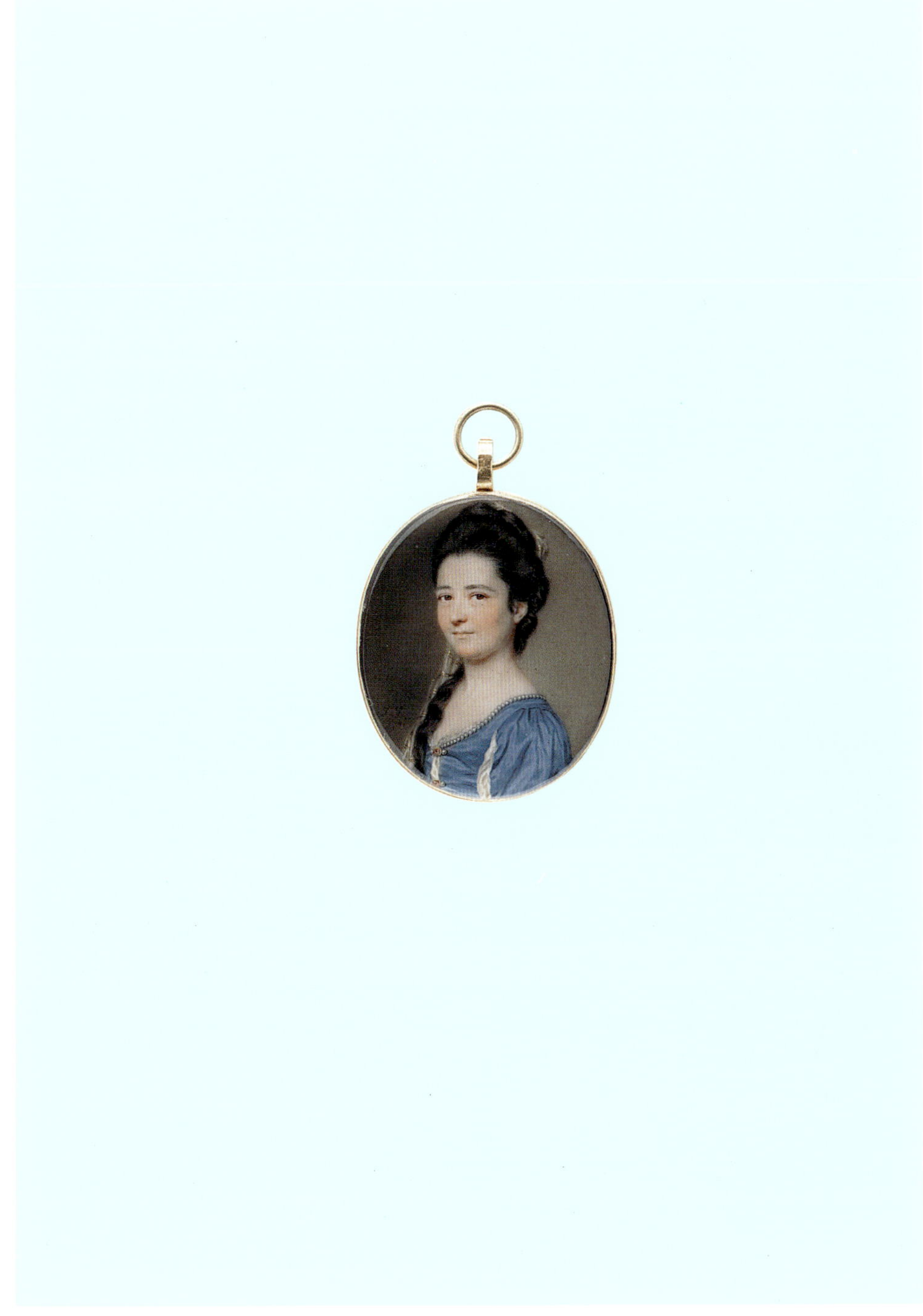

# John Smart

**41  Lord John Augustus Hervey (1757–96)**
Watercolour on ivory; gold setting in a tortoiseshell bonbonnière.
Signed lower left, *J.S./ 1782*.  Box engraved, *John Augustus Hervey.
Commander of / HMS Zealous died at Sea, 10th June 1766*  [*sic*]
Oval, 3.9 x 3.1 cm

By descent to G.E[llis?], 1917; Christie's 11 May 1994 (88);
purchased by the Draper estate; given to Kenwood, 1994
(88029820)

Lit.: Foskett, 1964, p. 68

Lord Hervey was the eldest son of the Earl-Bishop, 4th Earl of
Bristol, who was a great traveller and creator of the extraordinary
rotunda at Ickworth, Suffolk. Lord John is shown in the uniform of
a naval captain, for he took after his uncle, the third Earl, who was a
distinguished admiral. As the inaccurate inscription on the box
records, he died quite young, in action.
   This miniature shows Smart in his best, precise manner on a
small scale. The face is firmly modelled, without resorting to the
use of blue shading or heavy lines. He is also remarkably good at
rendering texture, so that the face has a lively, slightly shiny finish,
whereas the coat is matt except for the gold lace.

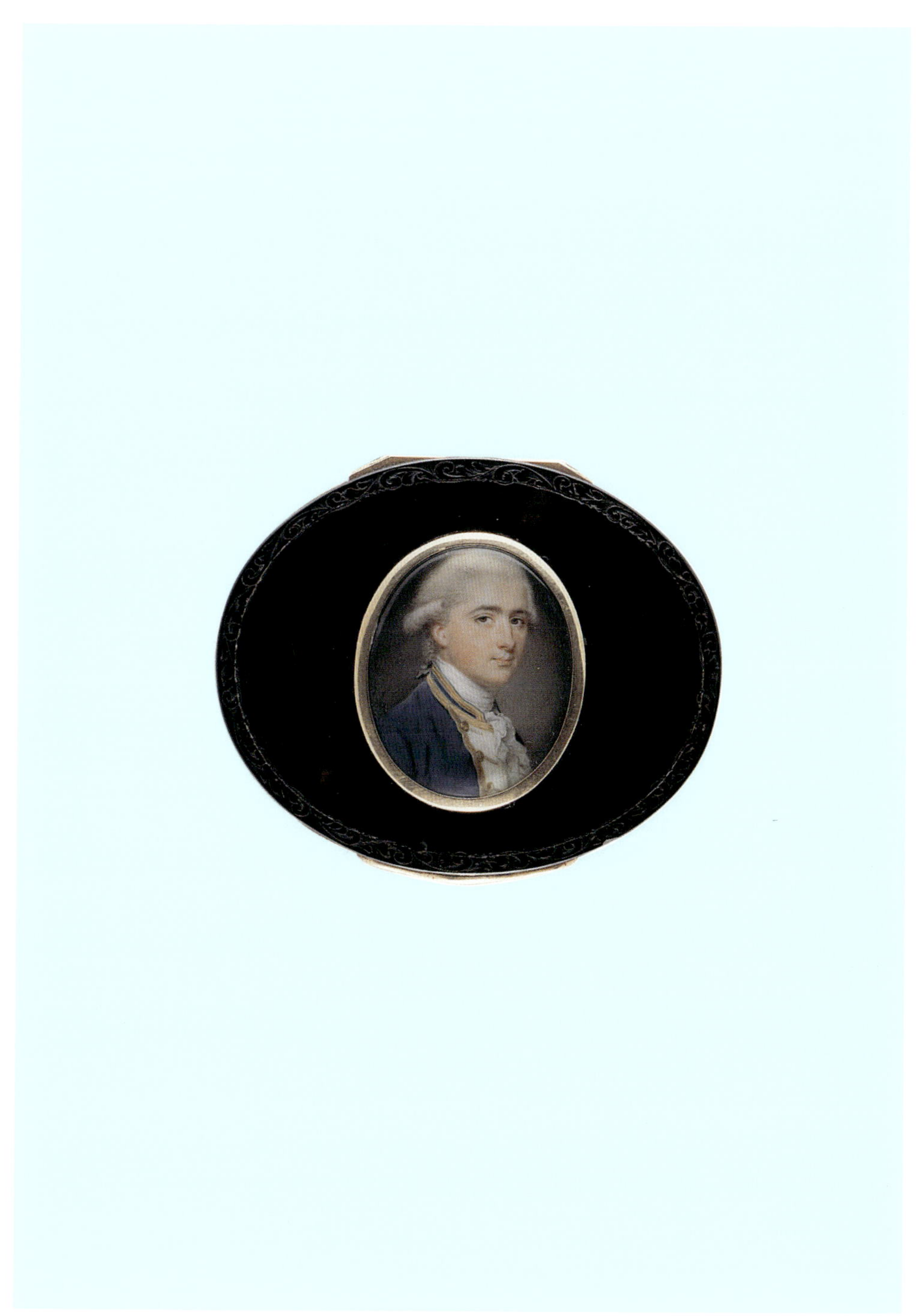

# Samuel Andrews (?1767–1807)

Reputedly an Irishman by birth, Samuel Andrews established himself in India painting members of the East India Company and the military, as well as wealthy Indians. He arrived in Madras in 1791 and by 1795 was living in John Smart's former home. He imitated and copied the work of his gifted predecessor, although his own work is less subtle and convincing. By 1798 Andrews had moved to Calcutta and his miniatures and grisaille profiles are often signed with the name of that city. His short life ended abroad at Patna.

### 42  Major Alexander Allan (1764–1820),
after John Smart
Watercolour on ivory; gilt metal mount in a japanned frame
Oval, 7.1 x 5.7 cm

R. L. Bayne-Powell; Sotheby's 11 Nov. 1994 (128); purchased by the Draper Estate; given to Kenwood, 1994  (88029832)

Lit.: Bayne-Powell, *Catalogue of Portrait Miniatures in the Fitzwilliam Museum*, Cambridge 1985 pp 200–201 for the Smart original

This is a fine copy of Smart's portrait of 1787, which is in the Fitzwilliam Museum, Cambridge (no. 3881). Major Allan was an East India Company director at Madras and deputy quartermaster-general during the Mysore War of 1799. He is shown wearing the coat of that rank, with a black neckband and pleated white jabot. The sitter was also MP for Berwick and made a baronet in 1819.

Andrews' copy is faithful to Smart's original, not only in detail but also in style of execution. Smart's portrait excellently captures the youthful, slightly plump face of his sitter and Andrews has successfully imitated his appearance. However, his style is distinguishable and is notably less refined and natural-looking, particularly around the sitter's mouth and in his powdered hair.

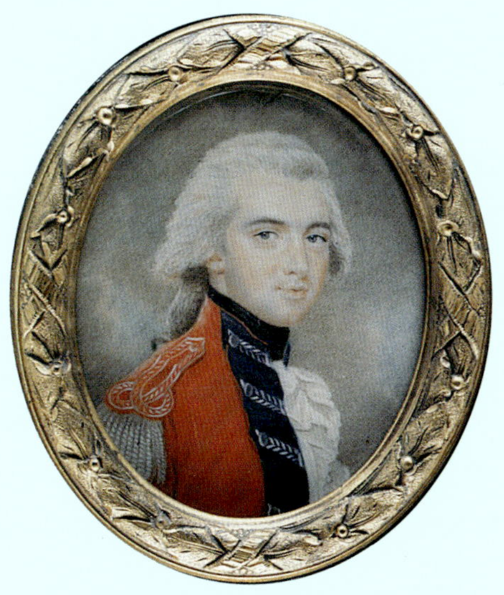

# Samuel Andrews

### 43  Harry Blunt

Watercolour and gouache on ivory; ebonised moulded frame.
Signed lower edge *S Andrews, Calcutta / Jan*. 1803
Oval, 8.5 x 6.5 cm

Limner Antiques, London; Marie Draper; given to Kenwood, 1989
(88029846)

This is a typical example of Andrews' grisaille portraits in profile, which he painted while in Calcutta. These are painted in grey watercolour against a smooth and opaque, brownish background. The technique was the artist's answer to the relatively inexpensive silhouettes of the period that were rapidly executed in both paint and cut-paper. The resulting image is in fact closer to the mass-produced portraits of more famous men made in stoneware and opaque glass by Josiah Wedgwood and James Tassie respectively.

Mr Blunt has the popular short hairstyle of the early nineteenth century and high stock and collar. While he may have appreciated the relatively low price such a portrait would have exacted, he no doubt also enjoyed the classical associations of the simulated relief bust, still a fashionable pretension at this time.

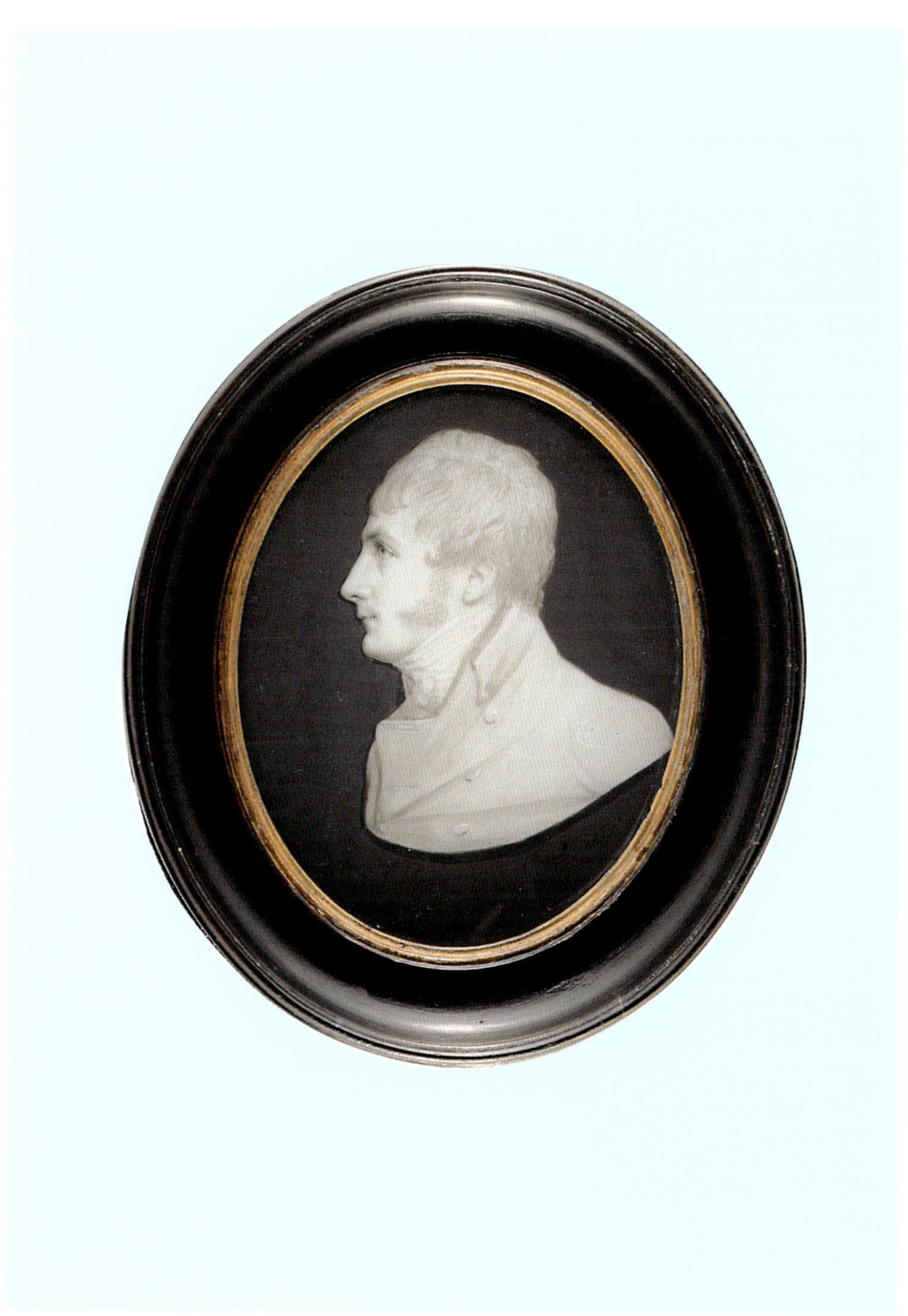

# Richard Bull  (fl 1777–1809)

A relatively minor Irish artist who studied in Dublin and exhibited there
between 1777 and 1780. Around 1790 Bull moved to London where he
worked and exhibited from 101 Pall Mall, from 1794 until 1809. His neat, linear
style attracted a distinguished clientele that included members of the royal
family, Admiral Lord Nelson and the actor Charles Kemble. He produced a
very good miniature of George, Prince of Wales, in profile, wearing the
uniform of his own, 10th Light Dragoon Regiment. Bull also painted a version
on paper with eighteen fellow officers (collection, HM the Queen).

### 44  Unknown Woman
Watercolour on ivory; gold bracelet frame with plaited hair and
seed-pearl surround, the verso with hair inset. Signed indistinctly
lower right with date *17[?88]*
Oval, 3.8 x 3.1 cm

Sotheby's 10 Mar. 1994 (27); purchased by the Draper estate; given
to Kenwood, 1994  (88029815)

This young woman wears her powdered hair loosely curled and
long about her shoulders, which corresponds with a date in the late
1780s (the inscribed date being now largely illegible). Her gown
follows the artistic convention of the period of a vaguely classical,
but ultimately timeless, form of dress.
   Bull's work here is heavily influenced by the great late
eighteenth-century miniaturists such as Cosway and Andrew Plimer.
The drawing is rather weak, but there is a certain decorative charm
in the fine brushwork seen in the sitter's hair and the carefully
hatched sky background. This artist also produced pictures using
hair, and it seems likely that he himself made the very fine wreath
of plaited hair and pearls surrounding the miniature.

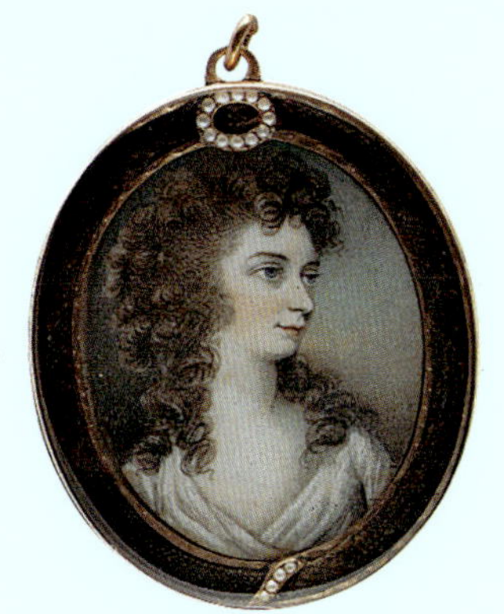

# Charles Shirreff (c1750–fl1809)

One of the more talented and individual miniaturists at the end of the
eighteenth century, Shirreff came from Scotland but was in London, attending
the Royal Academy Schools, in 1769. He won a prize in 1772 and exhibited
until 1831. Shirreff was deaf and dumb, which may have encouraged him to
take a great interest in theatre. This led him to paint some ambitious
miniatures of Mrs Siddons and also Charles Kemble in a stage setting. In 1795
he achieved his ambition to go to India as an artist and worked in Madras and
Calcutta before returning to London in 1809. He found a good clientele
during his long stay in India and one of the reasons for his return may have
been to make money from publication of his own 'finger alphabet'. Shirreff is
thought to have eventually retired to Bath.

Characteristics of his work are an often unflattering approach to his sitters
– sometimes with engaging results – and  very regular use of cross hatching
all over his pictures.

### 45 'Mrs Lothian'

Watercolour on ivory; gold *fausse-montre* frame with enamel and
(formerly) jewelled setting and hair verso. Recent label identifies
sitter
Oval, 5.8 x 4.8 cm

Bonham's, 22 March 1994 (191); purchased by the Draper estate;
given to Kenwood, 1994  (88029816)

Painted before Shirreff's Indian period, c1790, the sitter still has the
puffed up hairstyle of the end of the 1780s. Her simple dress
matches the exaggerated hair with a very large white fichu that
covers her shoulders.

Shirreff's use of watercolour cross hatching is apparent
throughout this miniature, especially in the shadow areas. Like
most artists of the period he has enlarged the eyes but generally
his modelling of the features is strong and effective. His intention
here seems to have been to create a good likeness rather than to
flatter.

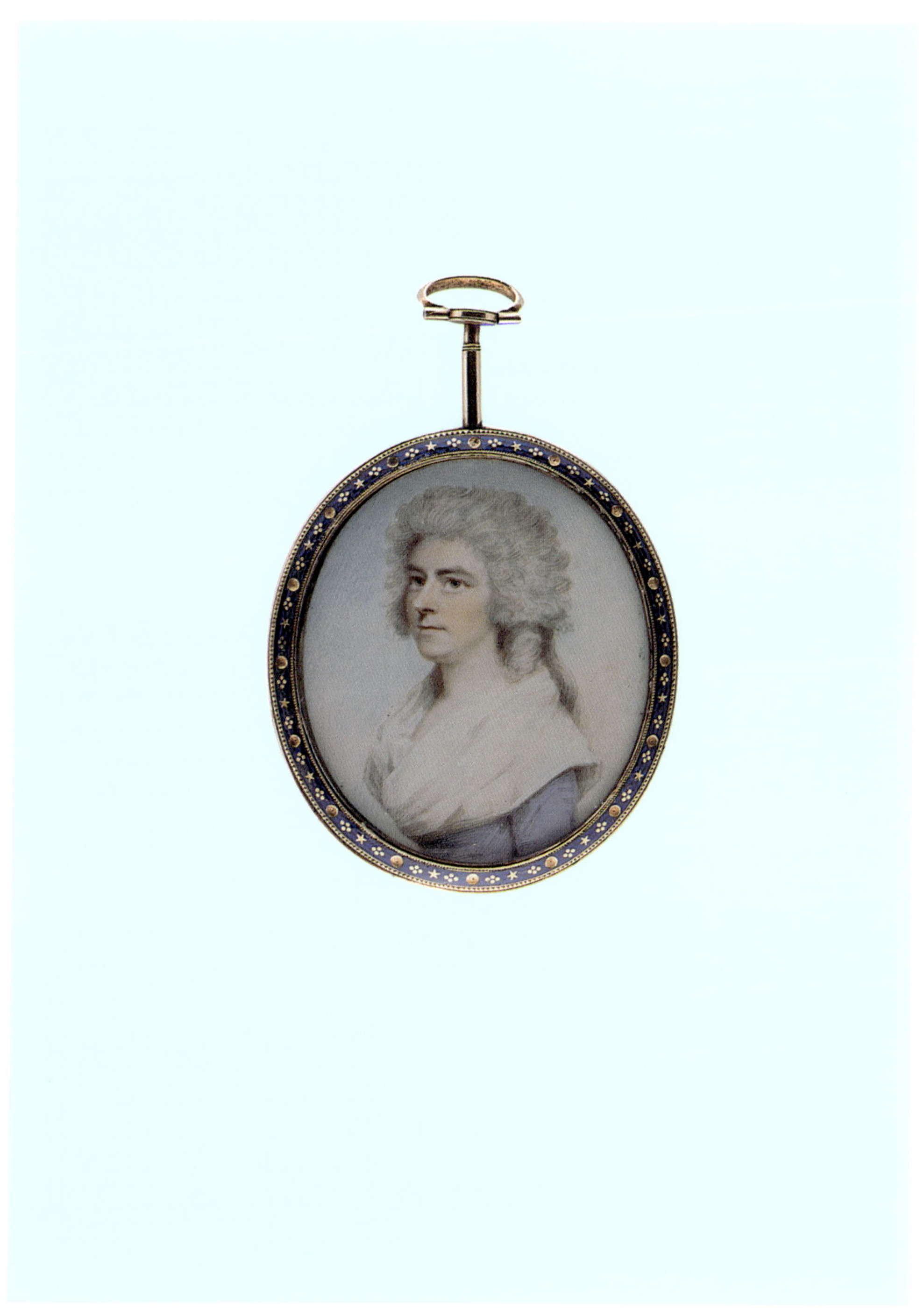

# William Grimaldi (1751–1830)

Born in Shoreditch, London, Grimaldi came from a European aristocratic family.  He studied under the portrait painter and miniaturist Thomas Worlidge and worked in Paris in the 1770s and 80s – a strong influence on his miniature painting. Grimaldi exhibited often, particularly at the Royal Academy and worked in the provinces as well as London. He was rewarded with patronage of the royal family, becoming Miniature Painter to the Duke and Duchess of York, Prince of Wales (1806) and George IV (1824), for whom he made several copies of full-sized portraits.

Grimaldi worked both in watercolour and enamel, and continental influences can be seen in his work. Blue and red shading were often employed for his sitters' faces. He worked in more than one distinctive style, but helpfully, often signed. At his best Grimaldi rivals the leading Regency miniaturists.

## Attributed to William Grimaldi

### 52  Unknown Officer
Watercolour on ivory; gilt metal mount
Oval, 7.3 x 6.0 cm

Bonham's 12 July 1993 (169); purchased by the Draper estate; given to Kenwood, 1993  (88029807)

This young subaltern is distinguished by the single epaulette. His uniform and the style of the miniature date the portrait to the end of the 1780s. His regiment may be one of the foot guards, but cannot be clearly identified, especially as the artist has left out the detail of his shoulder belt plate, which usually had a regimental badge.

The miniature has a lively surface with much blue shading to the face, both characteristics of Grimaldi. What is not so typical is the rather flat treatment of the officer's coat, with the coarse hatching used to shade it. Grimaldi tended to use blended stipple effects or worked-over washes for his backgrounds, rather than the cross hatching used here. It is possible that this miniature is unfinished, making an attempt at attribution more difficult.

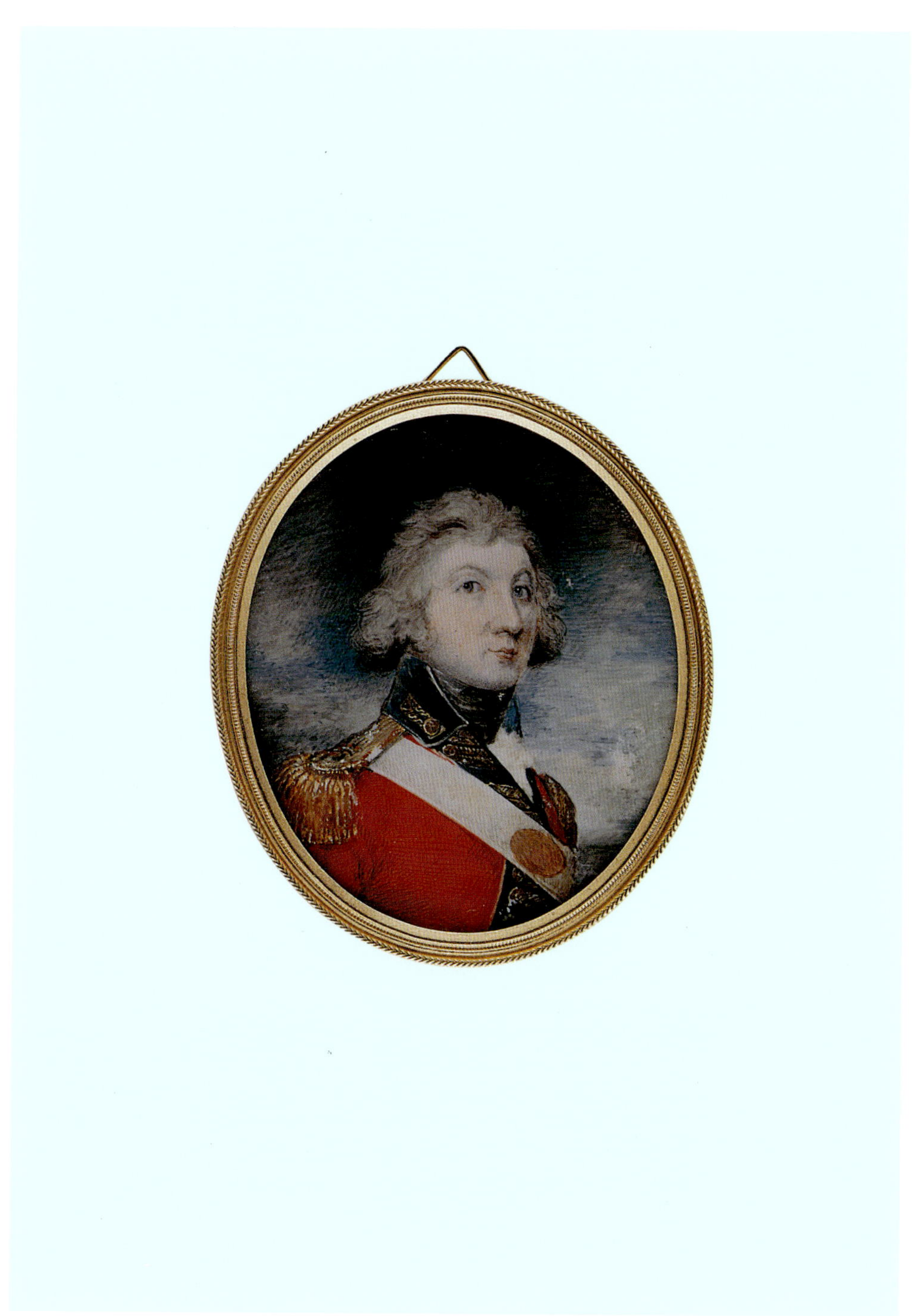

# Edward Miles  (1752–1828)

Miles was born in Yarmouth, Norfolk, and took up drawing at the Royal
Academy after the encouragement of his employer, a surgeon. As well as
London, he worked in Norwich (1779, 1782). He was made Miniature Painter
to the Duchess of York and, later, Queen Charlotte, and painted several royal
children. In 1797 he travelled to Russia, where he worked for the Tsar. In
1806, he went to Philadelphia, where he remained for the rest of his life,
becoming a teacher and founder of the Philadelphia Academy.

   Miles' works are not signed and have often been confused with Cosway's, as
they are of comparable quality if not originality. One common trait is a
yellowish cast found in the face and backgrounds.

### 53  Unknown Man

Watercolour on ivory; gold *fausse-montre* frame with plaited hair
verso
Oval, 5.9 x 4.9 cm

Christie's 4 March 1992 (81); purchased by the Draper estate; given
to Kenwood, 1992  (88029231)

This distinguished looking gentleman has a high, standing collared
coat and contrasting waistcoat, dating from the latter half of the
1780s. He appears to wear his own hair powdered, rather than a
wig, which would have been old-fashioned at this time.

   Miles paints the face with plenty of precise detail, using fine lines
with carefully blended hatching. The softness of his technique in
painting the hair contrasts with the flat and broadly hatched surface
of the sitter's coat. The lighter areas of the miniature all display
Miles' somewhat yellow palette, which appears to be a deliberate
effect of his.

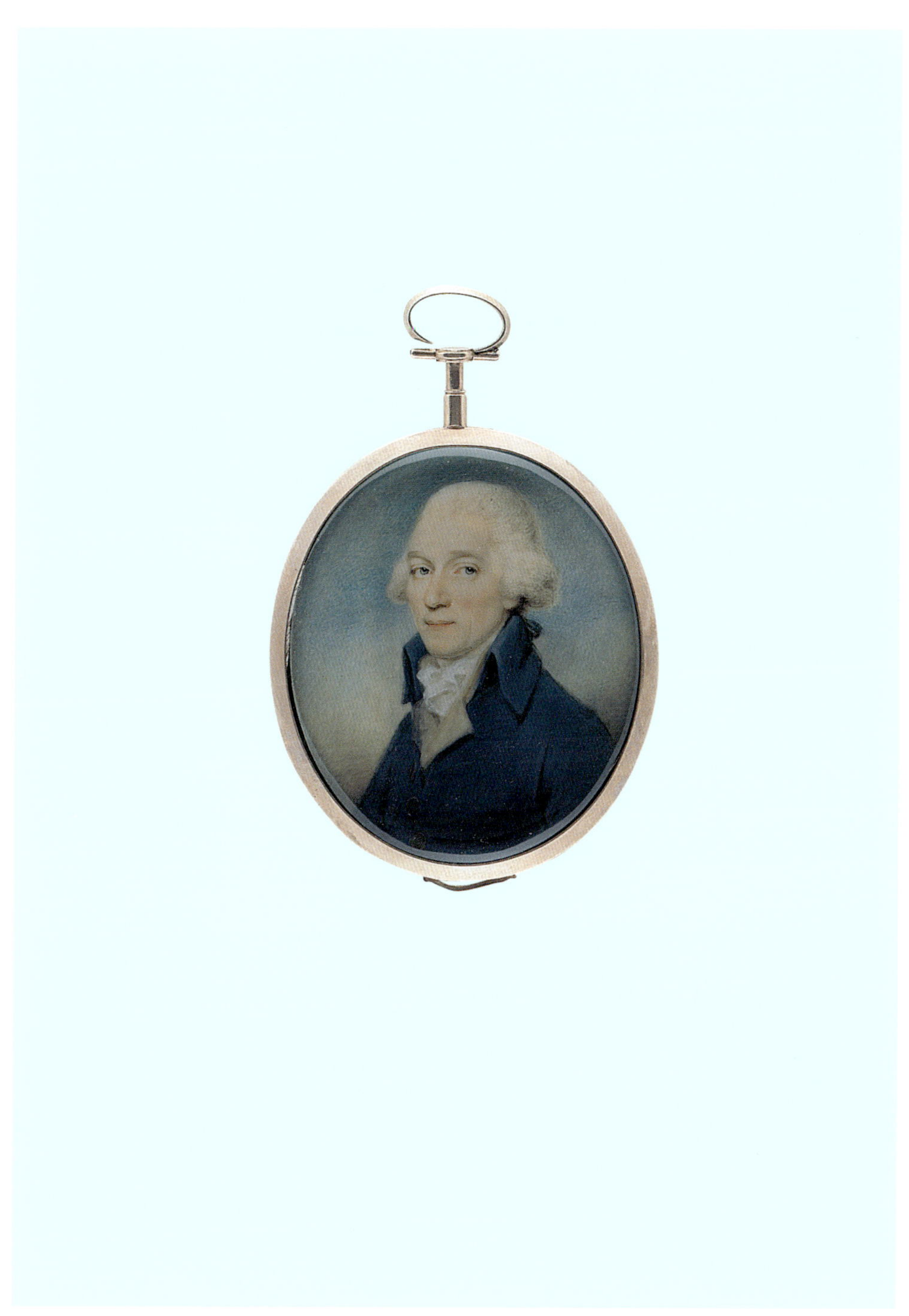

# George Engleheart (1752–1829)

One of the great miniaturists of the late Georgian period, Engleheart developed a rather decorative style which made the best of his sitters and created a great demand for his work. He was born in Kew, the son of a German plaster modeller. At the Royal Academy Schools he studied under Reynolds and the landscape painter George Barret and was appointed Miniature Painter to George III in 1789, following Jeremiah Meyer. For most of his life he worked in London and, after retirement to the outskirts of the city, he was buried at Kew.

Engleheart painted many miniatures over a long career: his fee books from 1775 to 1813 list 4,853 works, and he recorded many commissions with tracings. His style developed gradually over a long career, beginning with fairly modest works, often with a buff-coloured  background. By the 1780s his work is more characteristic. The eyes become rather large and deep, the hair is painted in strands and his flesh colouring is cool.  In the last years of the century he used a larger oval format and often modelled sitters' faces with brown paint. In the nineteenth century Engleheart began to be more honest in his likenesses and also used a larger, sometimes rectangular format.  Many of his miniatures are signed *GE* or *E* and in full on the verso.

### 54  Unknown Man, 'E.E.'

Watercolour on ivory; gold *fausse-montre* frame set with blue enamel and pearls, the verso with the monogram *EE* in diamonds on a silk ground
Oval, 4.8 x 3.3 cm

Limner Antiques, London; Marie Draper, 1972; given to Kenwood, 1988  (88029175)

This is a small-sized miniature characteristic of Engleheart's work during the late 1780s or early 90s. The sitter is painted as a fairly thickset man but our attention is drawn to the way the artist has handled his wig and clothing. The short, but rather full wig is painted in a mass of fine lines, in a manner completely different from the face and dress. Engleheart makes great play of the man's ruffled cravat with rapid, pencil-like brush strokes.

Although perhaps a little faded, Engleheart's use of brown and blue shading to the face is quite evident. He also uses pale blue for the whites of the eyes. These are typically drawn with particular emphasis, using shading to create their detail. While the sitter's coat is painted with opaque colour, his cravat is contrasted by leaving bare ivory outlined with grey watercolour. This miniature has a particularly fine enamel and jewelled frame.

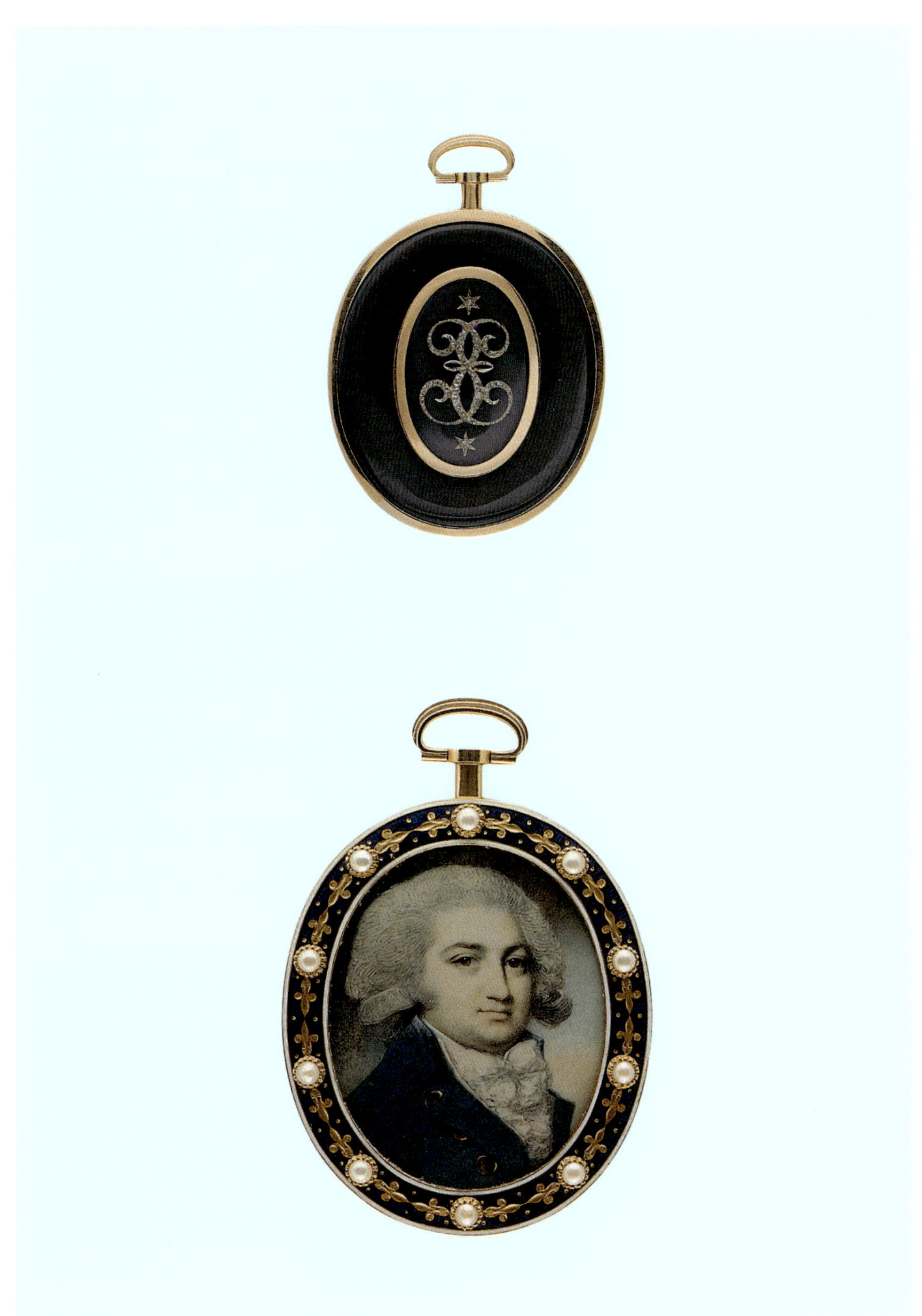

# George Engleheart

## 55 Unknown Woman

Watercolour on ivory; silver-gilt locket frame. Signed lower right
with initial *E*
Oval, 8.4 x 6.6 cm

Christie's 10 Nov. 1993 (59); purchased by the Draper estate; given
to Kenwood, 1993  (88029811)

In his slightly later and larger miniatures Engleheart was even less
likely to flatter his clients, as in this portrait of a young woman of c.
1805.  She is shown with her hair fashionably curled and cut short,
wearing a pretty embroidered muslin gown. While Engleheart
makes every effort to produce an elegant miniature, he has not
attempted to make his sitter less plain. Perhaps her neck was not
quite so long, but it was a good feature that he could emphasise
without resorting to invention.

This miniature shares the large eyes and decorative treatment of
the hair with the earlier Engleheart in the collection. It also shows
his effective use of short strokes of opaque white to draw the detail
of her dress. One idiosyncratic change in his later style is his
preference for grey-brown shading on the skin, which does not go
especially well with the sky background. A copy of this portrait,
attributed to W. Thick(e), was sold by Sotheby's in 1996 (6 June
1996, lot 55).

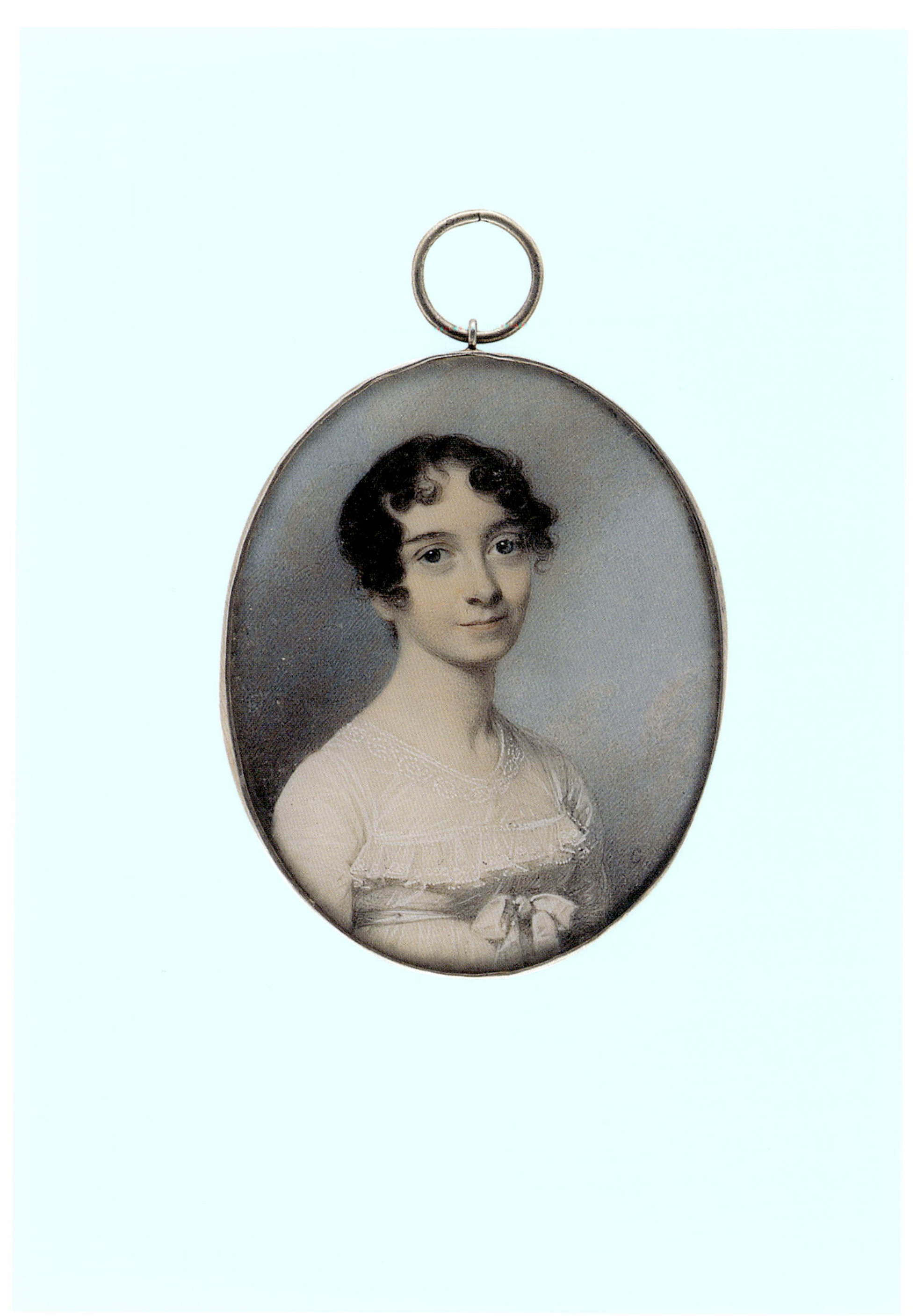

# Guy Head (1762–1800)

Head is better known as a copyist of old masters and painter of neo-classical subjects. He came from Carlisle and followed a conventional route through the Royal Academy Schools but then went abroad (c1781), via Cassel to Italy, where he worked for several years and also collected paintings and antiquities. He died shortly after his return to England in 1799.

Miniatures by Head are very rare. There are a couple of copies of Van Dyck portraits made in modern-day Germany, now in the Royal Collection. These are well painted in a manner founded on the style of mid-eighteenth-century English miniaturists.

### 56  Unknown Man, 'G.H.' or 'J.H.'

Watercolour on ivory; gold locket frame. Backing paper inscribed *Painted by/ G. Head/ this year 1784/ Amsterdam*. Locket engraved with interlocked monograms, *GH* and *JH*
Oval, 4.4 x 3.5 cm

Asprey's; Marie Draper, 1970–1; given to Kenwood, 1988
(88029180)

This young man in fairly conventional dress of the 1780s could either be Dutch or English. One unusual detail of dress is the large button on his collar, which may be for the storm flap hanging from the lapel. This would be eminently suitable for a cold, northern climate. It is quite possible that the work is a self-portrait or member of Head's family, going by the initials engraved on the frame.

This is a rare life portrait by Head, and important because of its unambiguous signature. The work is attractively painted with a careful technique that relies on the use of plenty of gum as a medium. His dependence on stippling and neat, close brush strokes suggest a fairly traditional teacher, when one considers that he is a contemporary of Andrew Plimer, who studied with Cosway.

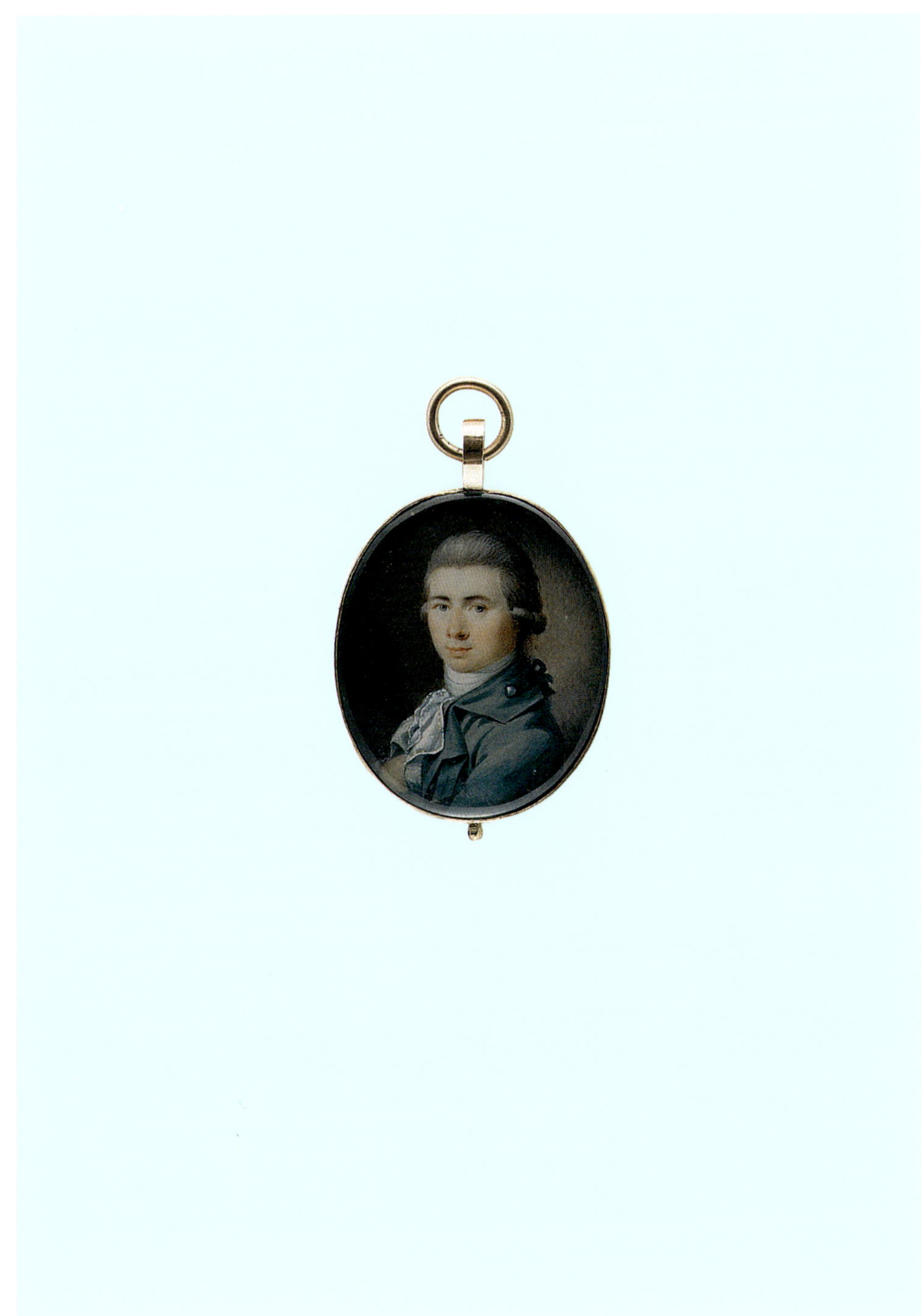

# James Nixon ARA  (c1741–1812)

The early years of Nixon's life remain unrecorded, but he is known to have worked in Edinburgh as well as London. He exhibited at the Society of Artists and attended the Royal Academy Schools in 1769. Nixon had great respect for the new Academy and imitated in little the manner of its president, Sir Joshua Reynolds, with some success. He was elected Associate in 1778.

Nixon also worked in oil and watercolour but it was with his miniatures that he made a living. He was appointed Miniature Painter to the Duchess of York (1792) and 'Limner to the Prince of Wales' (1803), sometime after moving to Edinburgh. His last years were spent in Devon. Nixon's works are often hard to identify, as he did not always sign. He painted with soft, sometimes quite broad, brush strokes and a subtle palette.

### 57  ? Lady Middleton

Watercolour on ivory; gilt metal locket frame. Inscribed on backing card *Lady Middlet[on]*
Oval, 3.3 x 2.8 cm

R.L. Bayne-Powell; given by him to Kenwood, 1993  (88029808)

This sitter is very likely to be Jane, Lady Middleton, wife of Henry Willoughby, 6th Baron Middleton (1761–1835), whom she married in 1793, probably not long after the portrait was painted. This miniature is a copy of a signed primary version (sold Christie's 10 July 1990, lot 142). The Kenwood version was probably a gift intended for another member of the family.

Lady Middleton is wearing a loose white turban, trimmed with gold lace and fringe, with a simple matching gown. Oriental influences in dress were fashionable in several periods of the eighteenth century, but the loose turban and hair seen here date from the end of the 1780s.

Nixon's accurate yet diffuse manner of painting is quite evident in this work. He has used a minimum of paint to build up the face, rather in the manner of Humphry (see cat. 37), and soft lines for the hair and dress. His debt to Reynolds is clear from the choice of dress and harmonious, warm colouring of the whole surface.

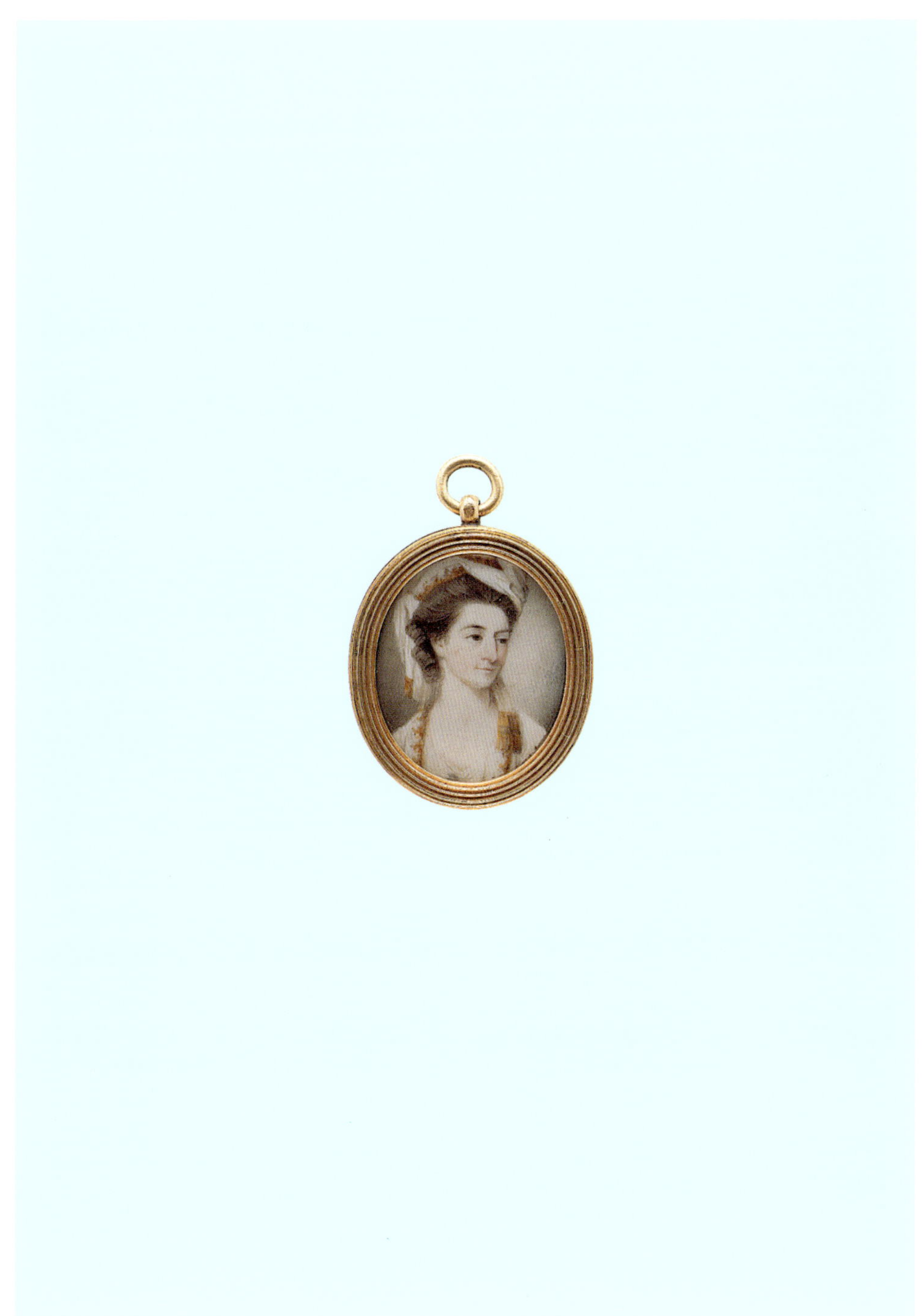

# Thomas Hull  (fl 1775–1827)

Hull is a lesser known artist of the late eighteenth century, but one of some ability and style. Little is known of him, other than that he exhibited at the Royal Academy between the above dates and placed occasional advertisements in newspapers. From these it is known that he moved from Clerkenwell to the artists' quarter around St Martin's Lane around 1795 and was in Leeds the following year.

His works appear softly painted, using stipple for facial details and fine hatching, but they are not over-laboured. He usually signed with his surname.

### 58  Unknown Woman, 'C.B.'

Watercolour on ivory; later gold swivel frame with gold-coloured initials on verso, *CB*
Oval, 4.2 x 3.3 cm

Christie's 10 July 1991 (163); purchased by the Draper estate; given to Kenwood, 1991  (88029870)

In this attractive miniature the sitter wears a dress trimmed in the Van Dyck fashion popular from the 1760s and 70s. The contrasting outer gown is used to good effect against this collar. Her wide, frizzed hairstyle is of the 1780s, the probable date of this miniature.

The artist builds up the face with delicate stipple on top of thin washes, avoiding the use of hard lines in the detail. Soft lines are used in a more decorative way to draw the sitter's hair.

The swivel frame must be a replacement of the mid-nineteenth century: however, its rococo revival details complement this decidedly unclassical portrait.

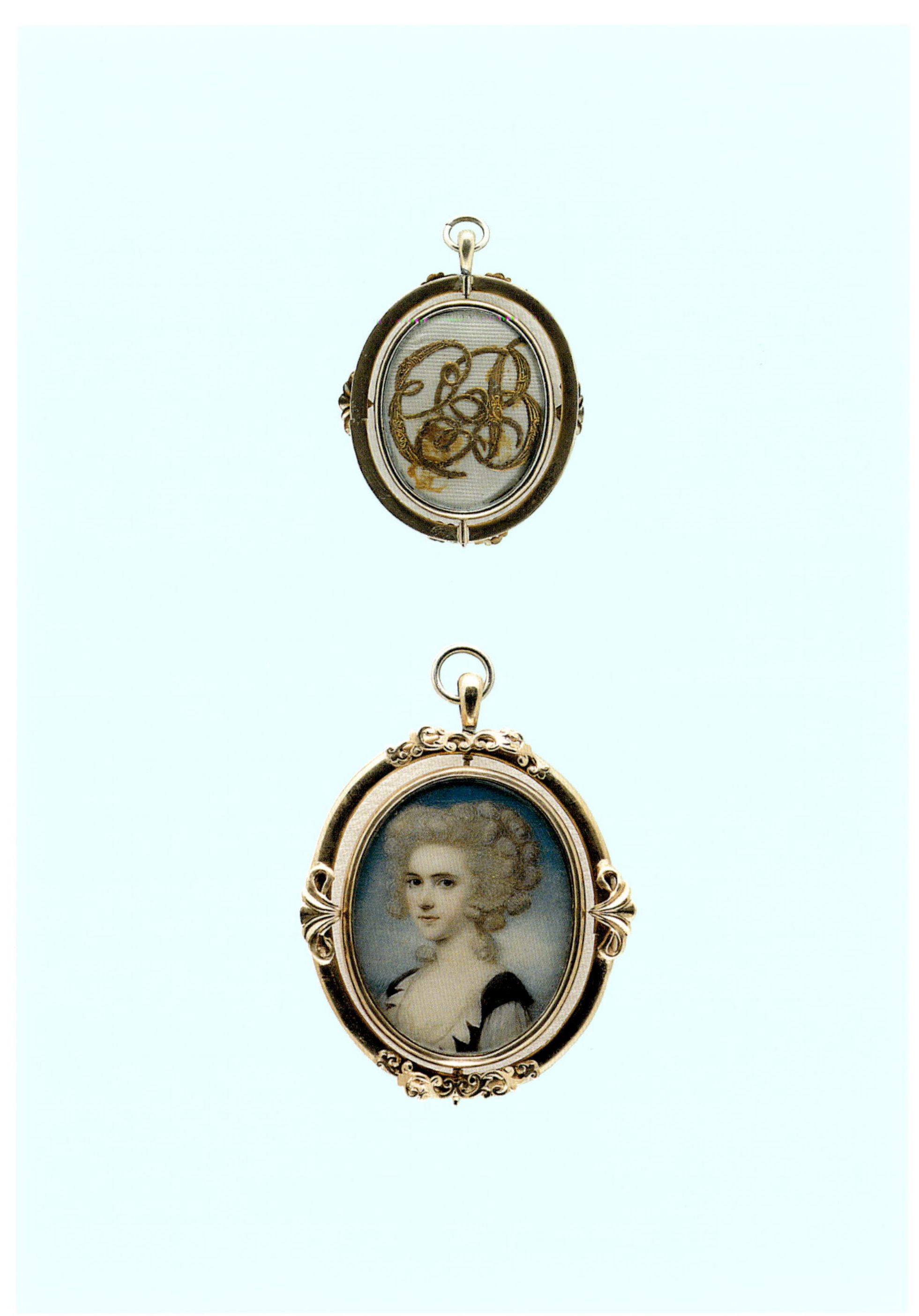

# John Bogle  (?1746–?1803)

A Scottish painter of disputed aristocratic descent, Bogle studied at a Glasgow drawing school and later found success in Edinburgh.  He sent works for exhibition to the Society of Artists between 1769 and 1770 and by 1772 was working in London and showing at the Royal Academy. Bogle worked from Panton Square, producing many miniatures, mostly small, in his rather idiosyncratic, soft stipple technique. Occasionally he produced larger ivories that show that he could rival the best miniaturists of the period.

He appears to have been friendly with the novelist Fanny Burney and painted her in a room interior (1783 – whereabouts unknown). By 1800 Bogle had returned to Edinburgh, where he died around 1803.

## 59  Unknown woman

Watercolour on ivory; modern gilt metal locket frame. Signed middle left *IB / 1799*
Oval, 4.1 x 3.1 cm

Limner Antiques, London; purchased by the Draper estate, 1991; given to Kenwood, 1991 (88029873)

This relatively modest miniature is characteristic of Bogle's work in the 1790s. The sitter has her hair loosely curled about her neck in a manner close to the short styles of the Regency period. Her simplified chemise dress may have a strand of pearls gathering up the sleeves.

Bogle's soft technique, relying almost entirely on stipple effects, is in marked contrast to the atmospheric, sometimes sketchy works of Cosway and his followers. The use of a dark background is another common trait and one which helps to give the figure a sense of solidity and presence. Bogle frequently signed his works with the monogram found on this example.

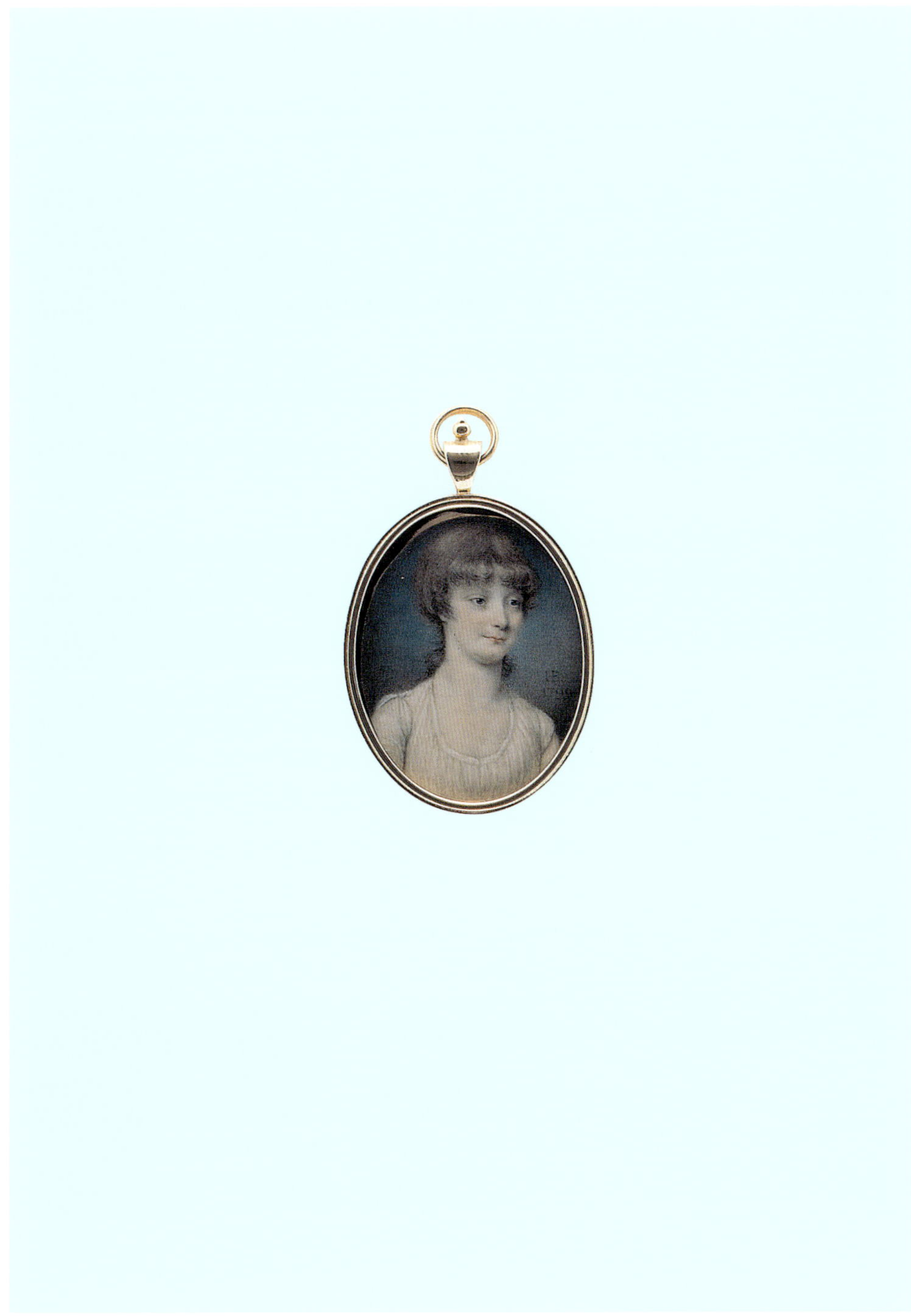

# John Bogle

## 60  Unknown man

Watercolour on ivory; gilt metal locket frame. Signed middle
left *IB / 1800*
Oval, 5.7 x 4.5 cm

E. Grosvenor Paine; R. L. Bayne-Powell, 1980; Sotheby's 11 Oct.
1994 (95); purchased by the Draper estate; given to Kenwood, 1994
(88029830)

As with many miniaturists of the eighteenth century, Bogle clearly
found more to portray with older sitters, especially, as in this case,
when he was using a larger size of ivory. The sitter is a distinguished
looking gentleman, wearing the sober grey and black clothing one
might expect of a professional man or wealthy merchant. His hair is
perhaps still  powdered and there are broad lapels to both his
striped waistcoat and coat.

Bogle uses fine, warm-coloured stipple on the face to build up a
quite naturalistic and convincing portrayal of the sitter. By avoiding
the use of lines even in the detail he creates an illusion of tangible
form, much in the way a photographic print is created from minute
grains of salts on paper.

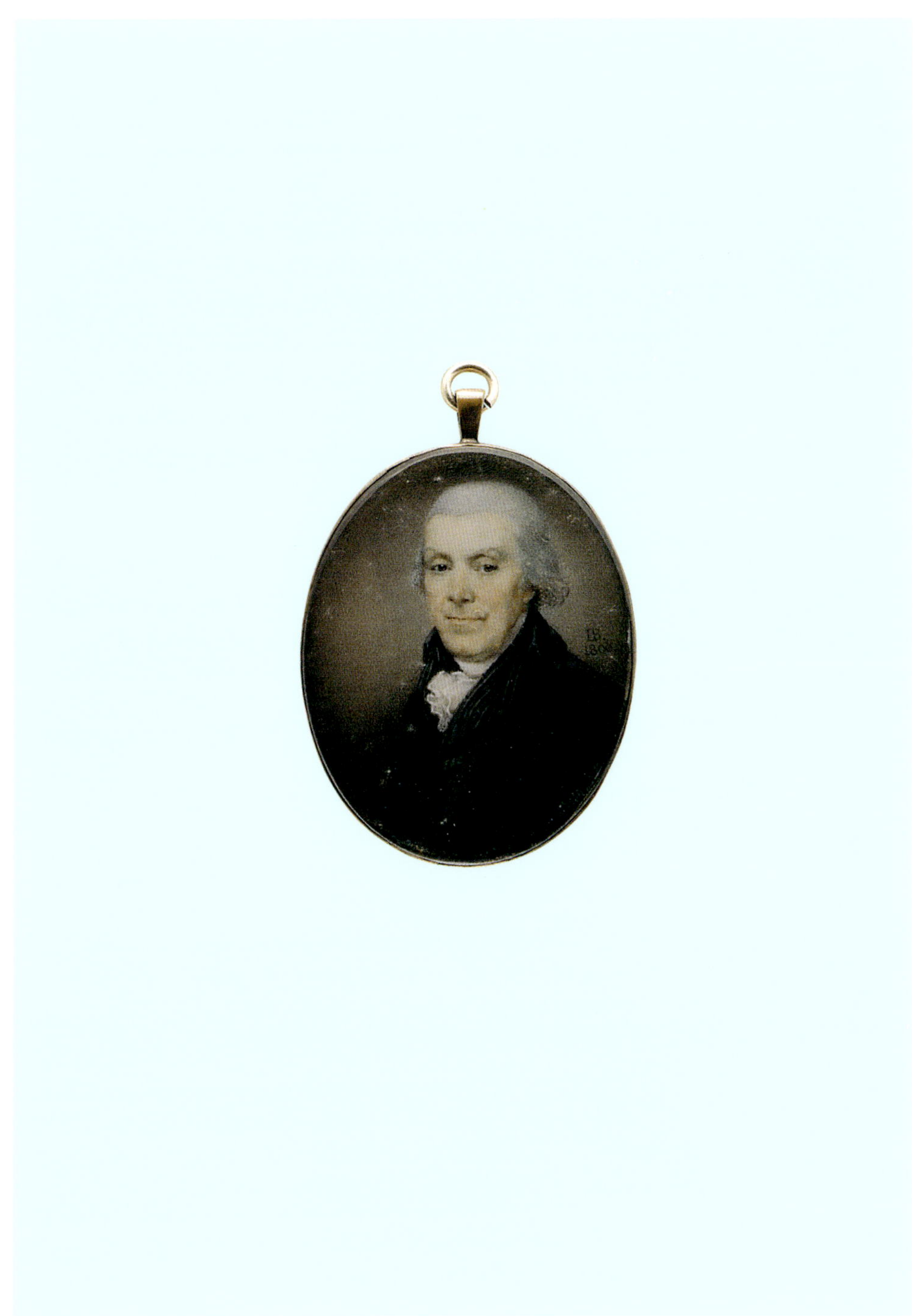

# Horace Hone ARA  (1754–1825)

Horace was the second son of Nathaniel Hone (see cats 12 – 14) who taught him before he entered the Royal Academy Schools in 1770. Whilst he exhibited at the Royal Academy for most of his life, he left London for Dublin in 1782, where he had a successful business for several years. He returned to London via Bath in 1804 and later suffered a gradual decline, from mental ill-health.

Hone was friendly with the artist and diarist Joseph Farington and became Miniature Painter to the Prince of Wales in 1795. His sitters included the celebrated actress, Mrs Siddons, as well as some of the highest members of the aristocracy. He painted equally well on ivory and in enamel, and used a variety of styles, all quite individual.

### 61  Captain Lambert Brabazon RN (c1740–1811)
Watercolour on ivory; gold locket frame. Signed lower right,
*HH/06  [1806]*
Oval, 4.5 x 3.8 cm

Limner Antiques, London; purchased by the Draper estate, 1990; given to Kenwood, 1990 (88029856)

The sitter was Flag Captain to Francis Drake, in the Leeward Islands, West Indies, after 1783. With the outbreak of war with France he was sent to Dublin to take charge of press gangs. At the time this portrait was made he was captain of the Royal Yacht *Dorset*, which he commanded from 1803 for the Lord Lieutenant of Ireland. The ship was built in 1753 and 'beautifully ornamented' with Irish motifs.

Hone paints his sitter with understanding in his late, distinctive style and produces a portrait that is full of bluff characterisation. The face is well painted, with warm colours. The eyes are emphasised but softly drawn. Captain Brabazon's hair and the background are neatly painted using parallel brush strokes, but the simple uniform is painted with little more than some impasted detail and hatched shadow, painted over solid areas of opaque colour.

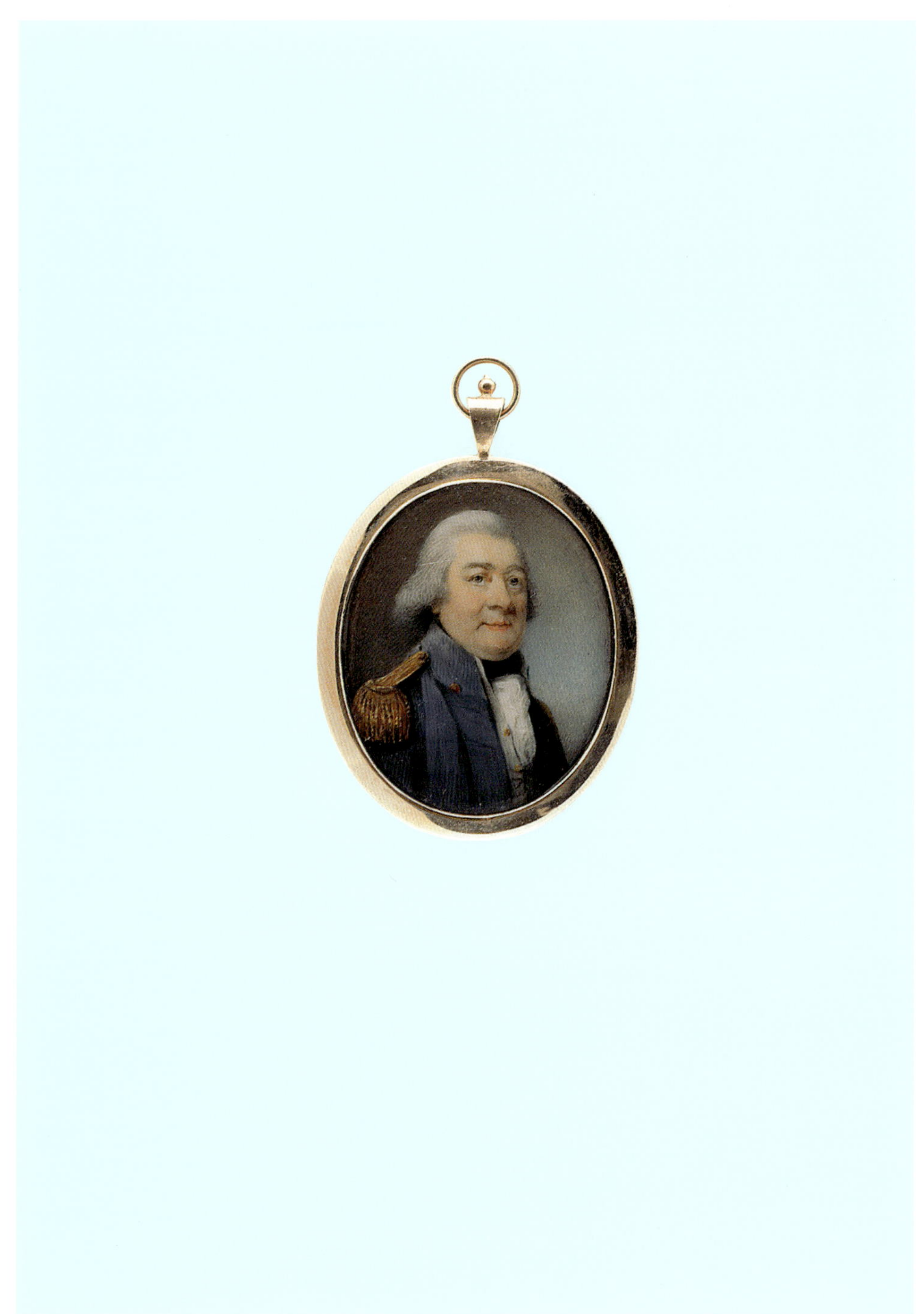

# Philip Jean  (1755–1802)

Jean was a Jerseyman, born at St Ouen. He first served in the Navy, under Admiral Rodney, before turning to painting in miniature and oil. He seems to have worked in London, where he exhibited at the Royal Academy from 1787 onwards. Here he used his good technique and drawing skills to assimilate the styles of leading artists, such as Cosway and Shelley. This ploy succeeded, and he gained the patronage of the Gloucester family at court and painted full lengths of the King and Queen. Two of his more illuminating subjects were the artists Paul Sandby and Dominic Serres (National Portrait Gallery).

Although he was something of a stylistic chameleon, Jean's works are recognisable and are mostly very well executed. He signed on occasion.

### 62  Unknown Man

Watercolour on ivory; gilt metal locket frame with hair verso
Oval, 6.7 x 5.5 cm

Sotheby's 1 Nov. 1990 (25); purchased by the Draper estate; given to Kenwood, 1990  (88029858)

This portrait is reminiscent of Cosway's work of c.1790 (see cat. 38). The man's powdered hair, tall coat collar with large buttons and the cravat frill are typical of this date. The sitter has chosen to be painted in the rather sombre-coloured clothing of an English gentleman, which seemed to be perennially fashionable for many years.

Jean's work is carefully drawn and worked up with dense, visible brush strokes. This can give his miniatures a slightly furry appearance. The sky is carefully hatched with long strokes – quite unlike Cosway, for instance – and only in the cravat does Jean make full use of the bare ivory for effect.

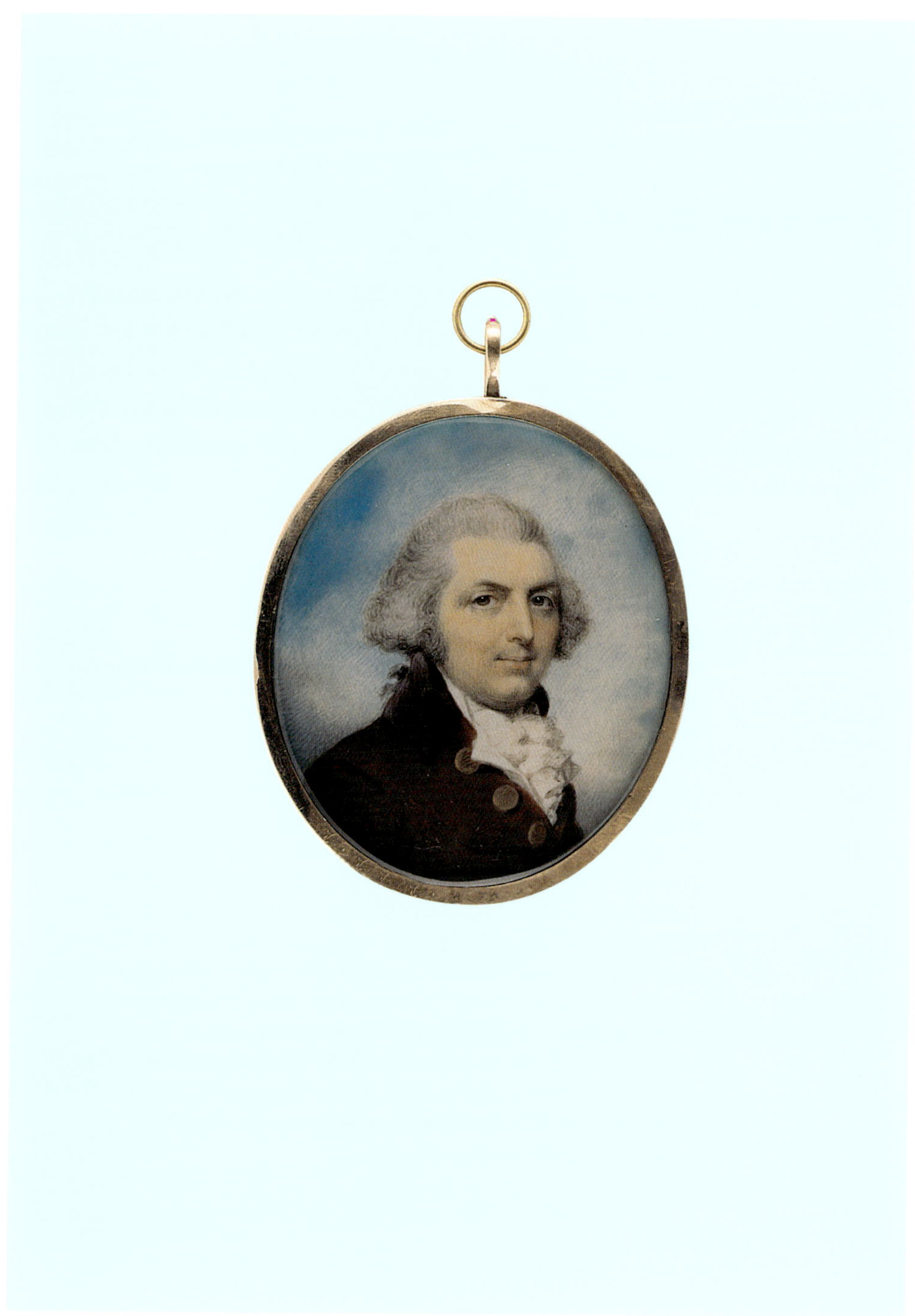

# Henry Bone RA (1755–1834)

Bone came from Cornwall and first worked painting china in Plymouth, before coming to London around 1779, where he created a new market for copies in enamel of full-scale easel paintings. He did also paint original portraits and worked occasionally on ivory. In 1801 George, Prince of Wales, made Bone his Painter in Enamel, a post he continued to hold under three monarchs in succession. His popularity led to election at the Royal Academy and an ability to command huge prices, especially for his large enamels after old master and contemporary subject paintings.

Predominantly Bone's works are copies, but they can be appreciated in their own right for his good drawing, sense of colour and technical accomplishment. His skill in enamel means that today many of his copies give a truer record of the colours of the originals than the actual oil paintings he worked from. Several of Bone's children became enamellists, most notably Henry Pierce Bone, who also went on to work for the royal family.

### 66  William Murray, 1st Earl of Mansfield (1705–93)

after Sir Joshua Reynolds, c1776
Enamel; gold locket frame, engraved on verso with monogram and inscription, *M/ Aetati sua 81, Pretor[a ]30/ Defecit Alter* and *LORD MANSFIELD BY H BONE*
Oval, 5.5 x 4.5 cm

Lavender Antiques, London; purchased by English Heritage for Kenwood, 1994 (88029822)

For a description of the sitter see cat. 64. Bone's copy was made about 1785–6, probably as a gift of the judge. The artist Joseph Farington mentions one of his copies in his diary in November 1802. Bone's drawing and technique are similar to William Russell Birch's, and it is tempting to think that he was working from one of the latter's copies, rather than the original oil. Coincidentally, he was born and died in the same year as Birch, who could possibly have instructed him on his arrival in London. His colour and modelling of the features are a little more robust than those of Birch's.

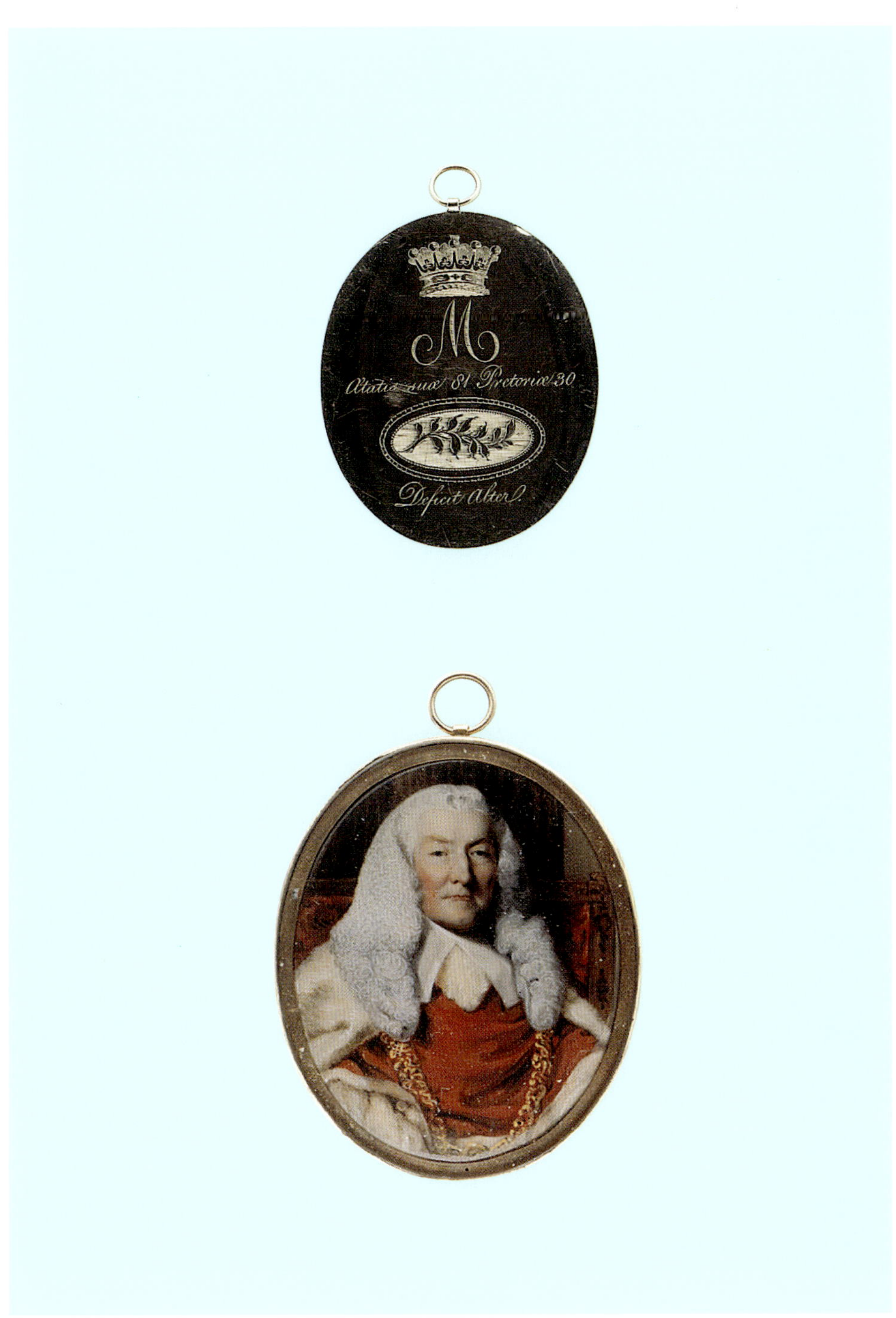

# Henry Bone RA

## 67 Charles Grey (1764–1845), later 2nd Earl Grey

after Sir Thomas Lawrence
Enamel; gilt metal locket frame. Signed recto, *HBone* and verso,
*Charles Grey Esq M.P./ Henry Bone pinx/ Sep$^{tr}$./1794*
Oval, 8.6 x 6.8 cm

Christie's 10 July 1991 (129); purchased by the Draper estate; given
to Kenwood, 1991 (88029868)

Lit.: K. Garlick, *Sir Thomas Lawrence*, 1989, cat. 353(a)

A reduced copy from Lawrence's three-quarter length portrait in oil
of 1793 (private collection), painted for the headmaster of Eton
College, Dr Heath. Charles Grey had already presented his portrait
by Romney on leaving Eton and nearly a decade later turned to the
rising star, Thomas Lawrence, to portray him as a Member of
Parliament. There he joined the supporters of Charles James Fox.
An astute politician, Grey became Prime Minister in 1831 and again
in 1832–4, when he successfully saw through the first Reform Act.
Away from public duties, Grey had liaisons with the notorious
Georgiana, Duchess of Devonshire.

Henry Bone manages to capture the warm colouring and sense
of immediacy of the young Lawrence's portrait. This is no mean
achievement considering the slow and gradual process of painting
in enamel. His skill using colours is amply displayed in the flesh
tones and he manages to emulate Lawrence's bold brush strokes in
the freely worked hair and highlights on the sitter's coat. Bone also
creates the effect of thickly impasted paint in the white highlights
on Grey's face and outline of the cravat.

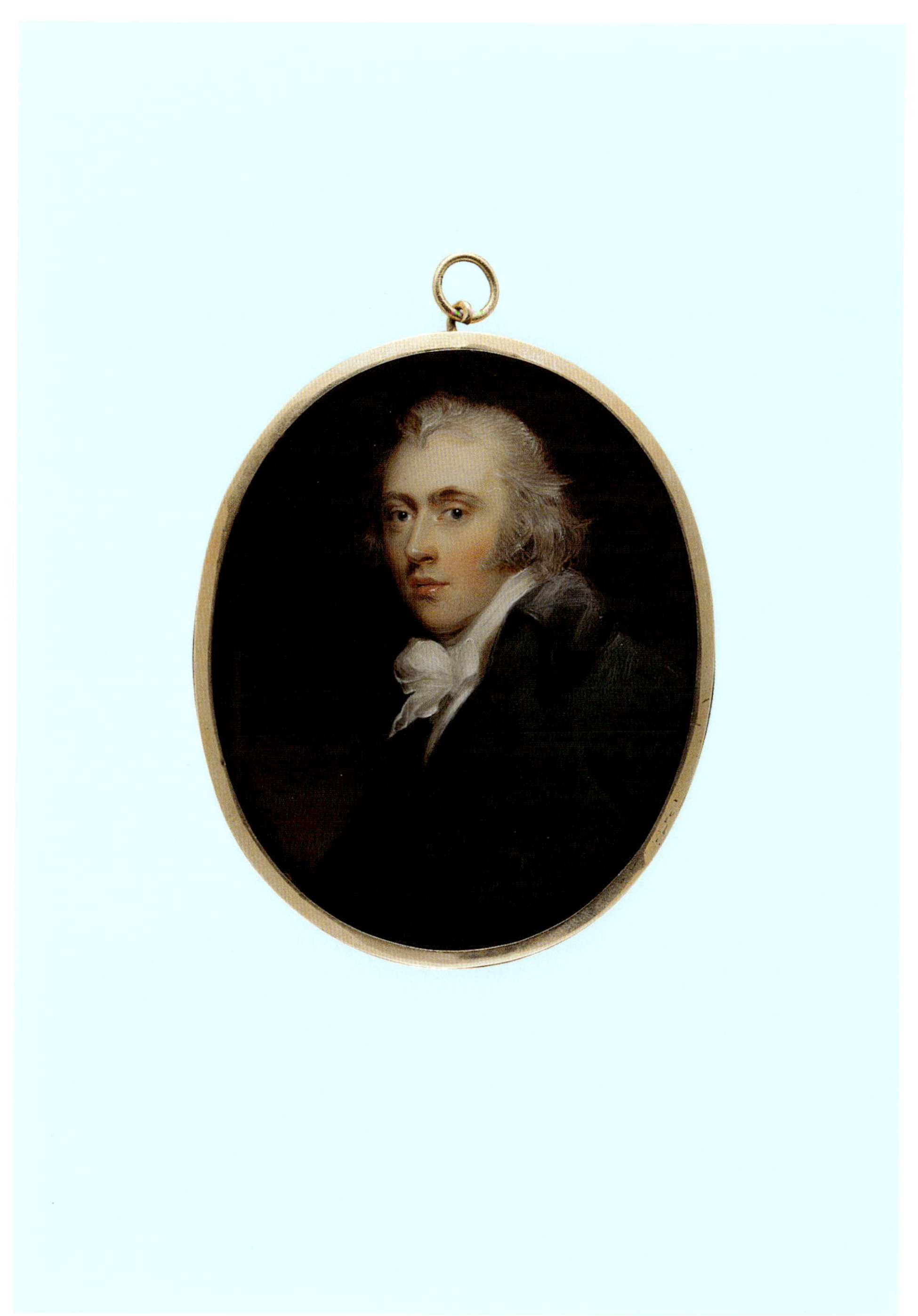

# Walter Robertson  (d1801)

The elder brother of Charles Robertson, Walter established himself in Dublin before moving to London around 1784. There he met the American portrait artist Gilbert Stuart and joined him in America between 1793 and 1795. In America, Robertson painted George Washington and copied Stuart's images, which were in great demand. In 1795 he went to India where he remained until his death.

Walter Robertson's work is often hard to distinguish from his brother's, and like Charles he did not sign his miniatures.  His sitters can appear more strongly modelled as he used blue lines around the eyes and other features. The dress is neatly drawn with an economy of brush strokes and paint, using plenty of line work.

### 68  Sir Henry Jebb (d1810)
Watercolour on ivory; gilt metal *fausse-montre* case
Oval, 6.7 x 5.2 cm

Bonham's, 13 June 1994 (96); purchased by the Draper estate; given to Kenwood, 1994  (88029823)

Sir Henry Jebb's clothes help date the miniature to about 1790, just before Robertson left for America. The artist has painted his shirt frill very effectively, using opaque white over the ivory ground, so that it stands out against the buff waistcoat lining.

The sitter's face is finely painted, using blue stipple and broken lines to model the features. This is typical of the elder Robertson. Flat gum colour is used to contrast the texture of the dress against the detail in the rest of the miniature. The stormy sky, with darker blues and browns, is another identifying feature.

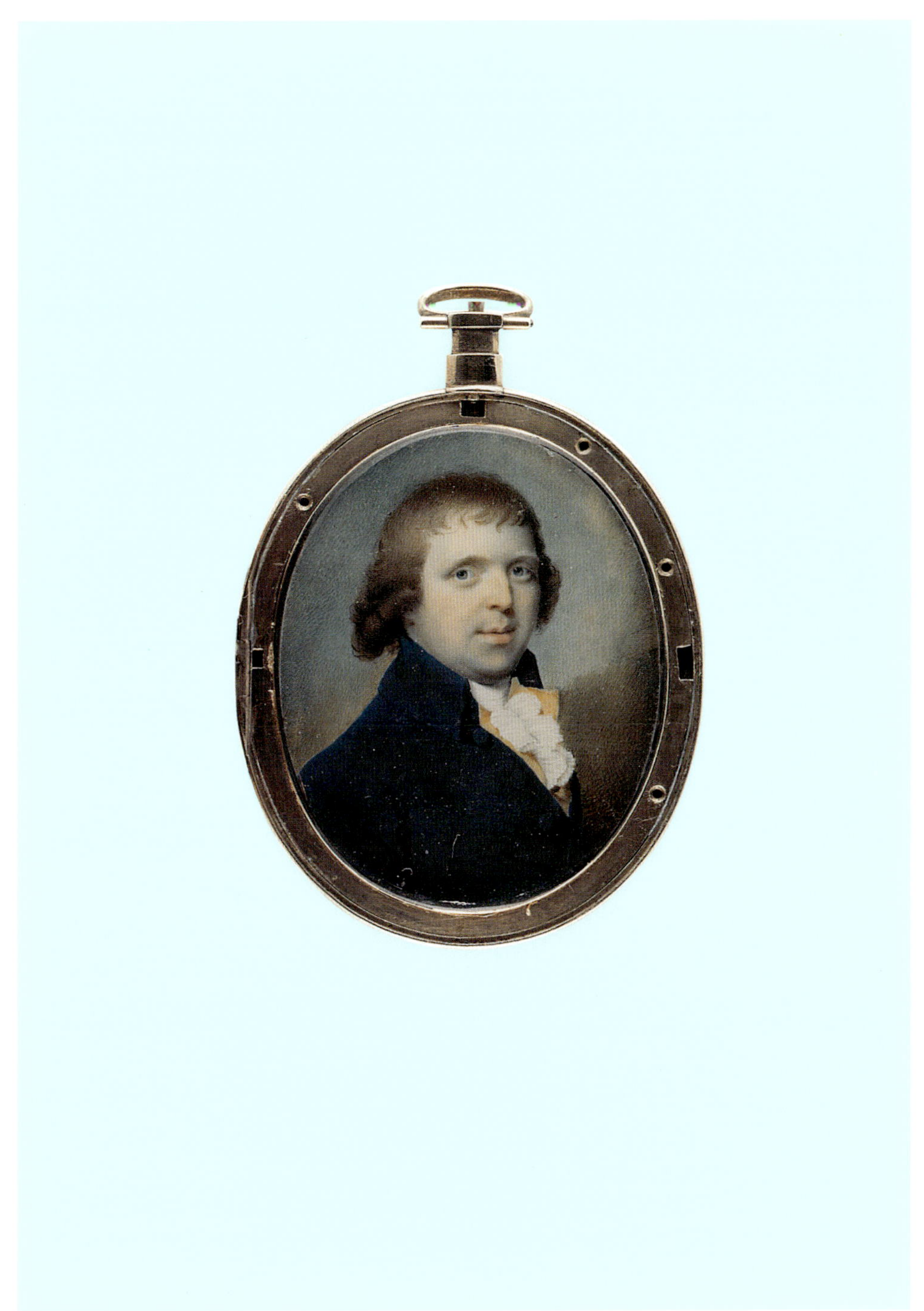

# Samuel Shelley  (1756–1808)

Shelley came from modest origins in the East End of London and reputedly taught himself to draw and paint. He attended the Royal Academy Schools from 1774 and exhibited regularly there until 1804. He worked in several media and copied Reynolds' paintings, but his real success was with miniatures. These are quite distinctive on account of his preference for using opaque paint with gum arabic (when pure watercolour was becoming popular) and a strong, yellow-green flesh colour. His draughtsmanship was very good, allowing him to capture character well — his portraits of women are especially successful.

Some of his best works have more than one sitter, using large and unusual shaped ivories.  He also attempted subject paintings in miniature for a period.

### 69  Unknown Man

Watercolour on ivory; gold locket frame with hair arrangement on verso, set with pearls on white glass and foil. Signed on backing, *Sam. SHELLEY/ 6 GEORGE STREET/ HANOVER/ SQUARE*
Oval, 6.6 x 5.5 cm

Limner Antiques, London; Marie Draper, 1970; given to Kenwood, 1988  (88029182)

This fashionable gentleman was painted in the very last years of the eighteenth century. He sports powdered hair with a pigtail and long sideburns and appears to have two waistcoats, the inner one of red material contrasting with the white of his outer and cravat.

Shelley's ability to create a very three-dimensional figure is apparent in this first-rate miniature. The face is built up of fine, dense brush strokes. Blue is intelligently used to create the beard, rather than as a general modelling tone, as with many other artists. On the body, washes of gum arabic are used to create mottled, sheen effect to simulate fine cloth.

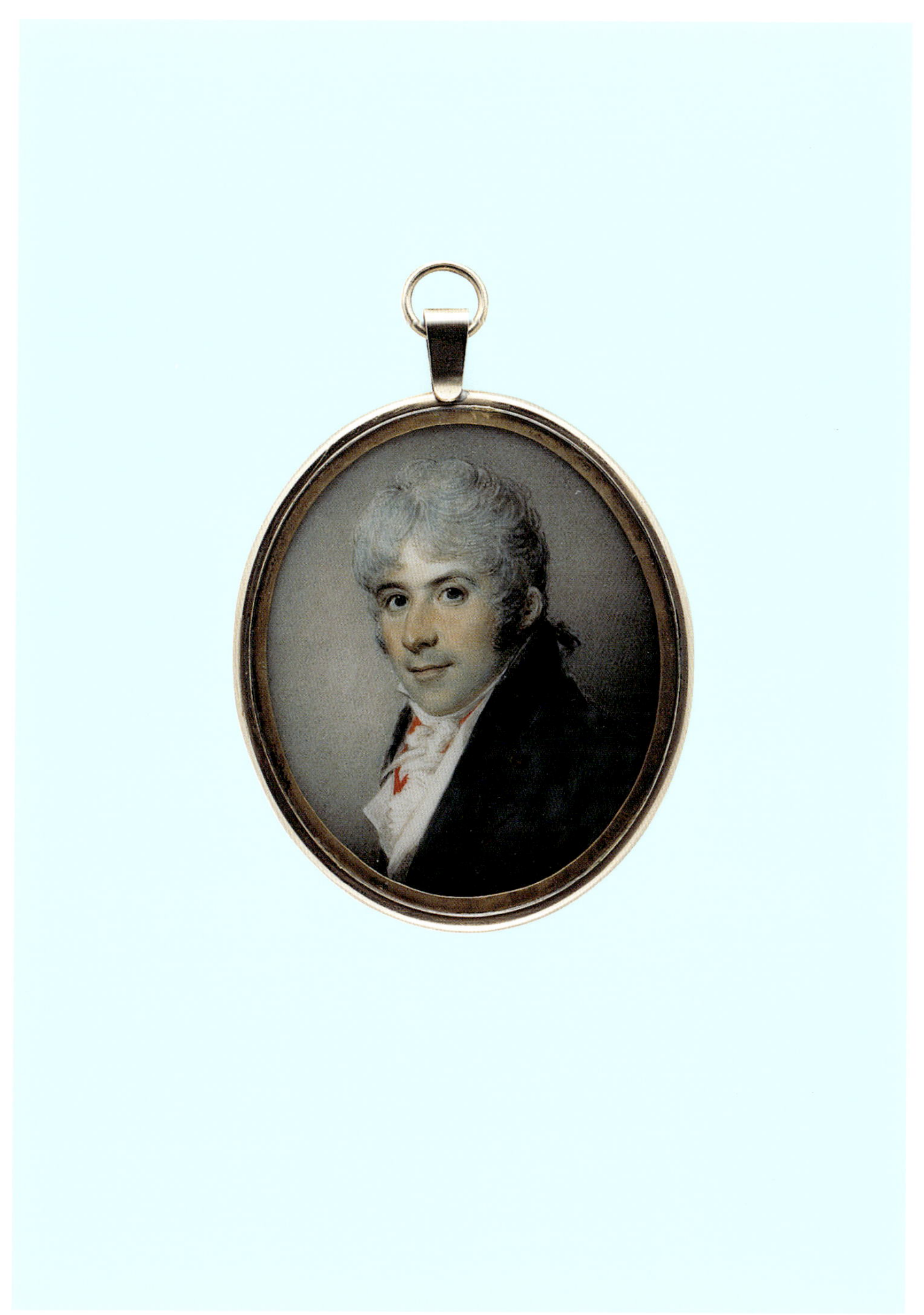

# Samuel Shelley

## 70  Marianne Nantes (c1772–1800)

Watercolour on ivory; set into a tortoiseshell and gold bonbonniere, inscribed inside, *Mrs Marianne Nantes d. 14 Feb^y 1800 Aetat 28 Years.* Signed on verso *Shelley/ Henrietta St./ Cov. Garden*
Oval, 6.0 x 4.5 cm

Limner Antiques, London; Marie Draper, 1970; given to Kenwood, 1988  (88029181)

Painted about 1790, and presumably made into a memento box after her death, this portrait of Mrs Nantes shows Shelley's attractive approach to female subjects. Her dress can be compared to that in Scouler's portrait (cat. 31) but is much more freely painted, using soft, decorative lines in the frills and hair.

In contrast to the dress and sky background, Shelley portrays the face with great pains, stippling and blending the paint, which is quite opaque and well-coloured. Often Shelley tended to follow fashion and exaggerate the eyes excessively, but this is not so in this instance.

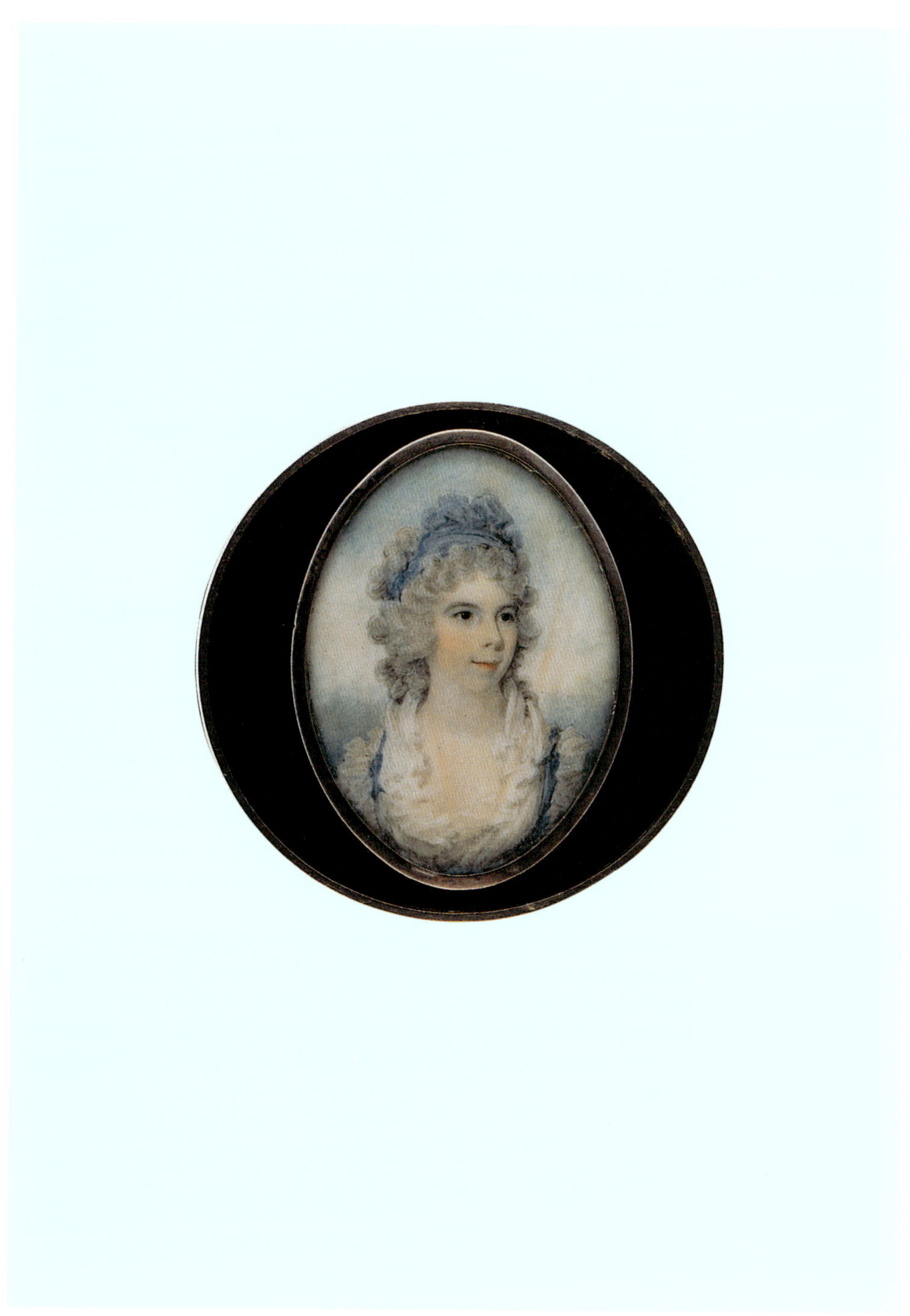

# Abraham (d1806) or Joseph Daniel (c1760–1803)

There still remains much confusion over the styles of the two brothers Daniel, who both worked in Bath at times and rarely signed their works. They came from a Jewish family in Somerset and are believed to have learned to paint from their mother. Both advertised as 'Daniel of Bath' from separate addresses and there is indeed little to distinguish their styles.

Abraham Daniel worked for most of his life and died in Plymouth. His miniatures are well drawn and often painted in almost sepia tones, although his brother also used this effect on occasion. Joseph was also a jeweller and worked in several other media besides painting miniatures, in Bristol and London as well as Bath. He remained in Bath from about 1786, where he suffered from ill-health.

It is now considered that Joseph was slightly the more gifted of the two brothers. He sometimes used a greyish shading on his sitters' faces and appears to have been more ambitious than his brother in attempts to render character.

### 74  Unknown Man

Watercolour on ivory; gold locket frame with hair inset verso and blue glass surround
Oval, 7.2 x 5.9 cm

Sotheby's 4 Dec. 1985 (104); Marie Draper; given to Kenwood, 1988 (88029179)

This portrait is almost devoid of colour apart from the eyes. The sitter wears a black coat and waistcoat with a white cravat . His dress features the high, upstanding collar of the mid-1790s.

The artist's use of sepia and grey tones to the face as well as background and a certain lack of finish might shift the question of attribution in favour of Abraham Daniel. However, the roundness of the figure, emphasised by the contrasting background, is also found in the work of his brother. The face almost has an element of caricature with the prominent eyebrows — another trait of both brothers.

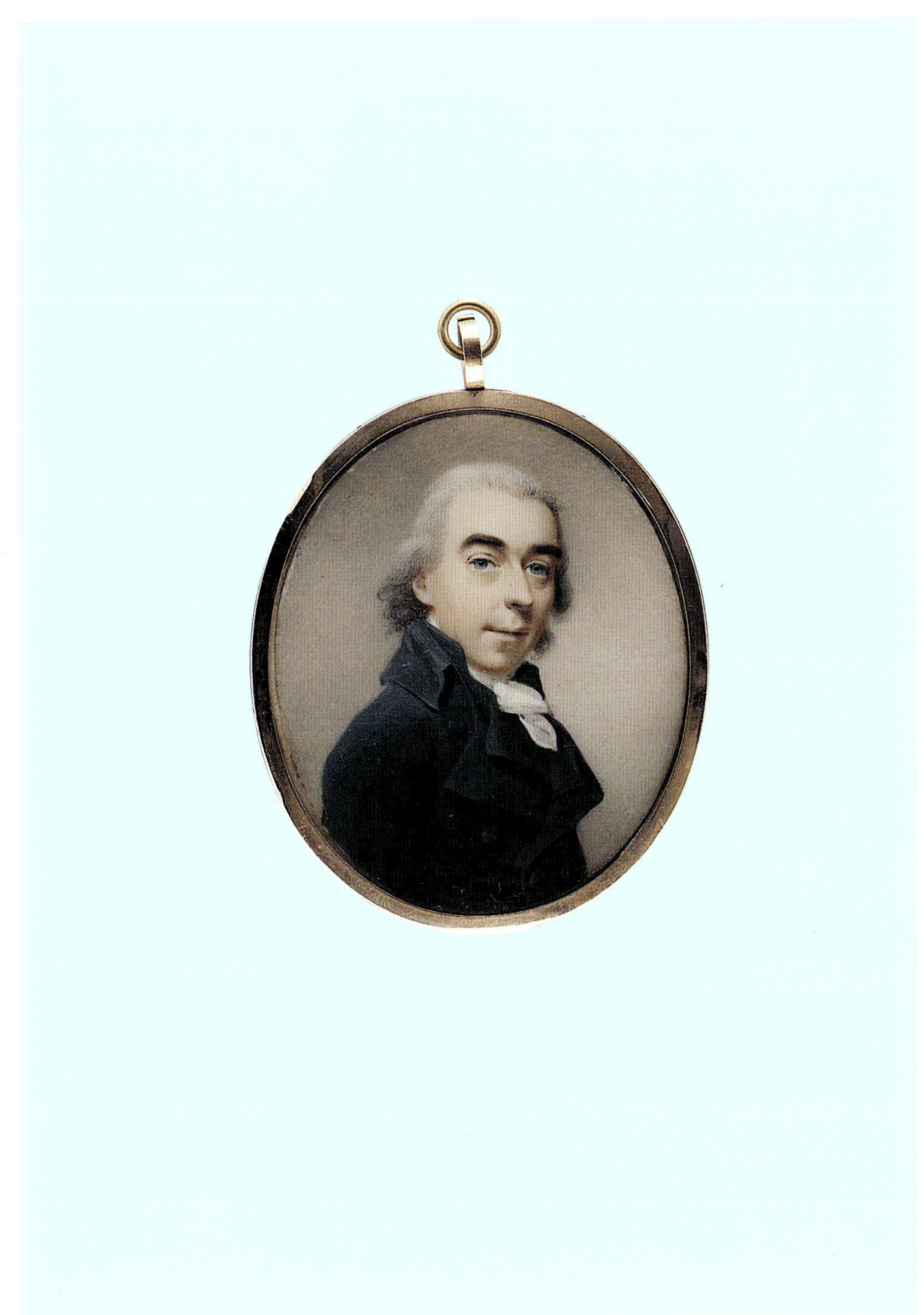

# Abraham or Joseph Daniel

**75  Mrs Margaret Roper**
Watercolour on ivory; gilt metal mount in a replacement ebonised
frame
Oval, 8.7 x 6.8 cm

Limner Antiques, London; purchased by the Draper estate; given to
Kenwood, 1990  (88029848)

The prominent bonnet worn by this somewhat matronly sitter
immediately draws attention. The sitter plainly decided that this
portrait would show her as a lady of fashion. The artist has again
chosen to limit the palette to almost grisaille tones through the
choice of clothing. Here the black coat and muslin shawl contrast
with the rather frivolous looking straw hat and white ribbon. It can
be dated to about 1795.

The reliance on a limited, brownish palette and the rather flat
appearance of the face suggest that this miniature is more likely to
be by Abraham rather than Joseph Daniel. This work shares much
in common with cat. 74.

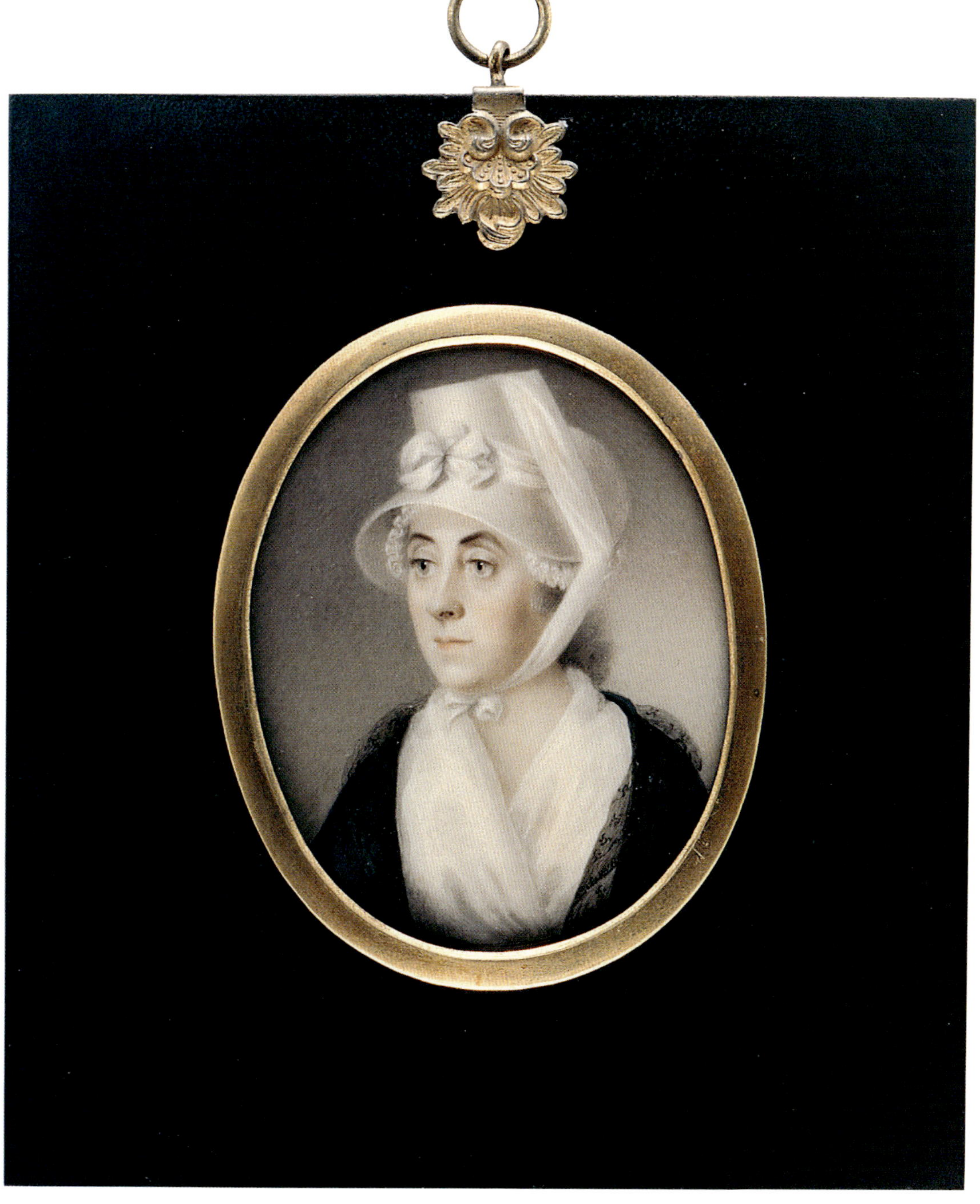

# Alexander Gallaway  (fl 1794–?1812)

Little is known about this able Scottish miniaturist, relatively few of whose
works are known. He shared a drawing academy in Glasgow from 1794 and
was working from St James's Square in Edinburgh from c.1810. Rather
unusually for the period in which he was working, he relied on very fine
stippling to draw and shade his miniatures, which he signed with initials. His
portraits of men sometimes exhibit an elongated head, with high forehead.

### 76  Unknown Man
Watercolour on ivory; gilt metal locket frame with hair work
wheatsheaf on verso, with blue glass border. Signed lower right *AG
/ 1796*
Oval, 6.7 x 5.3 cm

Sotheby's 28 Feb. 1977 (135); Limner Antiques, London; purchased
by the Draper estate; given to Kenwood, 1991  (88029875)

This plainly dressed gentleman was probably from the burgeoning
Scottish professional and merchant classes at the end of the
eighteenth century. He is wearing a high-collared brown cloth coat,
with a white waistcoat, cravat and shirt with frill.
   Most of the detail on the sitter's face and hair is built up using
very fine stipple, with plenty of blue in the shadow. This gives the
miniature a rather neat but hard-edged appearance. The
contrasting blue background is painted with very fine, blended
hatching in one direction. This technique is in marked contrast to
the more painterly effects of Gallaway's contemporaries in
England.

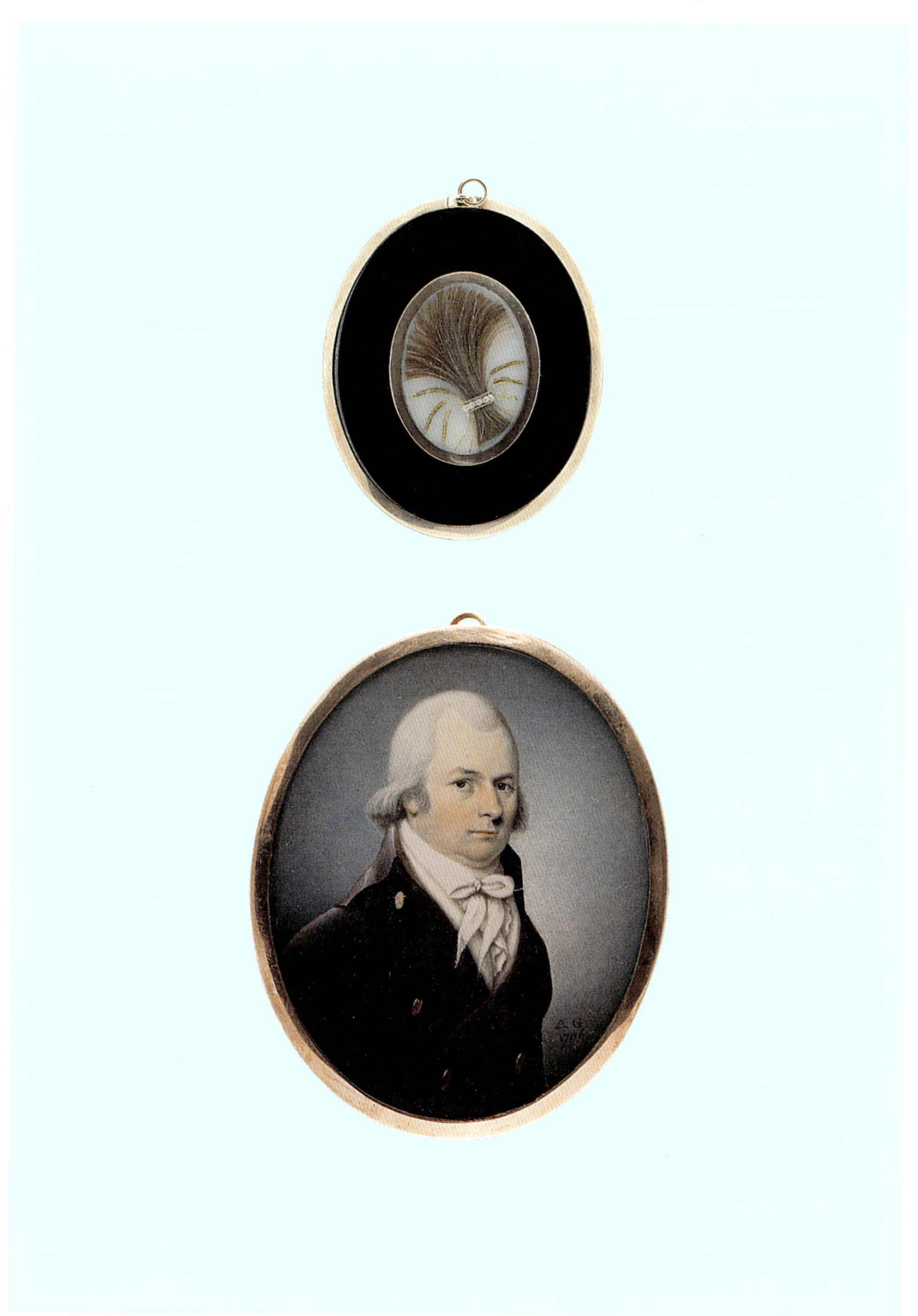

# George Place  (c1760–1805)

Place was born in Dublin, the son of a linen draper. He studied at the Dublin
Society Schools and painted both miniatures and oil portraits in Dublin for a
time, before moving to London around 1791. Place painted Queen Charlotte
and copied a portrait of George III by Beechey. In 1798 he reached Bengal
with his wife and set up business in Lucknow, where he found a lucrative
patron in the local nawab. His Indian works are supposed to have been
destroyed in the Indian mutiny (1857–8). He died in Lucknow.

Place's miniatures are painted with a good deal of detail in the faces, which
can have rather prominent eyes and a little too much blue in the shading.
Another characteristic is his use of long brush strokes in both the head and
background.

### 77  Unknown Man
Watercolour on ivory; modern gilt metal locket frame
Oval, 7.0 x 5.8 cm

R.L. Bayne-Powell; Sotheby's 11 Oct. 1994 (91); purchased by the
Draper estate; given to Kenwood, 1994  (88029829)

This gentleman, painted about 1795, is plainly but fashionably
dressed in a broad-lapelled white waistcoat and blue cloth coat
with a black, probably velvet, collar. Place has not flattered his sitter
by eliminating the mole on his cheek, which could not be
considered a beauty mark.

The quality of Place's drawing can clearly be seen in this work.
His peculiar mannerism of over-emphasising the eyes and mouth is
also displayed, as is his preference for plenty of blue in modelling
the face. Such features do help to define Place's work and might be
forgiven when one considers his degree of observation in the face
and the attractive use of opaque white and unpainted ivory on the
cravat and waistcoat.

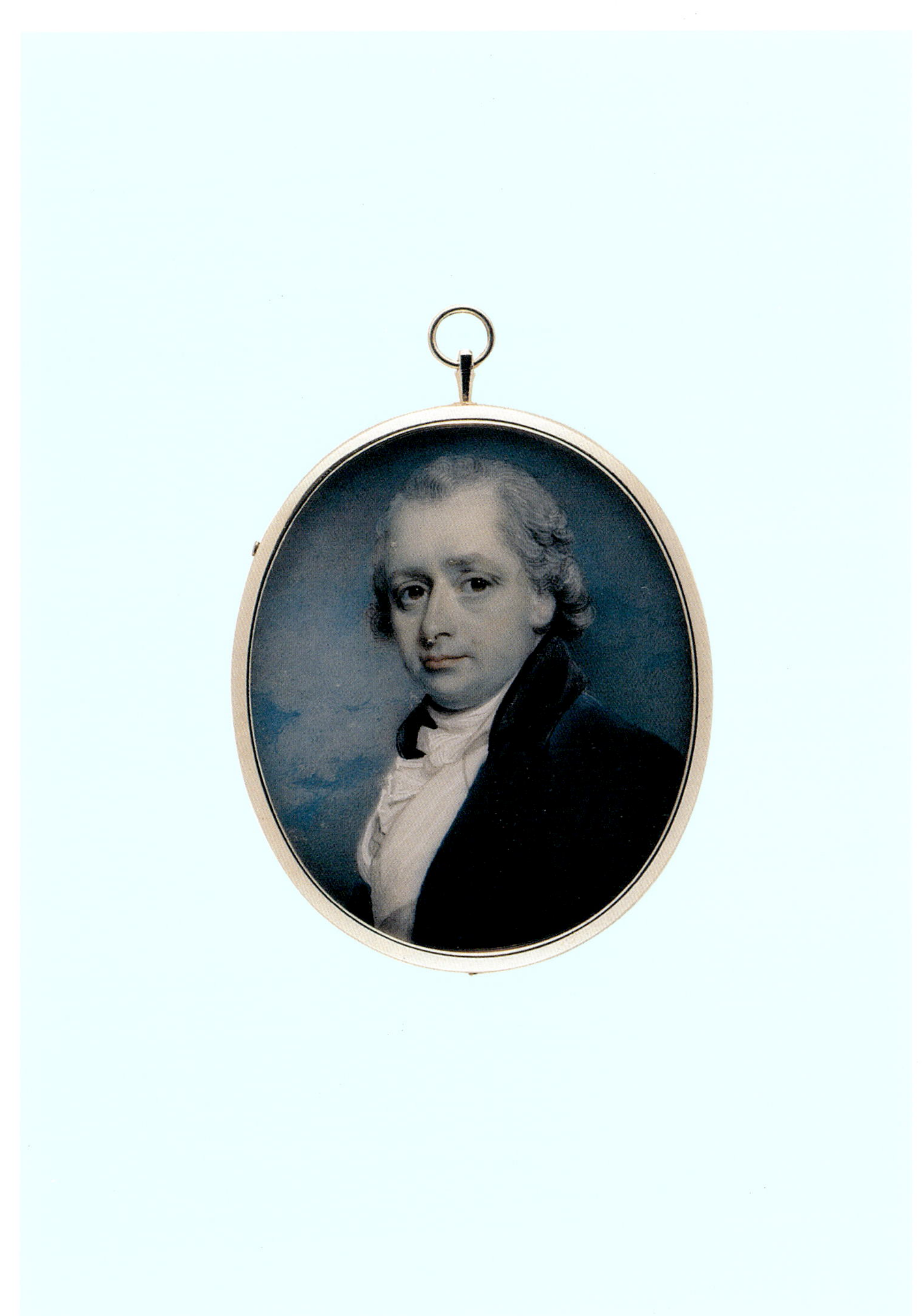

# Charles Robertson  (c1760–1821)

Robertson was a Dublin artist who worked making pictures in hair in his early
years. His elder brother Walter may have helped him as a painter. Charles
painted watercolours as well as miniatures and was exhibiting these in Dublin
by 1775. He worked in London from 1785 to 1792 and also in 1806, showing
at the Royal Academy. His daughter Clementina was also a miniaturist.

Robertson was a very good artist, but has often been overlooked because
he never signed his works. His style is characterised by a very soft overall
appearance, created by minute brush strokes, and neatly hatched, gradated
backgrounds. His choice of palette is often cool in tone.

### 78  James Alexander, 1st Earl of Caledon (1730–1802)

Watercolour on ivory; gold locket frame with glazed verso
Oval, 7.0 x 5.8 cm

Limner Antiques, London; purchased by the Draper estate, 1990;
given to Kenwood, 1990  (88029855)

James Alexander was a Londonderry MP and then Sheriff of Co.
Tyrone. His efforts as an Anglo-Irish politician were rewarded with
elevation to the peerage, and he rose from Baron to Earl between
1790 and 1800, about the date of this portrait. His son became the
first governor of the Cape of Good Hope. Caledon is conservatively
dressed, still wearing his hair curled and powdered at this late date.

Robertson's soft technique, giving a curiously far away look to his
sitters, is evident in this miniature. However, the face is nicely
modelled using quite thickly applied watercolour. The blue coat
appears almost to glow. This effect, shared by Walter Robertson, is
created by allowing a light ground to show through the edges of an
otherwise opaque area, painted very matt with plenty of gum arabic.

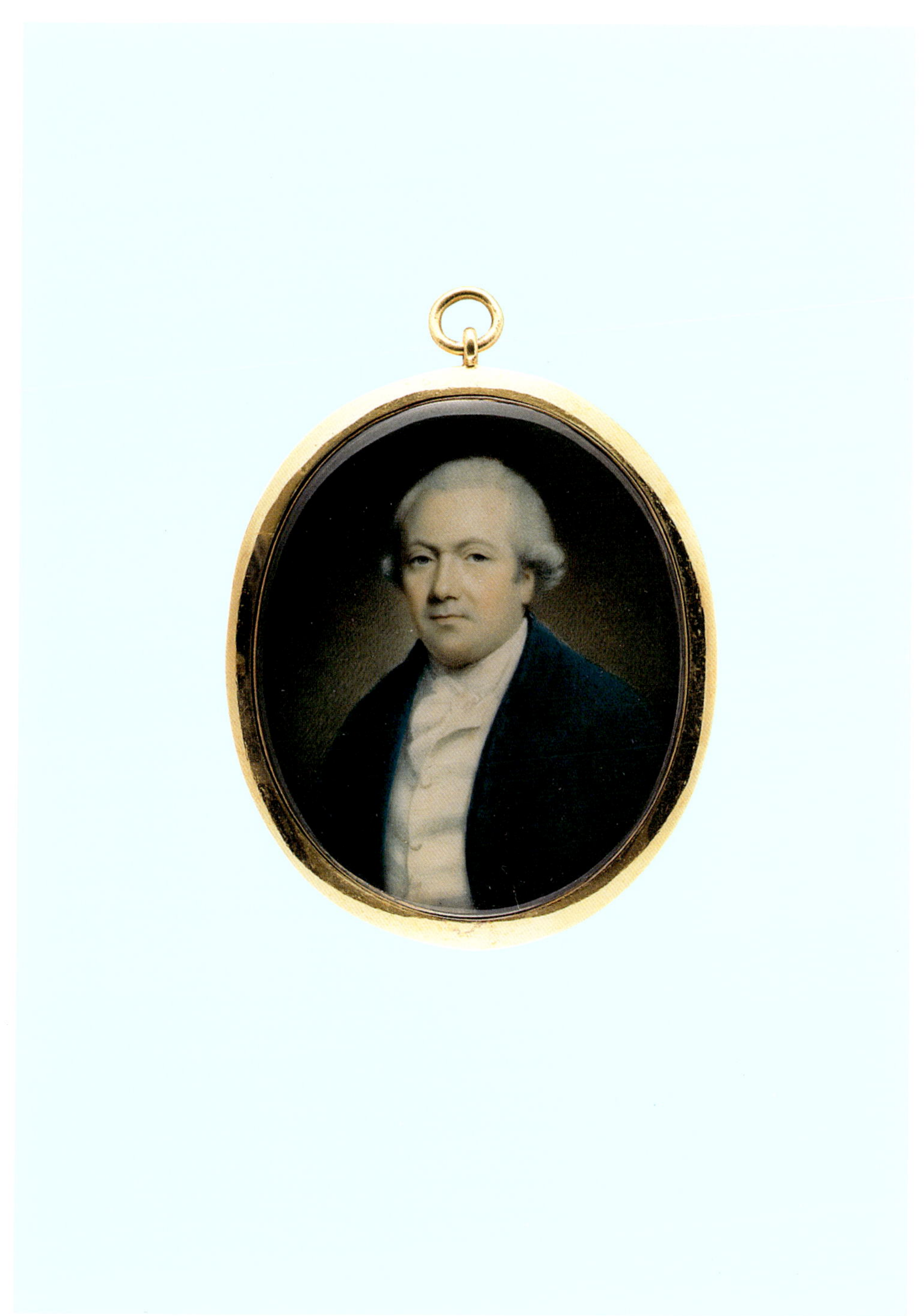

# Thomas Hazlehurst  (c1760–c1821)

Hazlehurst was one of the leading miniaturists from Liverpool active around the turn of the nineteenth century. It is possible that he studied with Reynolds, who exhibited in Liverpool in 1787, although by that date Hazlehurst would probably have already been well established. He did well as an artist but he was a poor businessman and died in poverty.

Hazlehurst's style varies over the years, from soft, muted early works to a rather harder and precise manner in later years. His drawing is quite good and he often combined soft lines, in the hair for example, with hatched or cross-hatched lines. Many of his portraits have sky backgrounds and are signed with his initials in neat, roman capitals.

### 79  Miss K. Blackburn

Watercolour on ivory; gold locket frame, the verso with seed pearl initials, *KB* with a plaited hair border. Signed lower left *TH*
Oval, 6.3 x 4.8 cm

Limner Antiques, London; purchased by the Draper estate, 1990; given to Kenwood, 1990  (88029847)

Miss Blackburn is shown wearing the simple but fashionable white gown of about 1790, tied with a blue sash. Her hair is long and probably powdered, but not quite so puffed out as it might have been a few years earlier.

This miniature is neatly drawn, especially round the eyes and mouth, but lacks the elegance of those by Hazlehurst's London rival, Cosway, and others. Whilst the hair is made up of spiralling lines with a hatched background, elsewhere on the body and in the sky Hazlehurst uses quite hard-edged lines, hatched in varying directions. This effect can make his works look rather angular and harsh. Works of this quality, with its up-to-date appearance, would have satisfied the majority of people wealthy enough to commission miniatures in and around Liverpool, who did not venture to London.

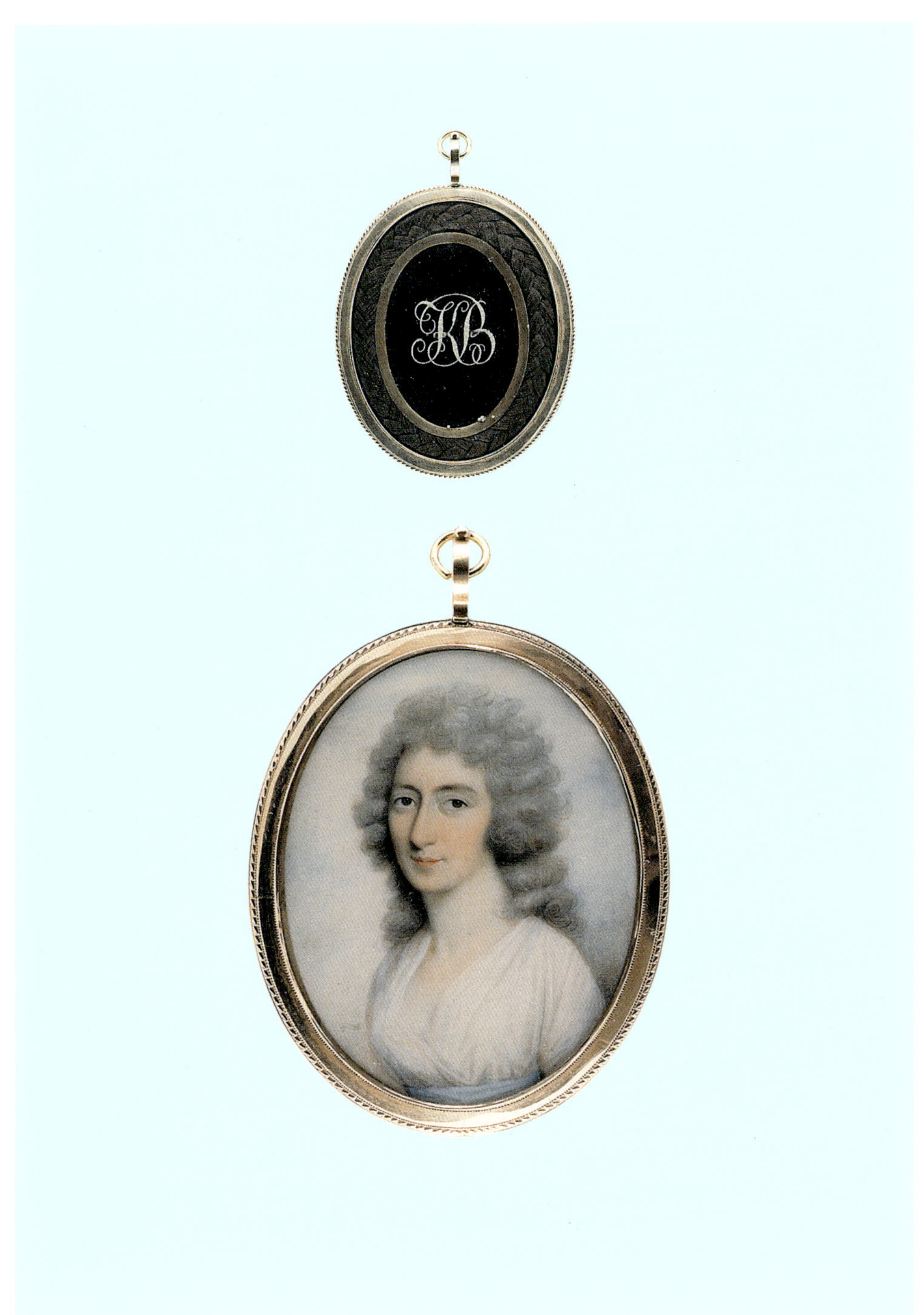

# William Armfield Hobday  (1771–1831)

The son of a Birmingham manufacturer, Hobday learned his art in London,
partly at the Royal Academy Schools. In addition to miniatures he painted a
variety of subject matter. Hobday also lived in Bath, and settled in Bristol,
where he admired the work of George Chinnery whom he met about 1796
(see cats 94,95). Here he set up a practice painting officers who were leaving
for duty in Spain. Hobday was always hopeless with money, presumably his
father's, and opened a gallery in Pall Mall, where he continued to lose money,
firstly with a panorama venture and then as a picture dealer. His works are
often no more than competent, but he managed to attract a good clientele,
suggesting perhaps that his charm was more persuasive than his pictures.

### 80  Unknown Woman, 'H.E.'

Watercolour on ivory; gilt metal locket, the verso set with gilt
initials *H.E.* , hair and seed pearl ornament, on white glass. Signed
lower right *Wm.·A. Hobday. 1797*
Oval, 6.9 x 5.6 cm

Limner Antiques, London; purchased by the Draper estate, 1992;
given to Kenwood, 1992  (88029235)

This miniature is particularly interesting because it shows the sitter
wearing another miniature, presumably of her husband, on a cord
around her neck. Her hair is curled and tied up with a band so as
to appear quite short. Over her dress is a black stole or cloak with
lace trimming.

At this date, 1797, Hobday employs mostly lines to build up his
miniature. These are neat and fused together on the face, but loose
in the hair and clothing. The dress is positively scribbled in places,
and indeed evidence of the use of a scraper may be seen in the
dark areas. He uses similarly uneven strokes in the sky background,
creating a lively surface over the whole miniature.

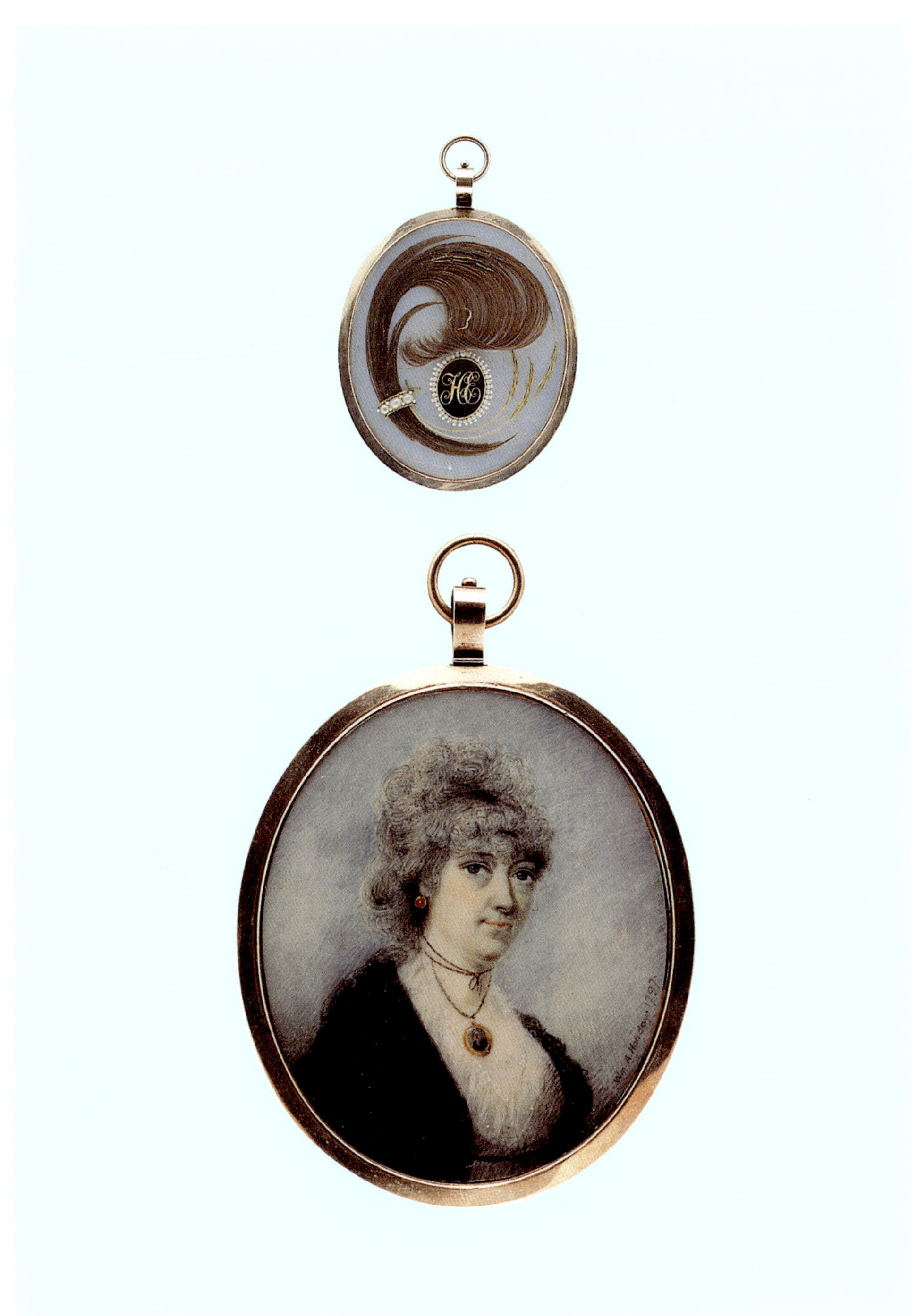

# William Wood  (1769–1810)

Wood came from Suffolk and it is not known where he learned to draw. In 1785 he attended the Royal Academy Schools and was soon painting successfully in a  manner which owed much to Cosway and Engleheart. He lived in Bristol and Gloucester as well as London and worked in watercolour and crayons in addition to painting miniatures.

As well as being an outstanding miniature painter who could rival Engleheart and Andrew Plimer on occasion, Wood is important because of the record of his practice he left in his ledgers with tracings (Victoria and Albert Museum). These also record his efforts to find more permanent pigments, the fruits of which are evident in his strongly coloured works. Wood was active in the early watercolour societies and joined the newly formed Artists Volunteer Corps (established by Charles Robertson). Wood's miniatures are distinctive for his manner of painting rather than any stylistic innovations. Without resource to minuscule brushwork, the figures appear solid and alive.

### 81  Unknown Man, 'J.N.'
Watercolour on ivory; gilt metal locket with plaited hair verso, set with gold initials, *JN*
Oval, 7.8 x 6.0 cm

Bonham's, 30 Nov. 1994 (1070); purchased by the Draper estate; given to Kenwood, 1994  (88029838)

A very good quality miniature and portrait, showing Wood's ability to capture character. The gentleman is dressed in the informal 'uniform' of the mid-1790s: high-collared dark coat, high neck band with white cravat and in this case two waistcoats. The inner of these is red, adding a note of colour to the sober dress.

Wood's miniature is like a less ephemeral looking Cosway. He relishes the use of paint and is not afraid to use visible brush strokes even on this larger scale. The flesh is built up with many marks in differing, mostly hot colours, whereas the coat and inner garments are floated on and hatched in a more conventional way.

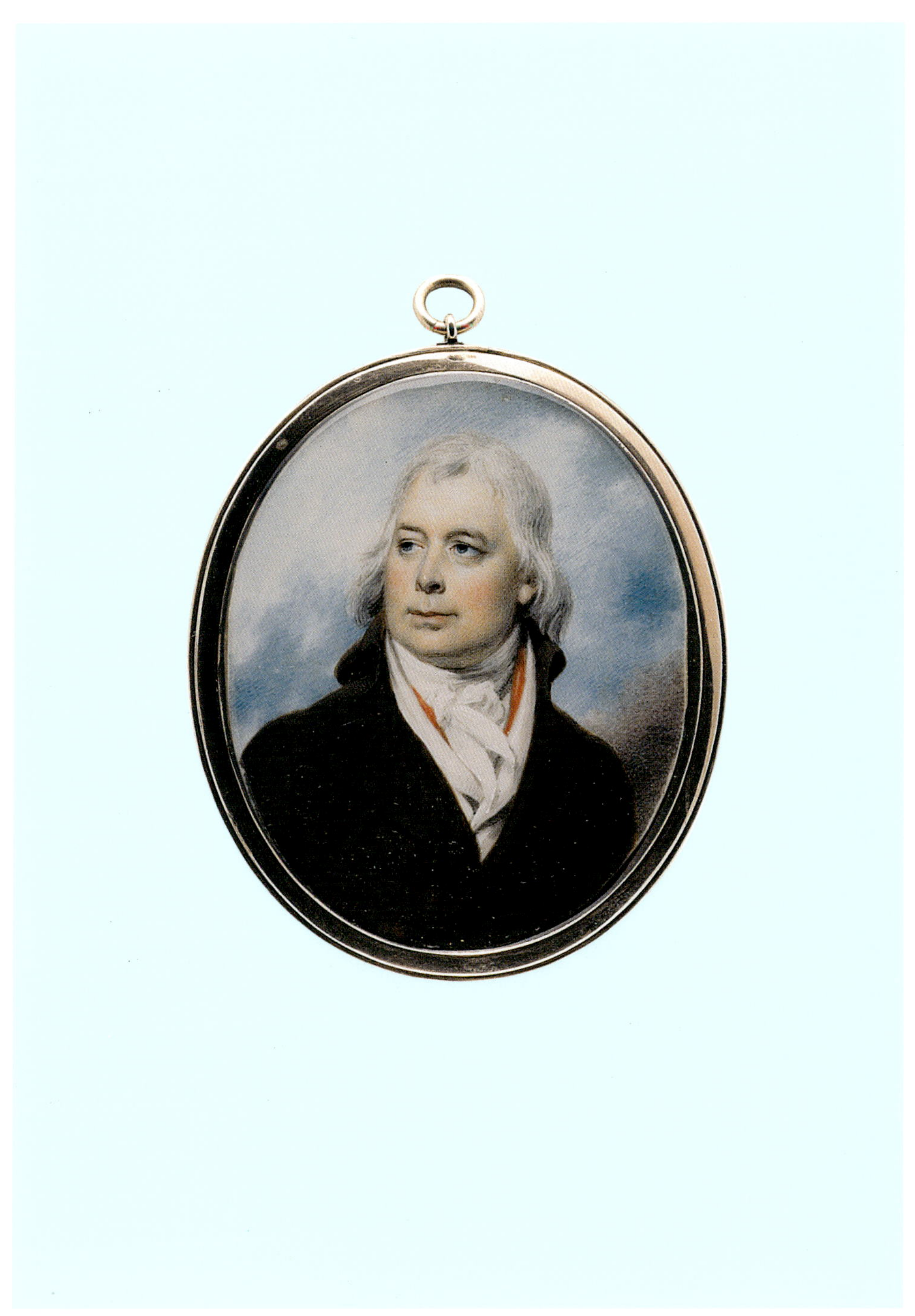

# William Wood

**82  ?Lady Eleanor Clifford**
Watercolour on ivory; gilt metal locket with plaited hair verso. Old
label on verso, *Eleanor Wife of Henry Clifford Earl of Cumberland*
etc.
Oval, 7.6 x 5.8 cm

Christie's, 20 March 1990 (122); purchased by the Draper estate;
given to Kenwood, 1992  (88029852)

The lady in this portrait of c.1805 may be Eleanor Mary, the
daughter of Henry, 8th Lord Arundell of Wardour and wife of
Charles, 6th Baron Clifford of Chudleigh. The traditional
identification on the label cannot be correct as the husband's title
given did not exist at the time of this portrait. She wears a coral
necklace, a popular form of jewellery at the time.

   Wood's characteristic use of warm colour, strong line and a
variety of bold brush strokes are all used with great success here.
One individual mannerism to note is the use of dotted lines, painted
fairly wet, seen in the shadow by the sitter's right shoulder.

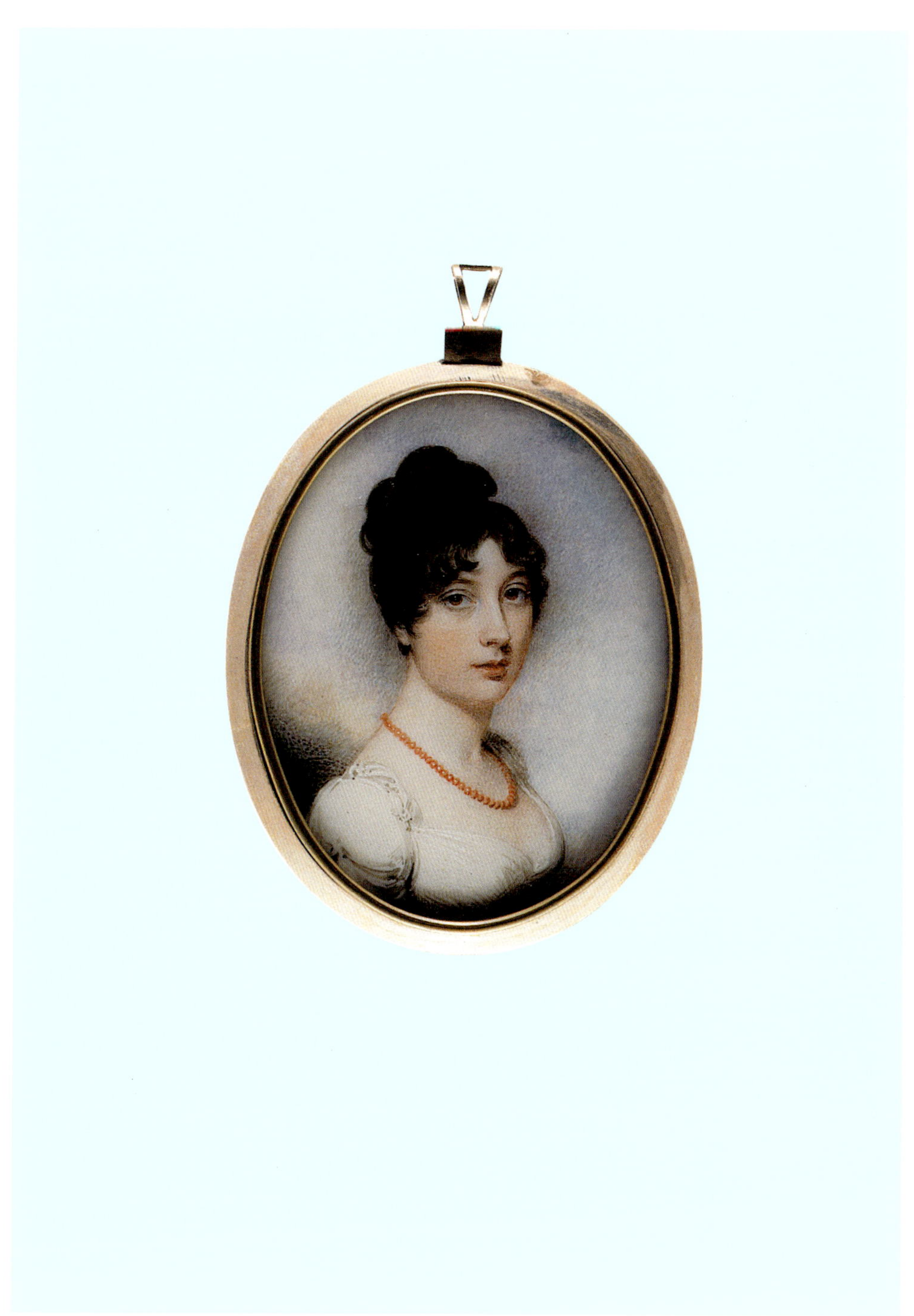

# Thomas Richmond  (1771–1837)

Thomas Richmond was the son of an innkeeper at Kew and was taught to paint by his cousin on his mother's side, George Engleheart. He also studied at the St Martin's Lane Academy. Richmond drew portraits on paper as well as miniatures, and regularly copied works of his contemporaries, including Engleheart. His own works compare with his cousin's, but lack their decorative effect and sometimes suffer from over-use of blue shading. However, they are generally well painted and show a good grasp of character. He also worked in Portsmouth (where he died) and regularly painted officers of the Army and Navy.

His sons Thomas and George also became artists. Thomas junior painted in similar manner to his father, but George produced some distinctive miniatures, somewhat influenced by the work of his friends William Blake and Samuel Palmer, as well as his more well-known portraits in chalk.

### 83  Unknown Man

Watercolour on ivory; gold locket with enamel verso set with hair arrangement in the form of a tree, inscribed *EVER THUS*
Oval, 7.2 x 5.6 cm

E.W.M.D. de la Hey; Sotheby's 4 July 1989 (288); purchased by the Draper estate; given to Kenwood, 1989  (88029845)

This young gentleman wears his own hair styled and powdered in the manner of the short wig that would probably have been worn by an officer or court official at the date of the miniature, c.1800, although he is not in uniform. The high collars of the shirt, stock, coat and waistcoat all correspond to male fashion at the turn of the nineteenth century. Richmond's choice of a nearly full-face pose is not so common for a male sitter and is made all the more effective by his emphatic painting of the eyes.

The miniature shares several traits with the contemporary work of Engleheart, in particular the large eyes with blue 'whites' and plenty of shading. The linear treatment of the hair is also similar. In contrast, Richmond's notably blue shading and quite heavily worked surface – seen in the long hatching of the background – are more peculiar to him. There is an oak tree motif on the back of the frame, perhaps suggesting steadfastness to the owner of the miniature.

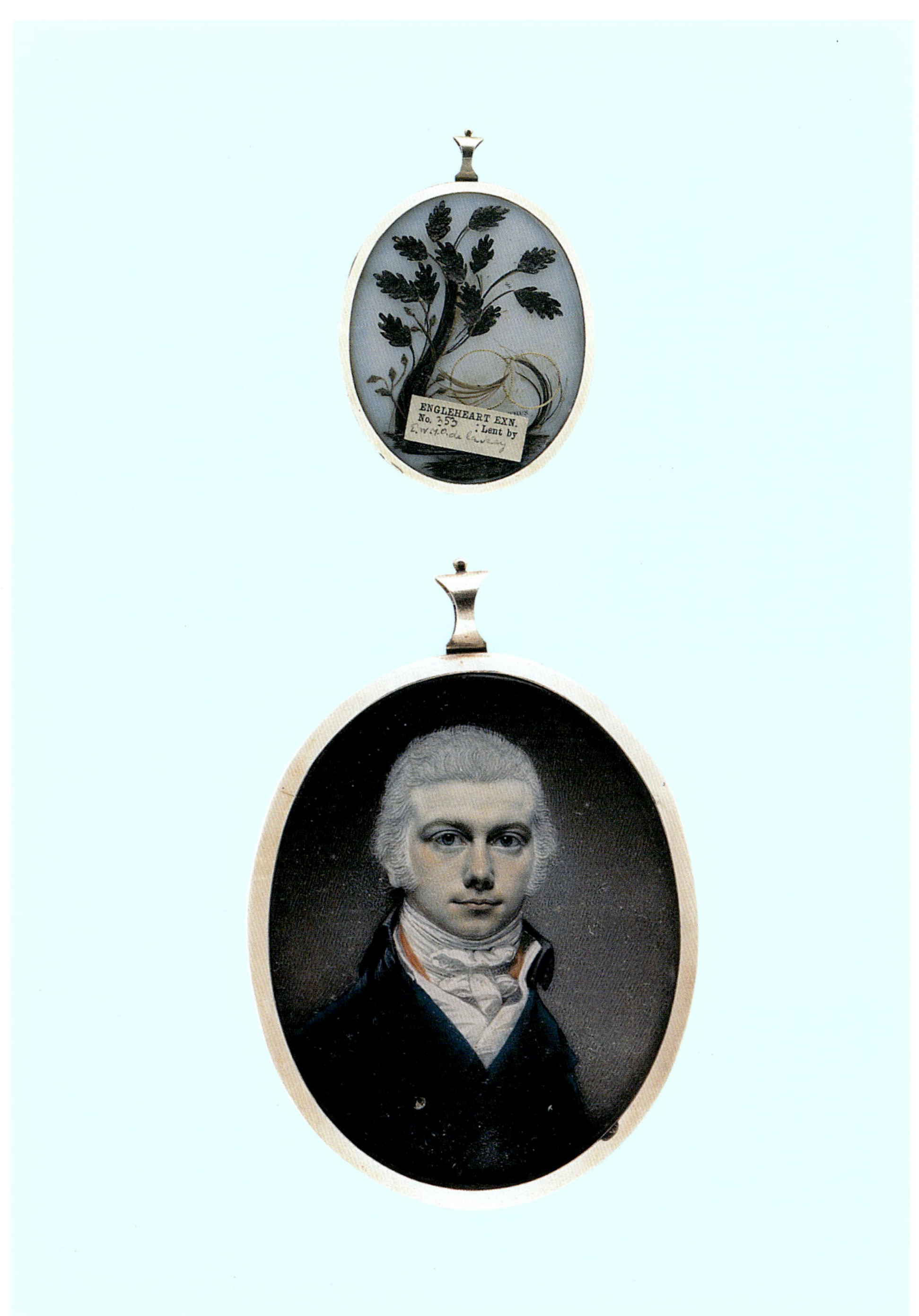

ENGLEHEART EXN.
No. 353 : Lent by

# Edward Nash  (1778–1821)

The son of a wealthy merchant of Kentish origins, Nash is thought to have
studied under Shelley. He exhibited at the Royal Academy between 1800 and
1820, but worked in Bombay from 1801 to 1810. He did well in India, working
in a manner not dissimilar to the popular Shelley. On returning to London he
lived for several years in Shelley's former home in George Street, Hanover
Square. During a period in the Lake District, Nash became acquainted with
Wordsworth and Coleridge.

### 84  Unknown Woman, 'K.P.'

Watercolour on ivory; gold locket frame with gold monogram on
verso, *KP* set on plaited hair verso. Signed on verso *Edward Nash
Bombay Feb. 7 1803*
Oval, 7.0 x 5.6 cm

Bonham's, 21 Feb. 1996 (97); purchased by the Draper estate; given
to Kenwood, 1996  (88029843)

This lady seems well wrapped up for the climate of the Indian
subcontinent. Her cap is trimmed with pink embroidered flowers
and her muslin gown has no less than two frilled collars. All this
gives her a rather matronly appearance.

Nash's debt to Shelley can be seen in his somewhat opaque
painting and yellowy-green colouring in the flesh and background.
However, the evening sky background, with a hint of landscape, is
his own, and his use of long, parallel brush strokes in the sky and
dress is distinctive.

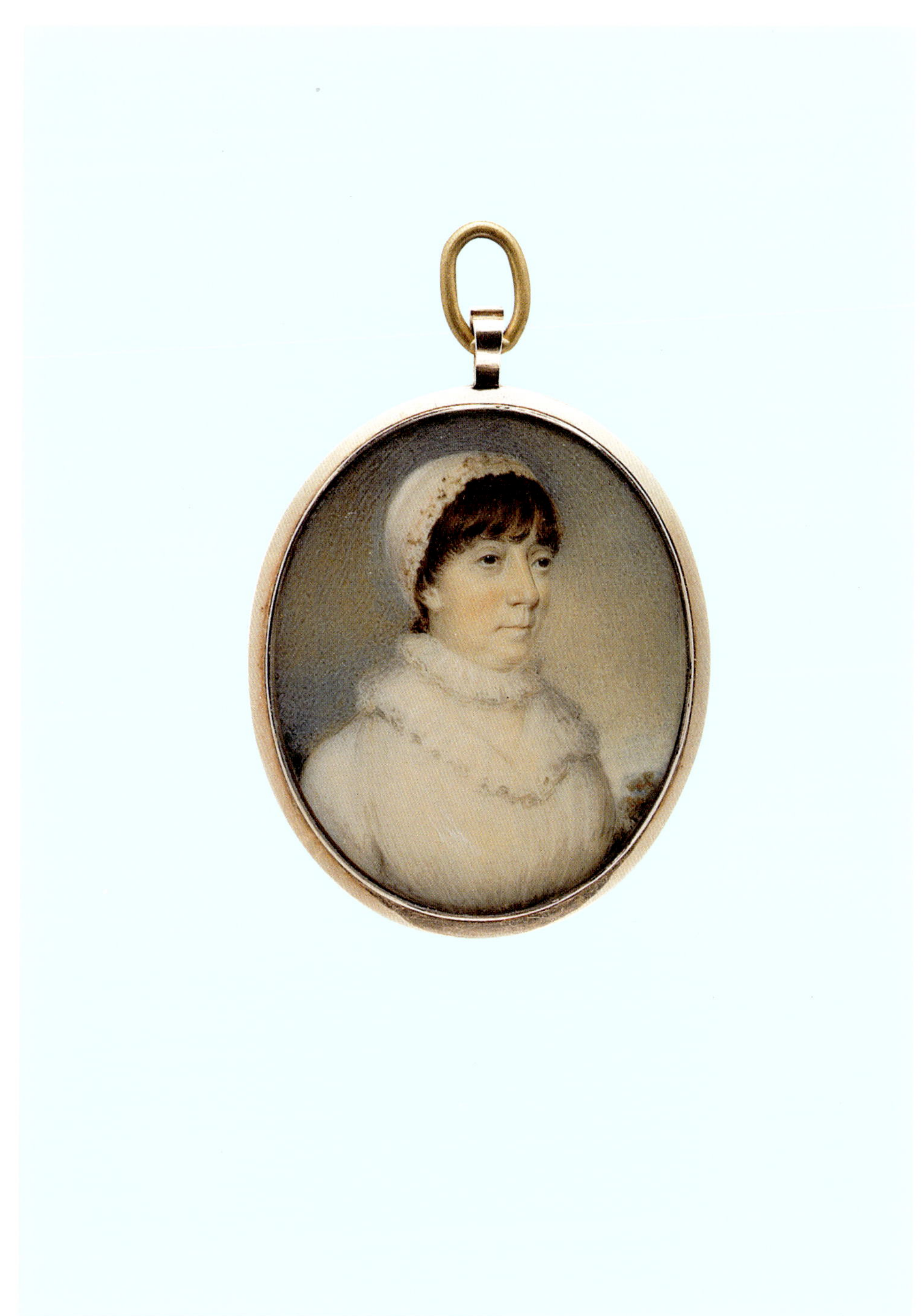

# John Comerford  (c1770–1832)

Comerford was from Kilkenny in Ireland, the son of a flax dresser. He is thought to have taught himself by copying paintings in oil from local collections. However, he found success by painting miniatures and exhibited regularly in Dublin until 1813. He also showed at the Royal Academy on two occasions. Encouragement came from George Chinnery (cats 94,95) and he may have also been influenced by the visiting American artist, Gilbert Stuart.

Comerford was able to make a good living through his talents in miniature and crayon. In 1811 he was made vice-president of Dublin Society of Artists, the main Irish association of artists before the establishment of a formal academy (the formation of which he opposed). His miniatures vary from the rather boldly painted to being very finely finished. A particular characteristic is red and grey hatching used on the face, giving rather a soft effect.

### 85  Paul Helsham

Watercolour on ivory; gold locket frame with gold monogram set on hair verso with blue glass surround. Signed lower right
*J. Comerford/ 1798*
Oval, 7.2 x 6.0 cm

Christie's 18 Dec. 1990 (148); purchased by the Draper estate; given to Kenwood, 1991  (88029862)

Helsham was ordained as a Deacon in 1781. At the time of this portrait he was Archdeacon of Ossory, and in 1800, after ordination as Priest, he became Vicar General of the Church of Ireland. Married to Rebecca Blunt, he had two children, and died in 1822. He was buried at St John's Church, Kilkenny.  He appears in secular dress consisting of a white stock and shirt ruffle, black waistcoat and double-breasted coat, with a high turned-over collar.

Comerford's more usual technique is clearly demonstrated in this work. The face is built up with fine soft hatching, alternating warm and cooler colouring. In the dress he uses flat areas of paint with lots of gum arabic — a common device at this time. The background is worked with bolder blue with yellow cross hatching, done very neatly, to create a lively surface.

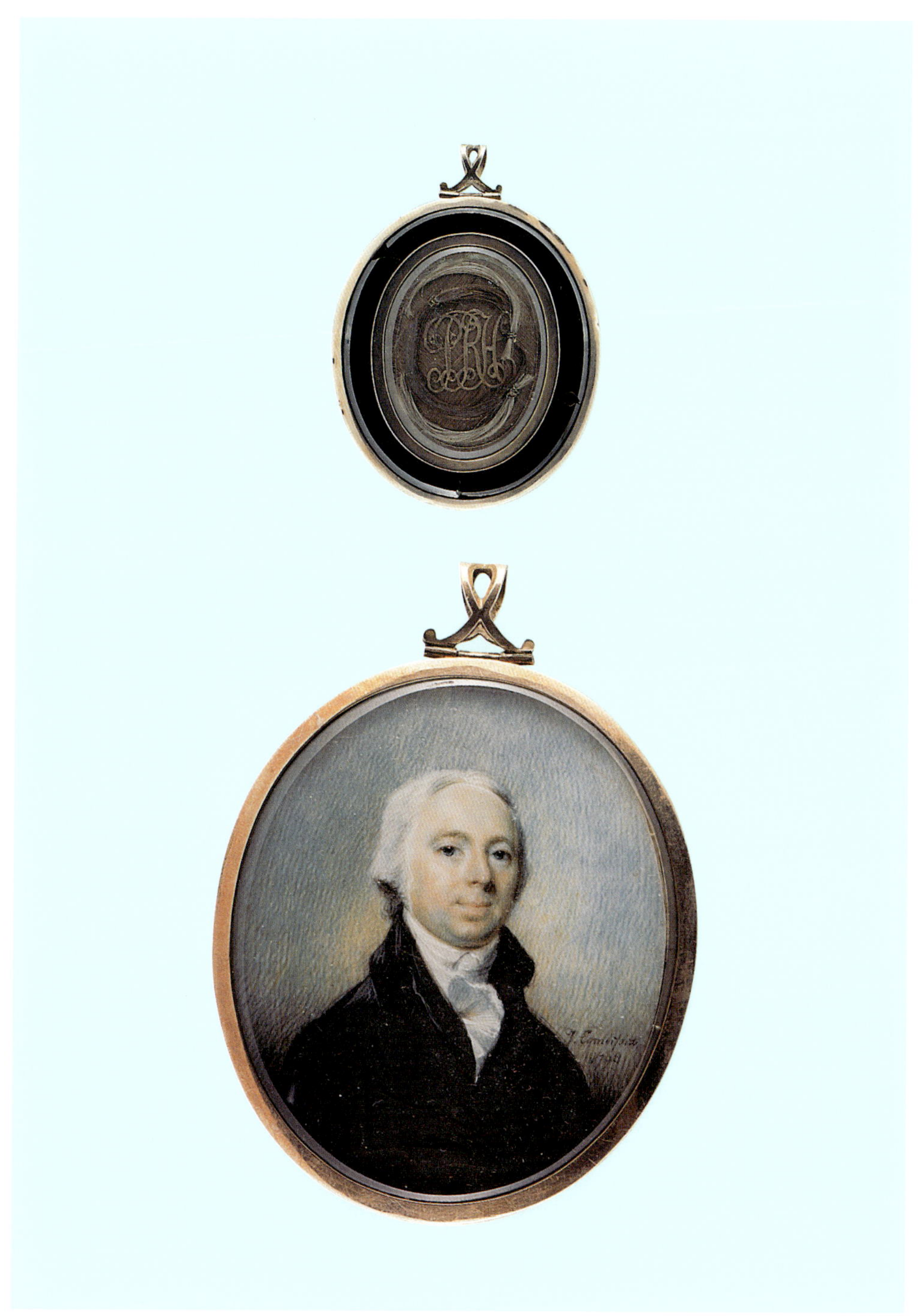

# Henry Edridge ARA (1768–1821)

Edridge was a Londoner who was apprenticed to the engraver William Pether and studied at the Royal Academy Schools, where he won a silver medal in 1786 and was to exhibit from then on. He was a skilled draughtsman and produced many portraits and landscapes in pencil and watercolour as well as in oil. His output of miniatures is relatively small and he abandoned the medium around 1800 because of his poor eyesight. From that date on he specialised in portrait drawings on paper, often set in a landscape.

His style varied between quite finished miniatures which have plenty of soft line work (especially in the hair) and more painterly works where the dress is laid on quickly with washes. Two notable characteristics are blue shading of the features and a deep shadow under the nose.

## 86  Unknown Woman

Watercolour on ivory; engraved gilt metal frame
Oval, 6.4 x 4.7 cm

Limner Antiques, London; purchased by the Draper estate; given to Kenwood, 1990  (88029854)

This miniature seems almost unfinished and shows Edridge's pencil-like technique to good effect. The perennially popular muslin dress of the turn of the century is seen in a more fussy guise here, with frills to the lady's *décolletage* and a large buffon neckerchief. The only colour is in her yellow waistband. Her two strands of very large pearls must have been highly prized.

In drawing this miniature Edridge has only worked up the face, using blue shadow. The hair is a mass of lines over a grey ground and the dress rapidly sketched in with much of the ivory left unpainted. It is as if he has taken Cosway's shorthand treatment of female dress and hair and decided that he can do away with much of the painstaking, traditional miniature technique. Edridge only succeeds in this because of his ability to draw well.

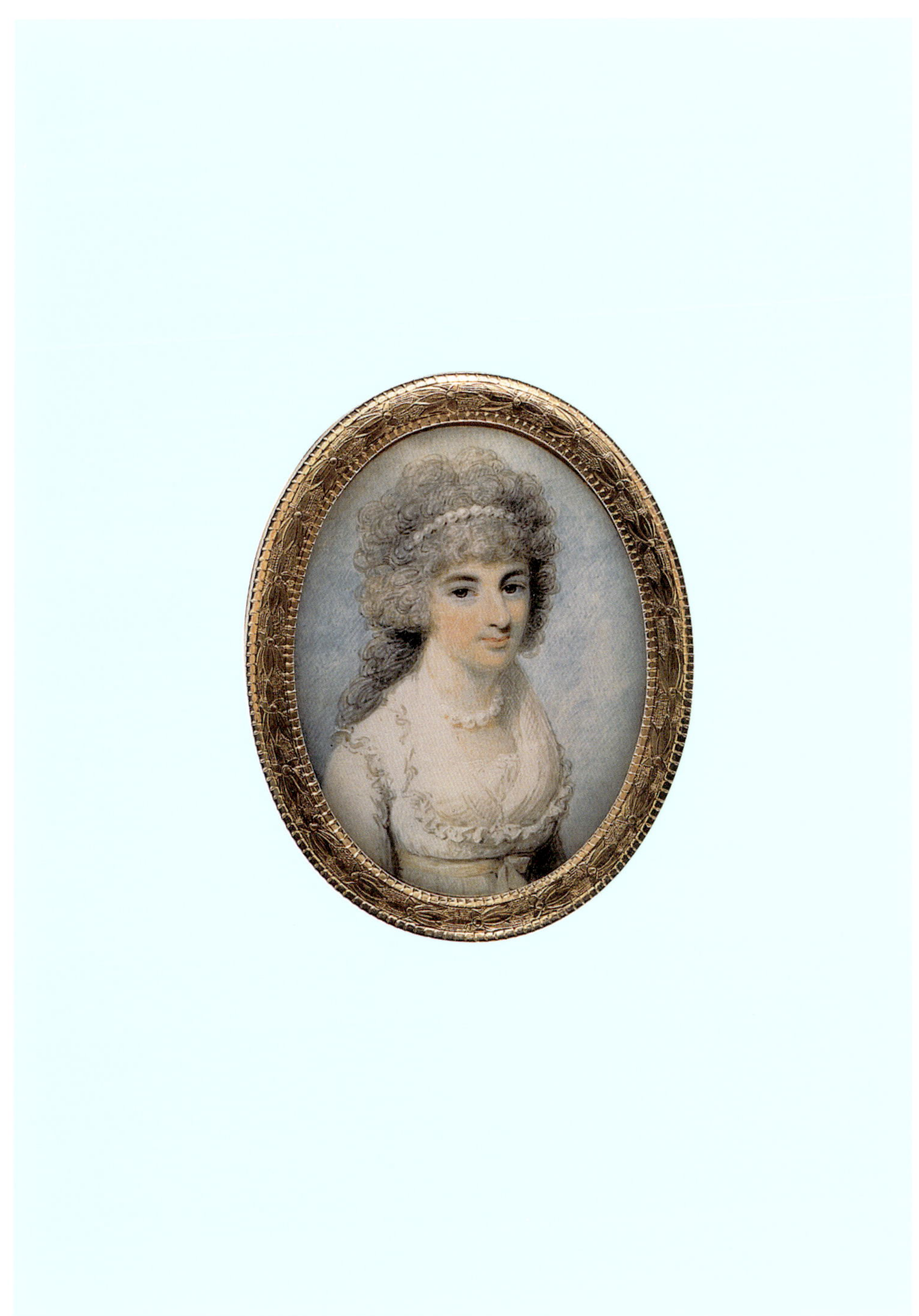

# Henry Edridge ARA

**87  A Naval Officer, 'J.C.'**
Watercolour on ivory; gilt metal locket, the verso set with gilt
initials *JC* on a hair verso, with blue glass border
Oval, 6.7 x 5.0 cm

R.L. Bayne-Powell; Sotheby's 11 Oct. 1994 (96); purchased by the
Draper estate; given to Kenwood, 1994  (88029831)

Painted about 1805, the sitter wears a light blue coat with gold
braid. The single epaulette distinguishes his rank as Commander.
His collar-length hair is simply dressed with powder.
　　This is quite a late miniature on ivory for Edridge, who was
suffering from eye strain by this date. The face is painted with his
characteristic blue-grey shading and use of deep shadow and
highlights on the nose. This is painted with fairly uneven, hatched
strokes. However, when it comes to the coat, Edridge employs thin
washes of colour and scrubby, rapid details that appear almost wet.
Such a lively use of watercolour on ivory was popular with a
number of miniaturists in the early nineteenth century, before a
return to a more meticulous finish.

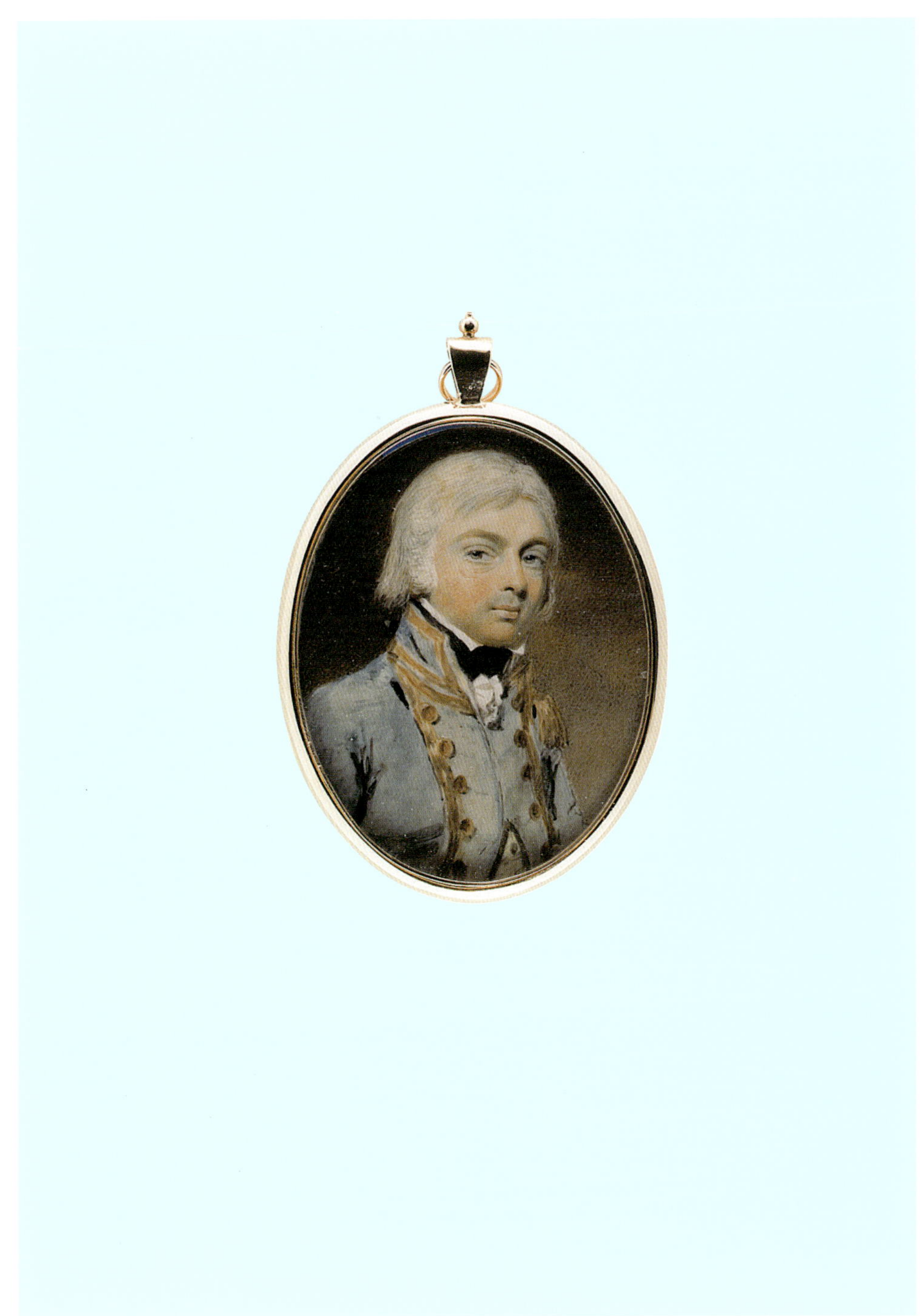

# Jean-Baptist Isabey (1767–1855)

Perhaps the greatest French miniaturist, Isabey was born in Nancy and was taught by Giradet and Claudot. His talent was recognised by Marie-Antoinette but his greatest success came later when he was brought into the circle of Napoleon. From then on he became Court Painter to four rulers of France and was eventually given an apartment at Versailles. As well as running a large studio, Isabey produced court ceremonies. He was reputedly in England between 1815 and 1820.

His technique was at first very fine, employing opaque colour on a dark background, but after about 1800 he often used a sky ground, after the English example, and thinly applied, transparent paint. In later years he successfully produced larger miniatures on paper, and worked in several other media.

### 88  Unknown Man
Watercolour on ivory; gilt metal mount
Circular, 3.7 cm

Bonham's, 12 June 1995; purchased by the Draper estate; given to Kenwood, 1995  (88029842)

The sitter's dress and the use of a dark, body colour background suggest that this is a work of the mid-1790s. His own hair is powdered and his grey coat with a high black silk or velvet collar and stock are the dress of an affluent but not particularly showy individual of the period.

Isabey's technique at this early point in his career owes much to his predecessors. This is apparent in his extensive use of opaque paint which is used in two different ways. The face is built up with a fine, soft stipple with subtle colour graduation; the clothing is broadly painted with brush strokes over a flat, solid ground. Even at this stage, his skill as a draughtsman in rendering the head in the round is outstanding.

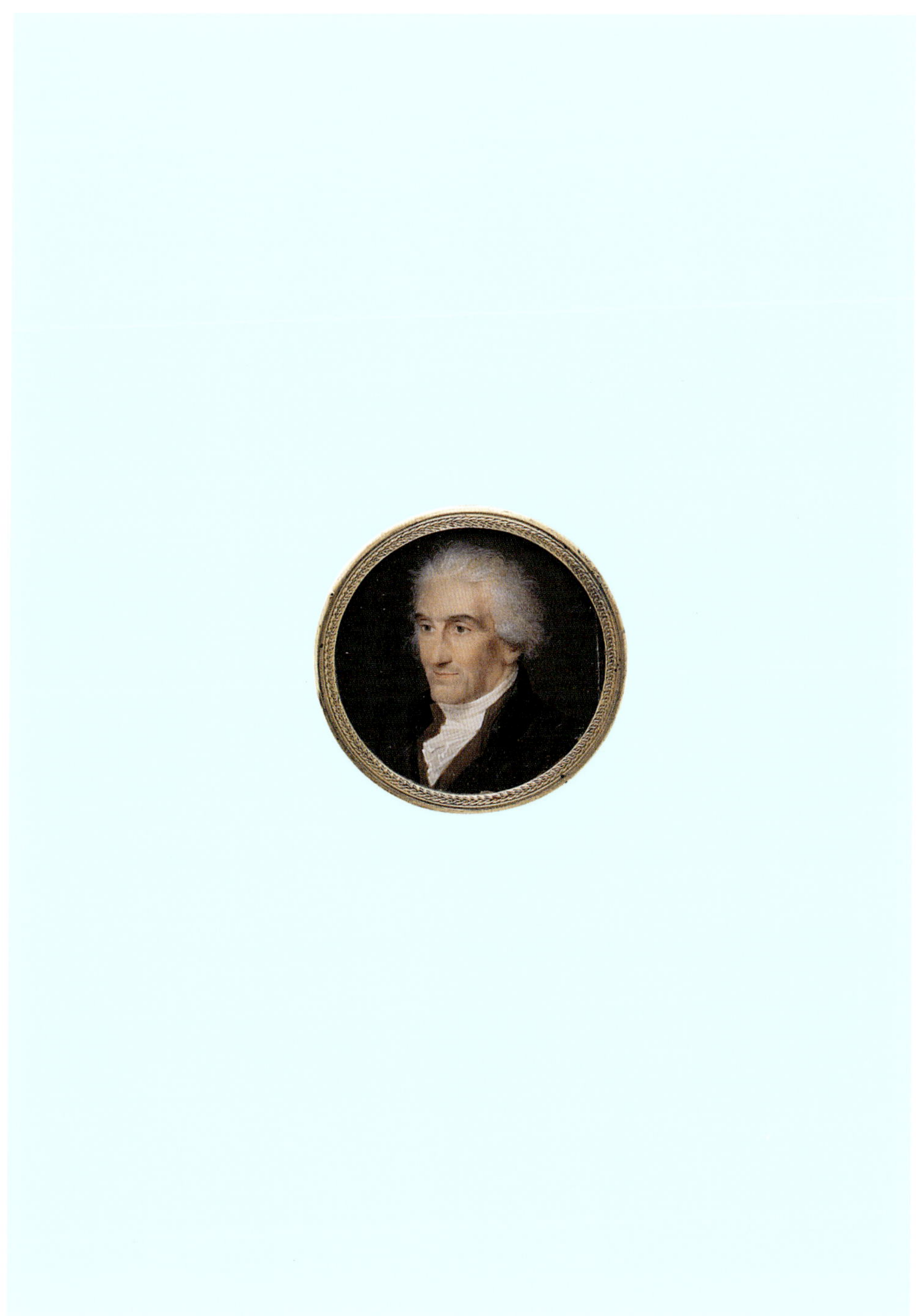

# Jean-Baptist Isabey

## 89  Unknown Young Woman

Watercolour on ivory; gold mount and gilt metal frame with velvet.
Signed lower right *Isabey*
Oval, 3.8 x 2.9 cm

Bonham's, 21 March 1995 (38); purchased by the Draper estate;
given to Kenwood, 1995 (88029836)

This young woman wears the low-cut, empire style dress that seems
to have swept Europe from the early 1790s, with the
complementary short-cut and curled hairstyle. Just as the eyes of
English artists like Cosway were on the latest developments in
France, where Isabey was rapidly coming to prominence, the eyes
of English men and women of fashion also turned to France at this
time.

Isabey's neat, unobtrusive technique is shown to good effect in
this simple miniature. The tiny, fused hatch strokes of the face and
delicate strands of hair are perfectly suited to the late neo-classical
style of the turn of the nineteenth century.

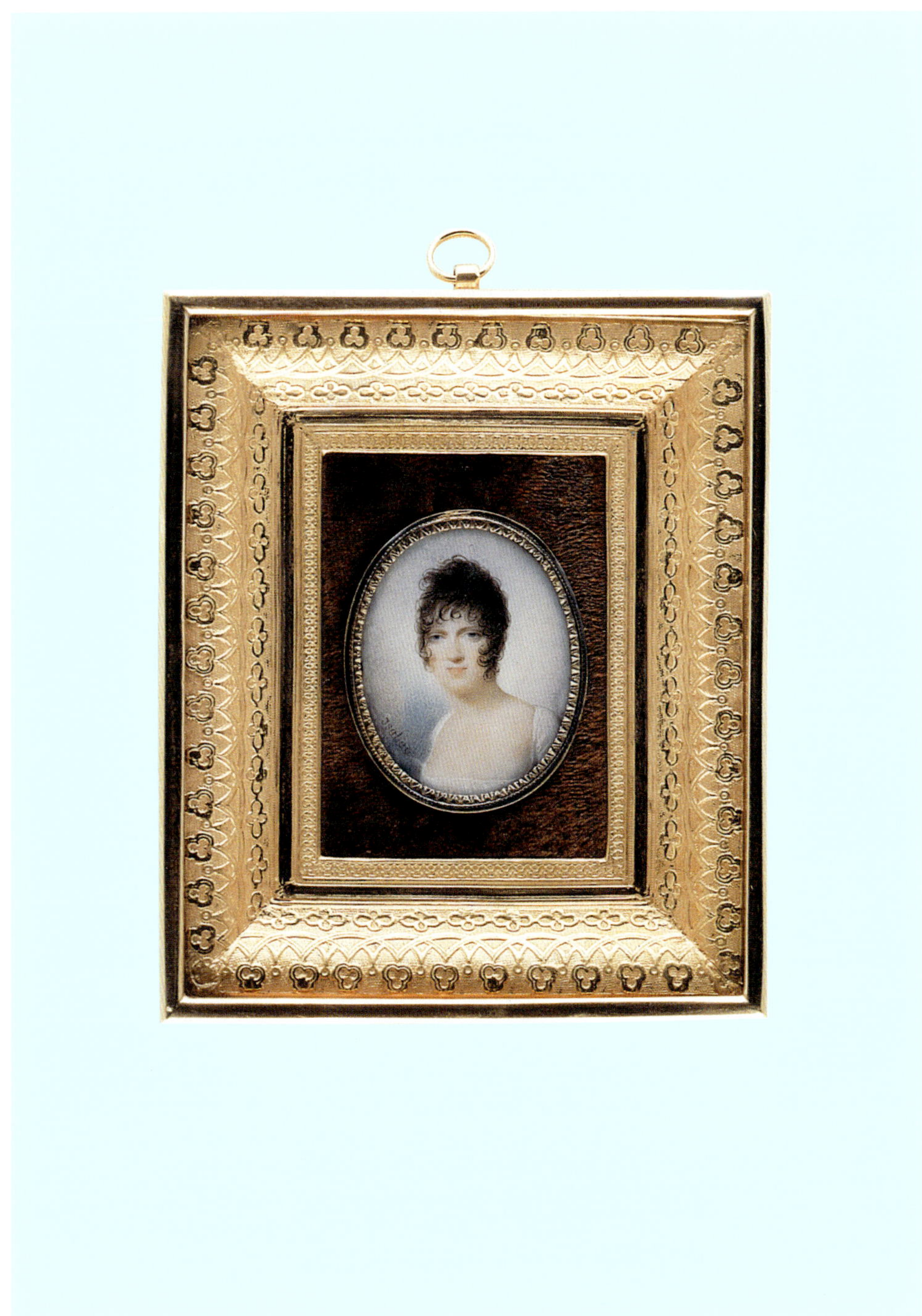

# Peter Edward Stroëhling (1768–after 1826)

Stroëhling, or Stroely (as he may have been known in England) was reputedly a Russian, born in Dusseldorf, who studied in Italy and then travelled Europe as an artist. He worked in England on two occasions: from 1803 to 1807 and 1819 to 1826. Stroëhling managed to adapt the continental style of painting to British tastes and found some important patrons, including the Prince Regent and Sir Walter Scott. His style is quite precise and he uses large areas of opaque colour, in common with many French miniaturists. One particular characteristic is his preference for grey in both the flesh colours and backgrounds.

### 90  Lucy Nelson

Watercolour on ivory; gilt metal mount
Oval, 6.9 x 5.5 cm

Hawtin Collection; Sotheby's 11 Nov. 1993 (54); purchased by the Draper estate; given to Kenwood, 1993  (88029813)

Miss Nelson's chemise dress and short hair, brushed forward, date this work to around the turn of the century, probably made not long after Stroëhling had arrived in London in 1803.

The face is very finely hatched, with rather cool colouring, while the hair is worked in opaque paint with very thin, even lines. Similar precision can be seen in the long cross hatches of the background, which, typically for this artist, is grey. Only the dress makes use of the ivory to create the appearance of transparent cloth: a nod, perhaps, to the leading artists of the time whom Stroëhling would have encountered on his arrival in England.

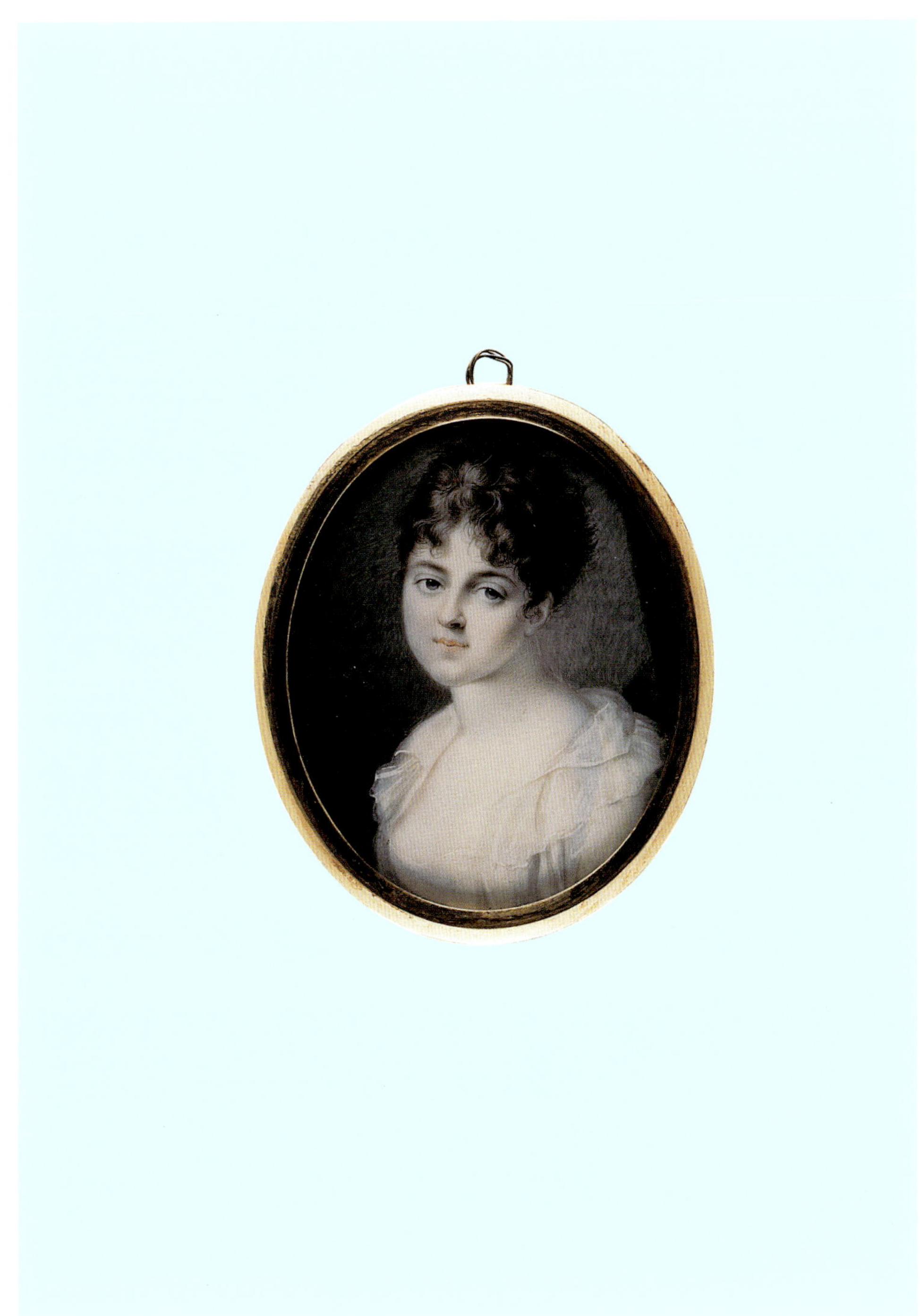

# Charles Hayter  (1761–1835)

Charles Hayter's chief achievement was to be the father of a great dynasty of painters, although he was a good artist in his own right, mostly working in pencil, crayon or watercolour on ivory. Hayter was born in Twickenham, studied at the Royal Academy Schools and worked in London and Winchester. He taught perspective to Princess Charlotte (daughter of George IV) and published books on perspective and colour theory.

Three of his children, George, Anne and John, were brought up as artists, with George becoming one of the leading British portrait painters in oil, as well as painting miniatures.

### 91  Unknown Woman

Watercolour on ivory; gilt metal locket. Signed left hand edge *C Hayter 1803*
Oval, 7.2 x 5.6 cm

Christie's 9 Nov. 1994 (36); purchased by the Draper estate; given to Kenwood, 1994  (88029835)

This lady has her hair tied up with a plait and curled all over, which Hayter has made play of by using highlights in the paint. Her white dress is made of two layers, the upper consisting of thin polka dot muslin, and she has a large neckerchief or buffon attached with a jewel.

Hayter's work here could be described as solid looking rather than elegant, although he does make the figure appear three-dimensional. His choice of blue to shade the face is unfortunate, given his rather furry looking hatching. This might look less disconcerting with a gentleman sitter. However, the dark sky background has plenty of colour in it and creates a romantic effect.

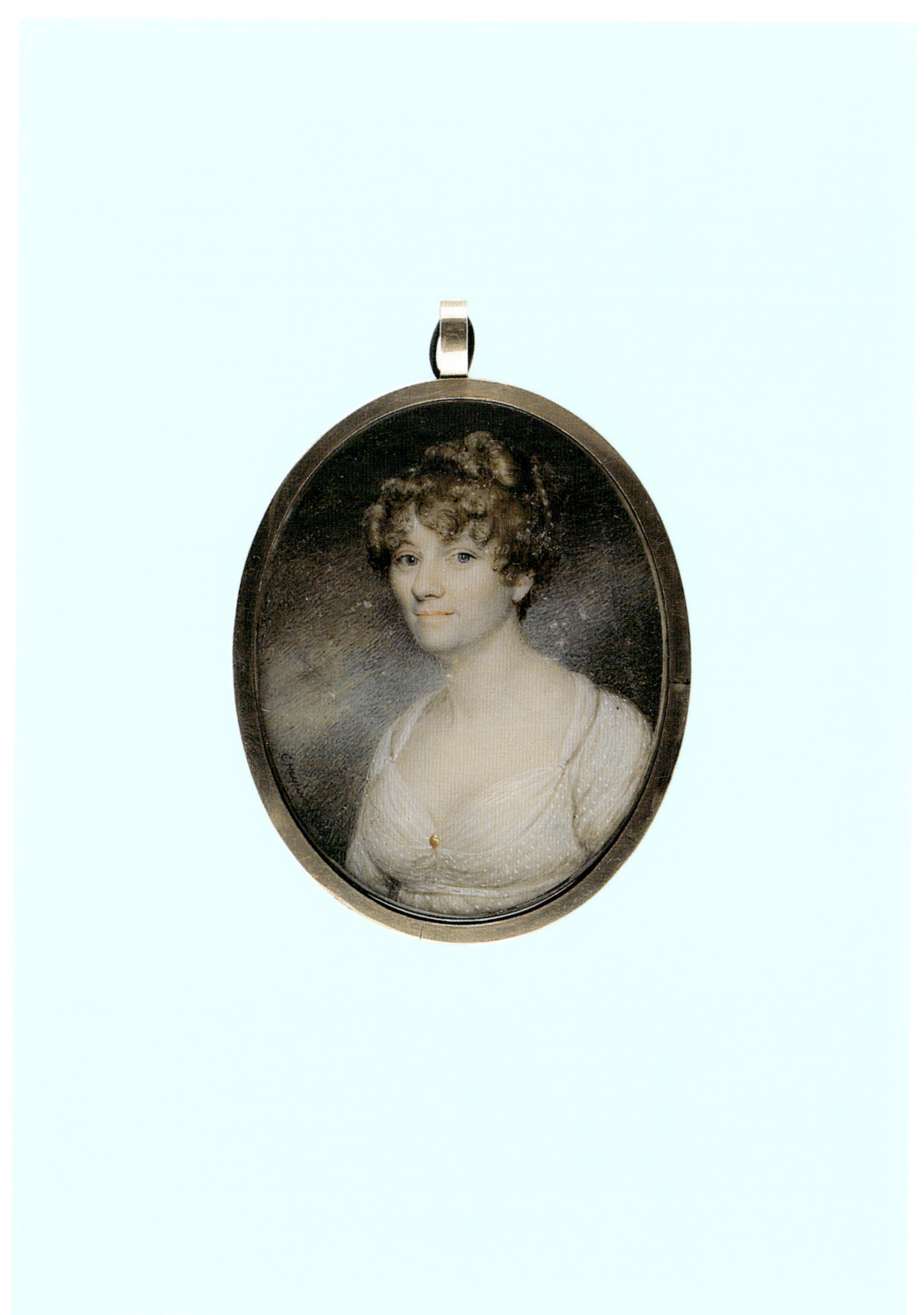

# Adam Buck (1759–1833)

The son of a silversmith from Cork and brother of the less-talented miniaturist, Frederick Buck, Adam Buck was a very able draughtsman and also worked in watercolour and produced designs for engravings. Like many contemporaries, he added to his income working as a drawing master. Buck was in London by 1795, where he exhibited regularly and worked from several addresses around Soho and Mayfair. He produced aquatint illustrations to the novelist Sterne's *Sentimental Journey*, and published his own work on Greek vase paintings in 1811.

Buck's miniature style varied, but his drawing was generally good and his works are always rather charming. They capture the spirit of informality of the early nineteenth century especially well. He often signed his works.

### 92  Unknown Woman
Watercolour on ivory; gold locket with the verso inset with plaited hair
Oval, 6.9 x 5.1 cm

Christie's 3 March 1993 (14); purchased by the Draper estate; given to Kenwood, 1993  (88029801)

This young woman wears a plain muslin chemise gown with ruffled edging, her hair curled and tied up with a band in a manner typical of the early years of the nineteenth century. This is the fashionable 'Grecian' style which swept Europe from France at the turn of the century. The work dates from around 1800 to 1805.

Although the sitter has presented few challenges to Buck, his precise drawing and observation of detail in the face are apparent in this miniature. The colouring is typically rather warm (so that his lady sitters often appear rather fresh-faced) and the visible brushwork seen on her face becomes even more bold in the sky background. This, too, is full of warm colour and laid with opaque paint.

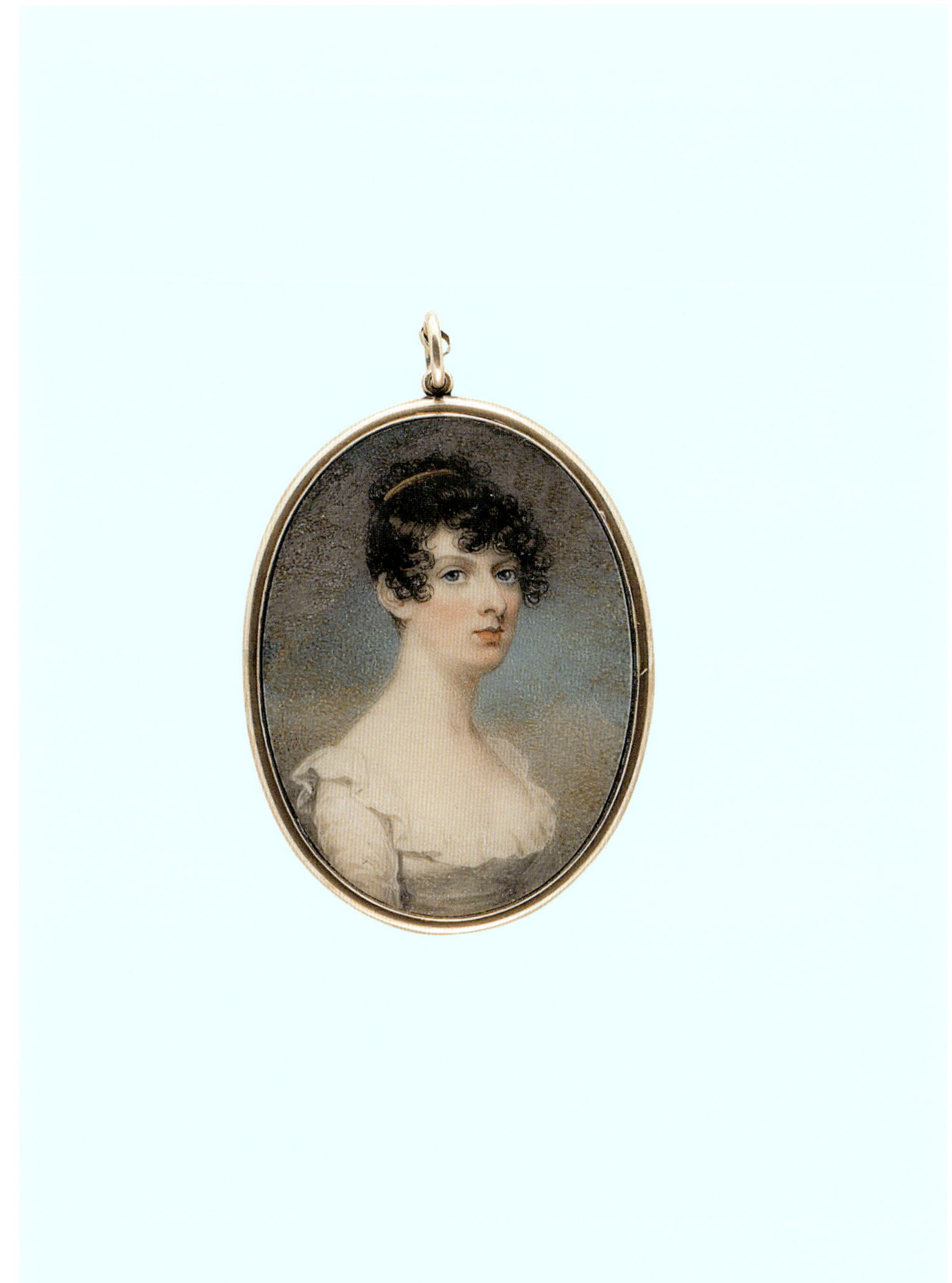

## Adam Buck

### 93  Mrs Robert Plampin, née Fanny Milchel

Watercolour on ivory; gold locket with glazed verso.
Backing paper inscribed *Fanny Milchel/ Wife of -/ Vice Admiral
Robert/ Plampin-*
Oval, 7.0 x 5.7 cm

R. L. Bayne-Powell; Sotheby's 11 Oct. 1994 (75); purchased by the
Draper estate; given to Kenwood, 1994  (88029828)

Exhib.: Holburne Museum, Bath, Nov. 1994

Fanny Milchel was married to Robert Plampin (1762–1834), a
distinguished naval officer in the French wars who became a vice-
admiral and later commander-in-chief in Ireland, 1825–8. Painted
around 1805, the sitter has her hair tied up with a plait in a Grecian
knot and Buck has loosely indicated a high-waisted dress of thin
white material, so commonly found during this period.

All the usual characteristics of Buck's miniatures of this date are
shown in this work: the warm colouring, rather coarse hatching and
almost stormy sky. Although the drawing is not especially good, this
work is notable for the profile pose, which is uncommon in
miniatures of women. Remembering Buck's interest in Greek vase
painting, which makes great use of figures in profile, it seems likely
that he was deliberately alluding to ancient art when he chose this
pose and perhaps directed Mrs Plampin in her choice of dress.

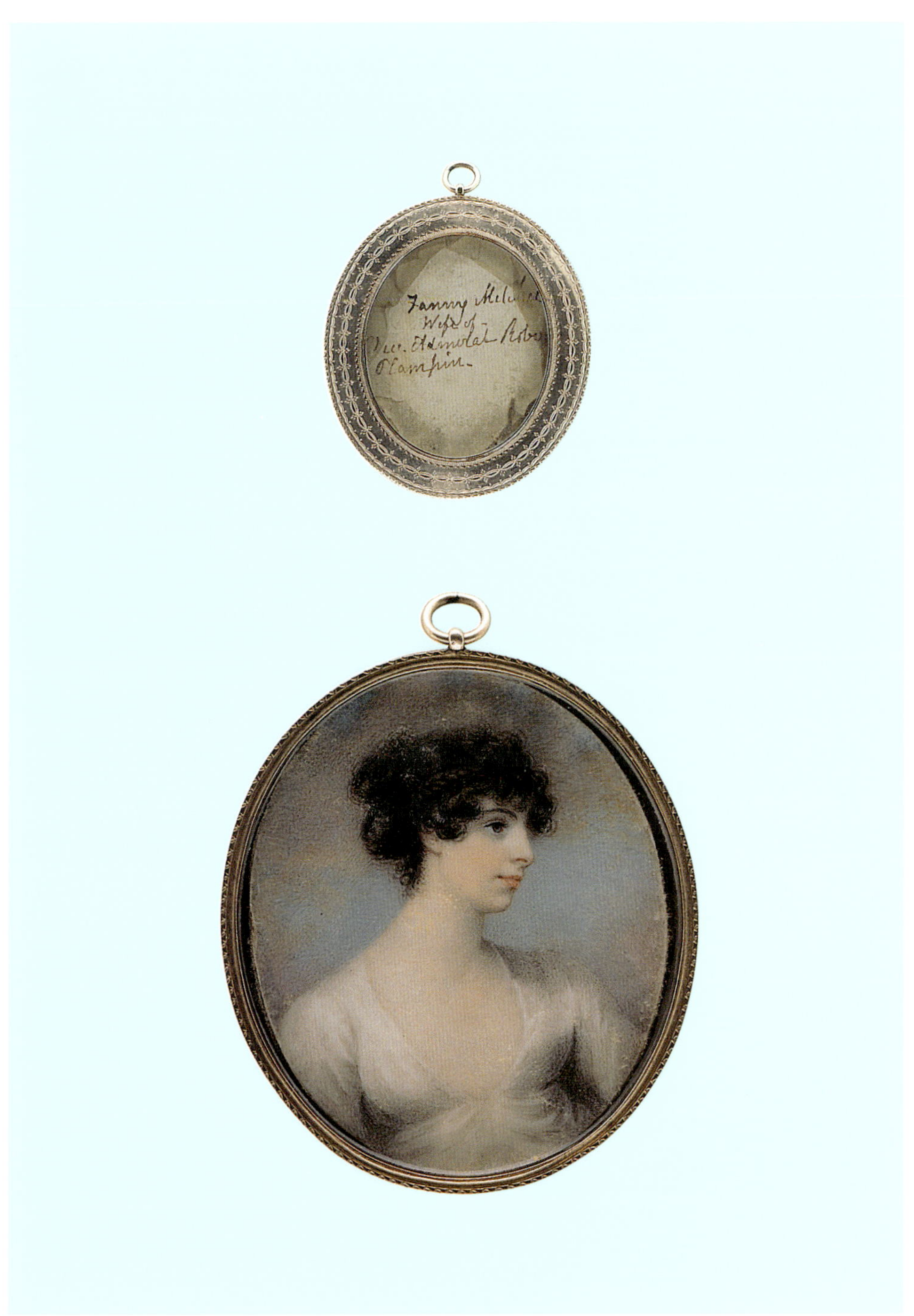

# George Chinnery  (1774–1852)

Chinnery was one of the most talented miniature painters of the turn of the nineteenth century, but his success in other media and a life spent in the Far East had deprived him of the recognition he deserved, until recent times. He was brought up in London, the son of an amateur artist of Anglo-Irish descent. His training was completed at the Royal Academy Schools from 1792, where his early works were compared to those of Cosway.

Around 1794 Chinnery moved to Ireland, looking for commercial success. There he encouraged John Comerford to take up miniature painting (cat. 85). An ill-fated marriage took place in Dublin, the first in a series of personal failures that brought him to lead an itinerant life. By the end of 1802 he was working in India, mostly in Madras, where he had a good clientele. However, his business acumen in no way matched his talents as an artist and by 1825 he had moved on again to Macao, China, after running up large debts. From this period on he no longer painted miniatures, but worked in oils and produced topographical watercolours, full of local detail.

Chinnery's style varied from something akin to that of Engleheart's in his early years, to a more personal manner developed in India. These works are often boldly painted, with strong colours in the face and backgrounds and coarse, yet  neat hatching. Even with the discipline of working on ivory, he gives a sense of his skill as a rapid and accurate draughtsman. Another reason for his lack of full recognition is that his works are rarely signed.

### 94  Unknown Woman, 'R.M.E.'

Watercolour on ivory; gilt metal locket, the verso with gilt initials *RME* set on opaque white glass with plaited hair border
Oval, 6.9 x 5.4 cm

Christie's 11 May 1994 (80); purchased by the Draper estate; given to Kenwood, 1994  (88029819)

This portrait of an Anglo-Indian lady was probably painted when Chinnery was in Madras, about 1805. Her thick hair is dressed with pearl ornaments and she wears coral and pearl necklaces, suggesting a person of some rank. The sketchily painted dress has a ruffled, lace collar that recalls the periodic interest in Van Dyck-inspired dress of the late eighteenth and early nineteenth centuries.

It is interesting to note how Chinnery alters his typically ruddy palette, using more brown paint to reflect the sitter's complexion, which is darker than that of his European lady clients. The long parallel hatching on the face and background commonly found in his work gives way to loose wash with opaque white highlights in the areas of dress.

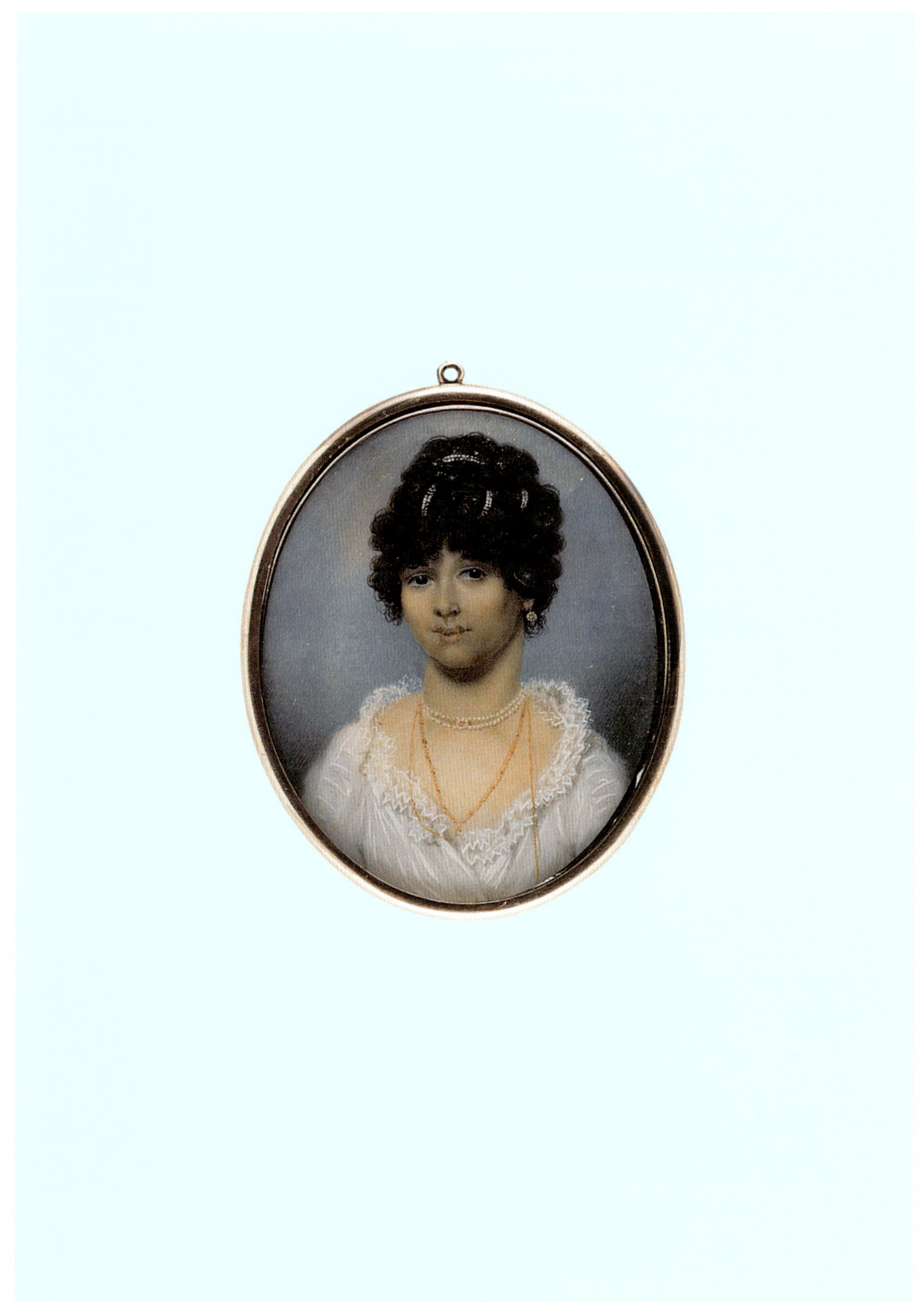

# George Chinnery

## 95 Unknown Man

Watercolour on ivory; ivory case with velvet-lined cover (not illustrated)
Oval, 8.7 x 6.8cm

Christie's 3 Mar. 1993 (65); purchased by the Draper estate; given to Kenwood, 1993 (88029803)

The style and framing of this portrait suggest that it was made in India c.1805-10, when some of Chinnery's best miniatures were made. The sitter is wearing the ubiquitous dress of an English gentleman that varied little over two or more decades: high, upstanding shirt collar with stock and cravat; dark-coloured double-breasted coat, with a high collar. The buttons are monogrammed with the letters 'C.P.R.' which may refer to the sitter's position in India.

This is an excellent example of Chinnery's skill in watercolour. The face is strongly modelled with hatching, using plenty of local colour. The hair is very freely painted and the coat quickly laid on with flat washes. Chinnery has painted an almost stormy sky, through the use of a varied palette and dark shading toward the lower half.

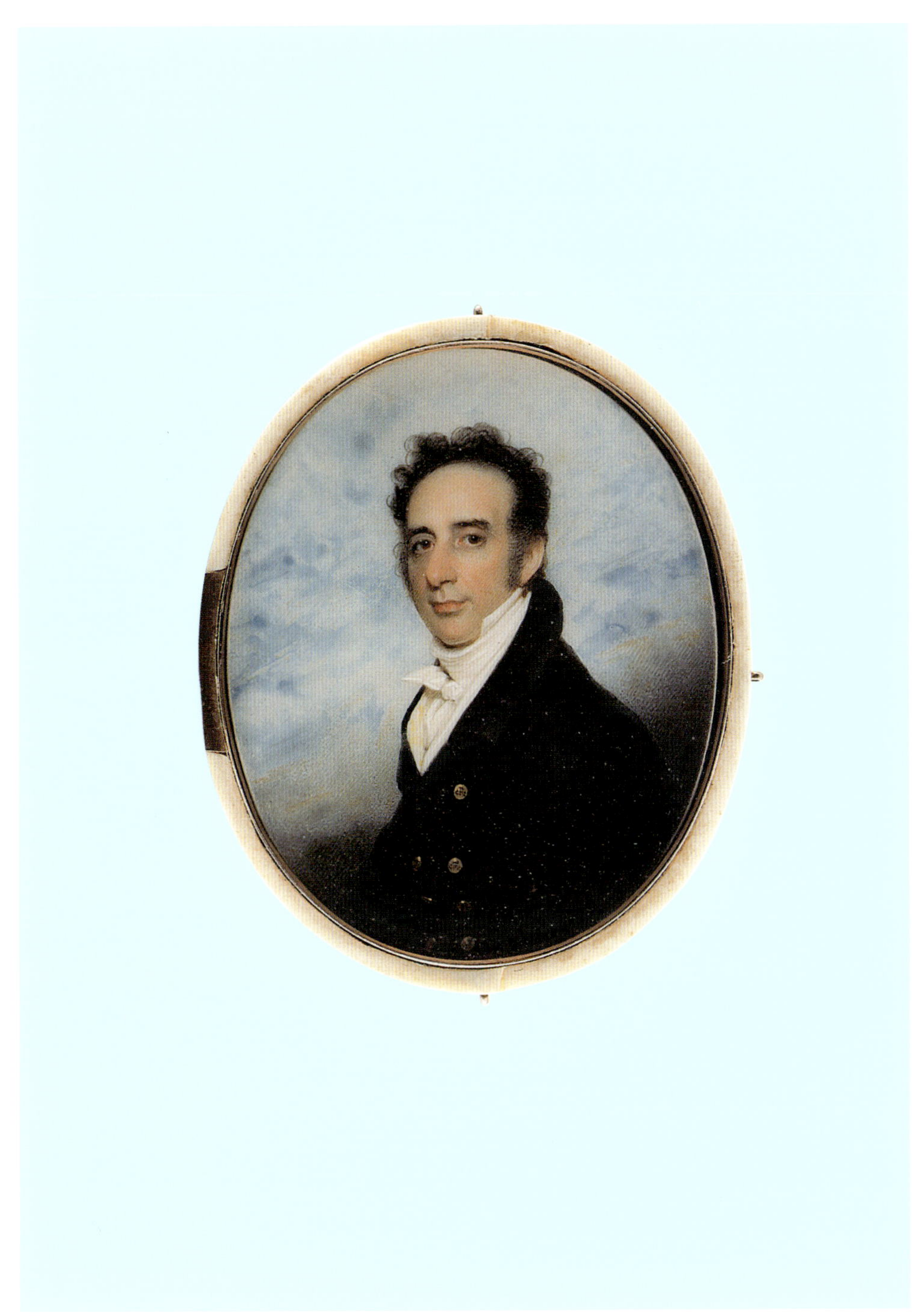

# English School, early nineteenth century

### 96  A Woman's Eye
Watercolour on ivory; gold brooch frame
Almond-shaped, 1.1 x 2.3 cm (shown opposite at actual size
(above) and twice actual size (below))

Limner Antiques, London; purchased by the Draper estate; given to
Kenwood, 1990  (88029857)

The peculiar fashion for making sentimental jewellery of a single
eye – usually a lady's – was started by George Engleheart when he
painted the eye of Mrs Fitzherbert, the morganatic wife of George,
Prince of Wales.  The fashion proved to be short-lived and such
miniatures ceased to be produced after about 1820. Ironically, this
very fact has made them attractive to some collectors, with the
result that fakes have been made by cutting up complete
miniatures. This (genuine) example was painted around 1810,
going by the broad, washy technique and the fact that the hair is
curled right around the eyes.

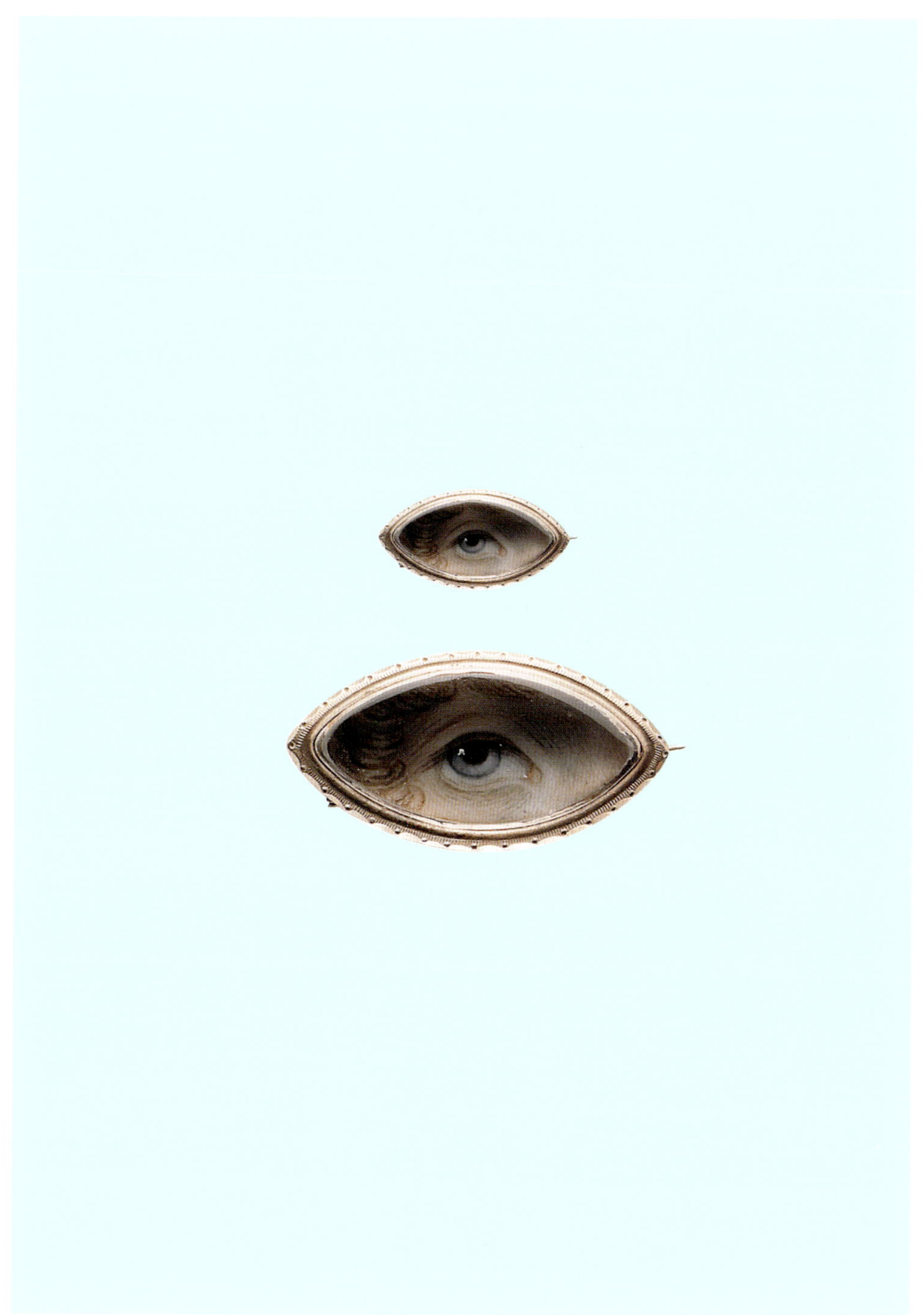

# Walter Stephens Lethbridge  (1771/2–?1831)

A Devon farmer's son, Lethbridge probably learned his skills from itinerant artists. He is recorded showing at the Royal Academy from 1801 until just before his death. In 1805 he advertised in Canterbury: 'Likenesses painted in miniature. Mr Lethbridge is just arrived in Canterbury. Price 3 guineas and upwards'. His works are often signed on the verso in full with his addresses in the Strand. Lethbridge died in Plymouth.

Lethbridge's technique could be described as robust but effective. He employed broad, even coarse hatching, scratching and strong colours, but was able to capture character without painstaking effort.

### 97  A Naval Officer

Watercolour on ivory; gold locket, plaited hair verso with blue glass border. Signed on verso *W S Lethbridge/ 96 Strand London*
Oval, 6.6 x 5.5 cm

Bonham's, 12 July 1993 (162); purchased by the Draper estate; given to Kenwood, 1993  (88029806)

This miniature is remarkable for the inclusion of the sitter's bicorn hat, which dominates the portrait. The naval uniform bears no distinctions to help identify the sitter, who was probably a fairly junior captain. The style of hair and dress suggest a date of about 1810.

The hat is used to good effect, giving a sense of movement to the pose of the sitter. Lethbridge has drawn the features with a series of short, straight lines which are then modelled using uneven hatching of grey with a notably reddish flesh colour. The hat and coat are laid on with flat, gum-based washes and roughly shaded with scratchy line work in black paint.

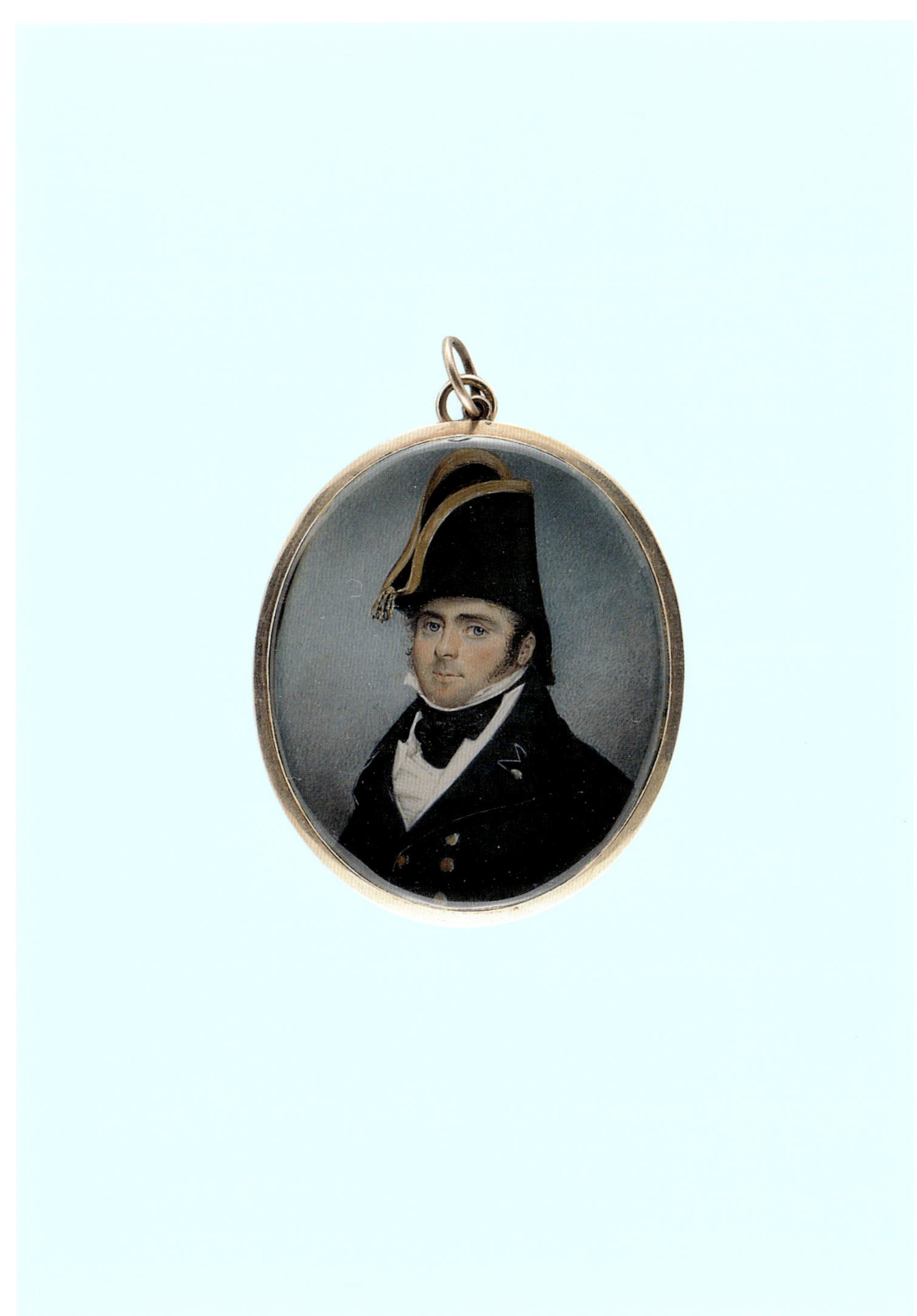

# Charles Jagger  (c1770–1827)

Jagger was one of the leading miniature painters in Bath during the late
eighteenth to early nineteenth-century period. Few details of his life are
known. He worked in Green Street and Milsom Street, painting local
residents and visiting gentry who came to Bath for the waters.

His miniatures are well observed and carefully painted with fairly opaque
colours, often employing fine hatching and stippling techniques. This can
give them a quite hard-edged appearance. Sometimes the backgrounds have
a gradated tone, which has the effect of creating a space around the sitter.

### 98  Unknown Woman

Watercolour on ivory; gilt metal locket frame with glazed verso.
Signed on backing paper *C Jagger*
Oval, 8.2 x 6.6 cm

Sotheby's, 11 Nov. 1993 (53); purchased by the Draper estate; given
to Kenwood, 1993 (88029180)

This fashionable lady wears a rather showy dress of about 1810. Her
hair is elaborately dressed in the Grecian style, that is tied with
plaits and pearls and dropping down in ringlets around her ears.
She has more pearls on her earrings and necklace. A dark maroon
dress, with high bust, complements her hair and is set off with
white lace edging, arm bands and shawl.

Although not similar in execution, this portrait has something in
common with Smart's late works of young women. It may be that
Jagger or a client had seen and admired an example. Jagger's own
technique relies on fine stipple and broken lines on the face. The
dress is painted with quite hard lines with much gum and white
gouache detail. As with many miniaturists of the period, he
enlarges the eyes to flatter the sitter: these are rather almond
shaped in this case.

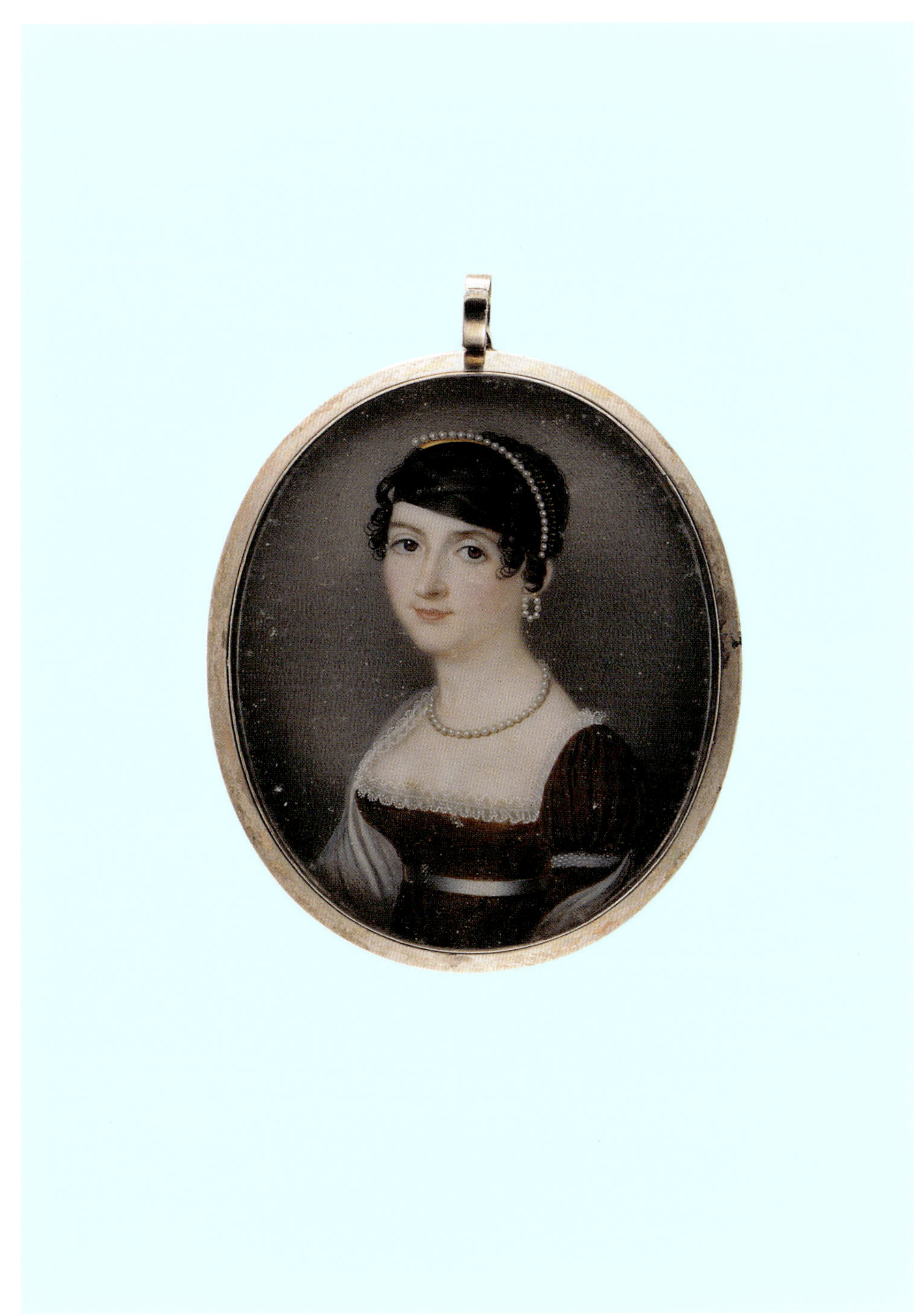

# John Wright  (fl 1780–d 1820)

Little is known about the early life of this talented artist, who produced some
good cabinet-sized works in the 1800s. He was friendly with Thomas
Lawrence and John Hoppner, among other portraitists, and made copies in
miniature of their work. He painted the Duke of Kent, George III's fourth
son, and consequently styled himself Miniature Painter to the Duke. His style
is certainly influenced by the painters in oil with whom he associated, and
like other miniaturists of the period, he used plenty of gum arabic with his
colours to create the appearance of miniature paintings in oil. His drawing
was good and his figures well modelled.

### 99  Captain George Scott RN (1783– ?)
Watercolour on ivory; gilt metal mount in modern papier mâché
frame. Backing paper inscribed, 1. *John Wright/ pinx/* [ *]Burlington
Garde* [ ][ ] *of Old/* [ ] *St/ 1812*    2. [Later hand on label] *George
Scott R.N/* [ ] *and Vice-admiral*
Oval, 7.8 x 6.5 cm

Christie's 3 March 1993 (15); purchased by the Draper estate; given
to Kenwood, 1993  (88029802)

George Scott joined the Navy in 1798, had been shipwrecked near
Cape St Vincent and served as master's mate on the *Victory*
(Nelson's flagship) before receiving his commission as a first
lieutenant in 1811. A year later he was made a captain after taking
active command of the *Renomé* at Java. His service took him from
Greenland to the East Indies.  In this miniature Captain Scott wears
a plain navy-blue uniform with simple gold lace trimming, which
denotes a junior officer. Note his upstanding collar with a military
stock. The choice of a dark sky background is very appropriate for
such a dashing naval officer.

   Wright's use of opaque paint with plenty of gum allows him to
use dense, bold brush strokes to create a rich depth of colour. The
face and details of the dress are especially painterly, whereas the
background is painted in a more traditional way, with neat,
directional hatching.

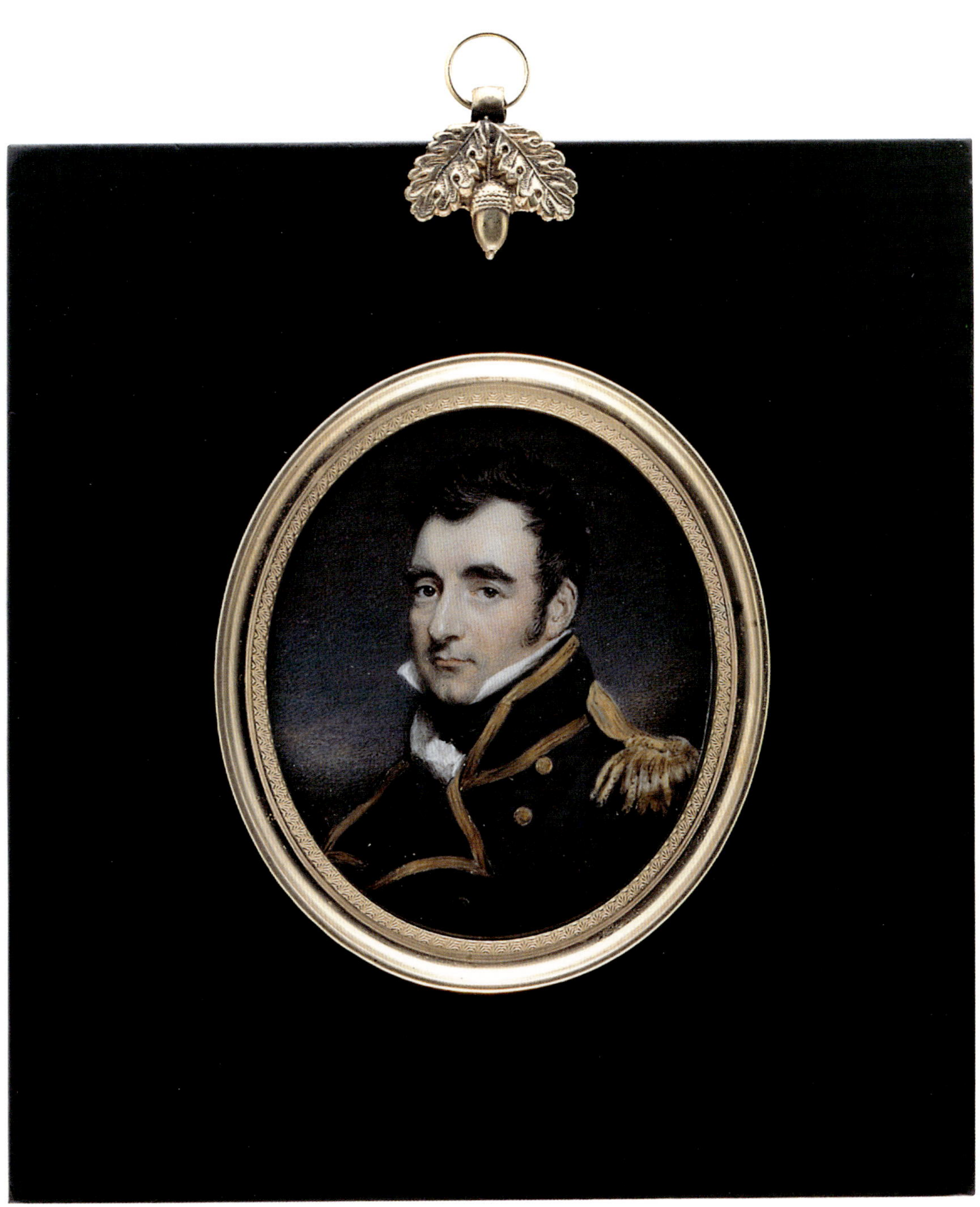

# James Leakey  (1775–1865)

Leakey was born in Exeter and for much of his life worked in the West
Country, painting all subjects in a variety of media. He was most successful
with his miniatures and landscapes. In London he was acquainted with
Constable, Lawrence and Wilkie and painted a miniature of Joseph Farington.
The biographer of his neighbour in London, the artist John Raphael Smith,
claimed he was known as 'Young Virtue', while Smith was 'Old Vice'.
Certainly he was a godly man and is reported to have taken up preaching in
later years.

Leakey worked with a distinctive, opaque technique that relies heavily on
the use of gum as a medium. He drew well with a soft brush and tended to
give his sitters a pinkish complexion. Attribution is often difficult as he is not
thought to have signed any of his works.

## 100  Unknown Man

Oil on ivory; gold locket frame with blue glass verso
Oval, 7.3 x 5.7 cm

Limner Antiques, London; purchased by the Draper estate, 1992;
given to Kenwood, 1992  (88029233)

The sitter wears his hair cut quite short and brushed forward, in the
manner influenced by antique art popular in the early nineteenth
century. His high-collared coat and stock with cravat help to date
the work to around 1810.

Leakey's technique, which has been likened to oil painting, is
seen to good advantage here. The face is very well painted using
blended opaque paint, without a need for hard-edged lines for the
detail. Slightly more transparent paint is used for the softly painted
hair and the cravat. The overall effect is of a well-rounded portrait,
painted without too much labour, which indeed was the effect
Leakey's contemporaries were achieving with their full-sized works.

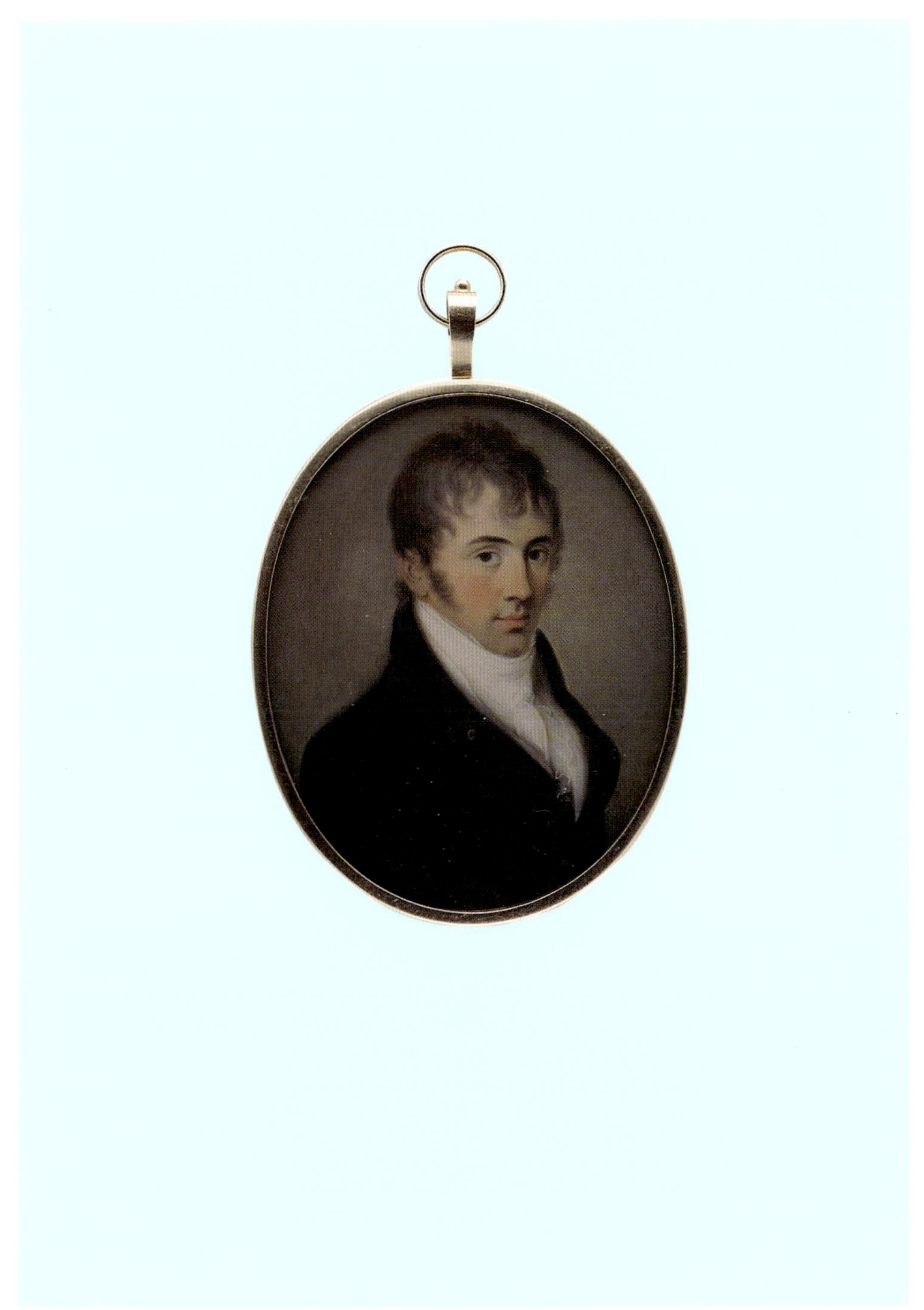

## Samuel John Stump  (1778–1863)

Stump is believed to have been born in America, but came to England and
was studying at the Royal Academy in 1796. He showed at several exhibiting
societies until 1849 and joined one of the new sketching societies. He worked
in watercolour and oil and produced engravings as well as miniatures, both in
Brighton and London. His many works included people from the theatre such
as Dora Jordan and Edmund Kean. They are well drawn and painted using
plenty of gum, but are not often very exciting.

### 101  Unknown Man, 'A.J.'

Watercolour on ivory; gold locket frame with hair verso, with
initials set on blue and white glass, *AJ*. Signed lower right *Stump pt*
Oval, 7.3 x 5.8 cm

Limner Antiques, London; purchased by the Draper estate, 1992;
given to Kenwood, 1992  (88029234)

This gentleman is plainly dressed in the fashion of the years
1810–15, although men's everyday dress in town changed little
after about 1795. His neck band and collar have not yet reached
the great heights of George IV's reign. Stump paints with even, fine
hatching which is blended to a certain extent. The overall effect is
rather solid looking. He uses red and blue together in the face,
which creates quite a pink complexion on this sitter.

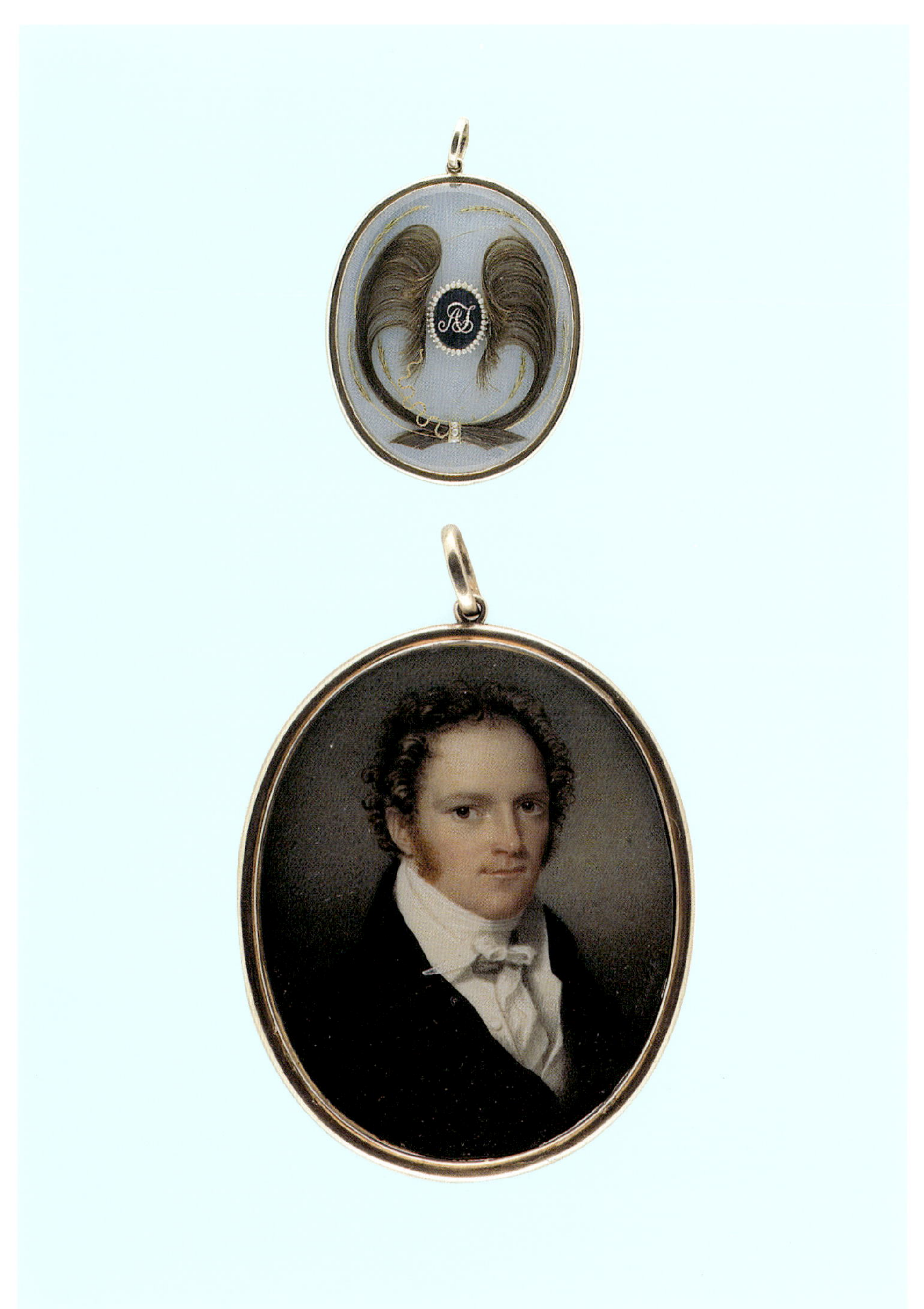

# William John Thomson RSA (1771/3–1845)

Thomson came from Savannah, in America, the son of a colonial official from Scotland. His father returned to England with no living and William probably supported him with his painting. He exhibited at the Royal Academy and several other artists' groups throughout his life. Married in Edinburgh, he returned to live in his family's home in 1812. Thomson's style was conventional for the period and he was very capable of producing larger-scale miniatures with attractively painted dress. As a result, he became a Royal Society of Arts member in 1829 and was in a position to turn down a knighthood.

### 102  Mrs Anne Hathorn

Watercolour on ivory; modern gilt metal mount. Inscribed on backing card, *Painted by/ W.J. Thomson/ June 1820/ Edinburgh,* with later label, *Ann Hathorn/ married Dec*[ ]*23rd/* [...] *Fletcher* [...]
Rectangular, 7.8 x 5.8 cm

Sotheby's 3 June 1992 (704); purchased by the Draper estate; given to Kenwood, 1992  (88029236)

Mrs Hathorn or Fletcher has her hair tightly curled with a centre parting, in the fashion of the Regency period. Her black gown with contrasting stole illustrates the return of strong colour to women's dress after nearly three decades during which white gowns dominated the day clothes seen in portraiture. The bust remains high and the short sleeves puffed.

Thomson's work here is fairly run-of-the-mill. He has concentrated his efforts on the face with soft, gum-rich paint strokes, using the warm palette advocated by Andrew Robertson, the leading Scottish miniaturist of the time (who worked mostly in London). The dress is more loosely painted.

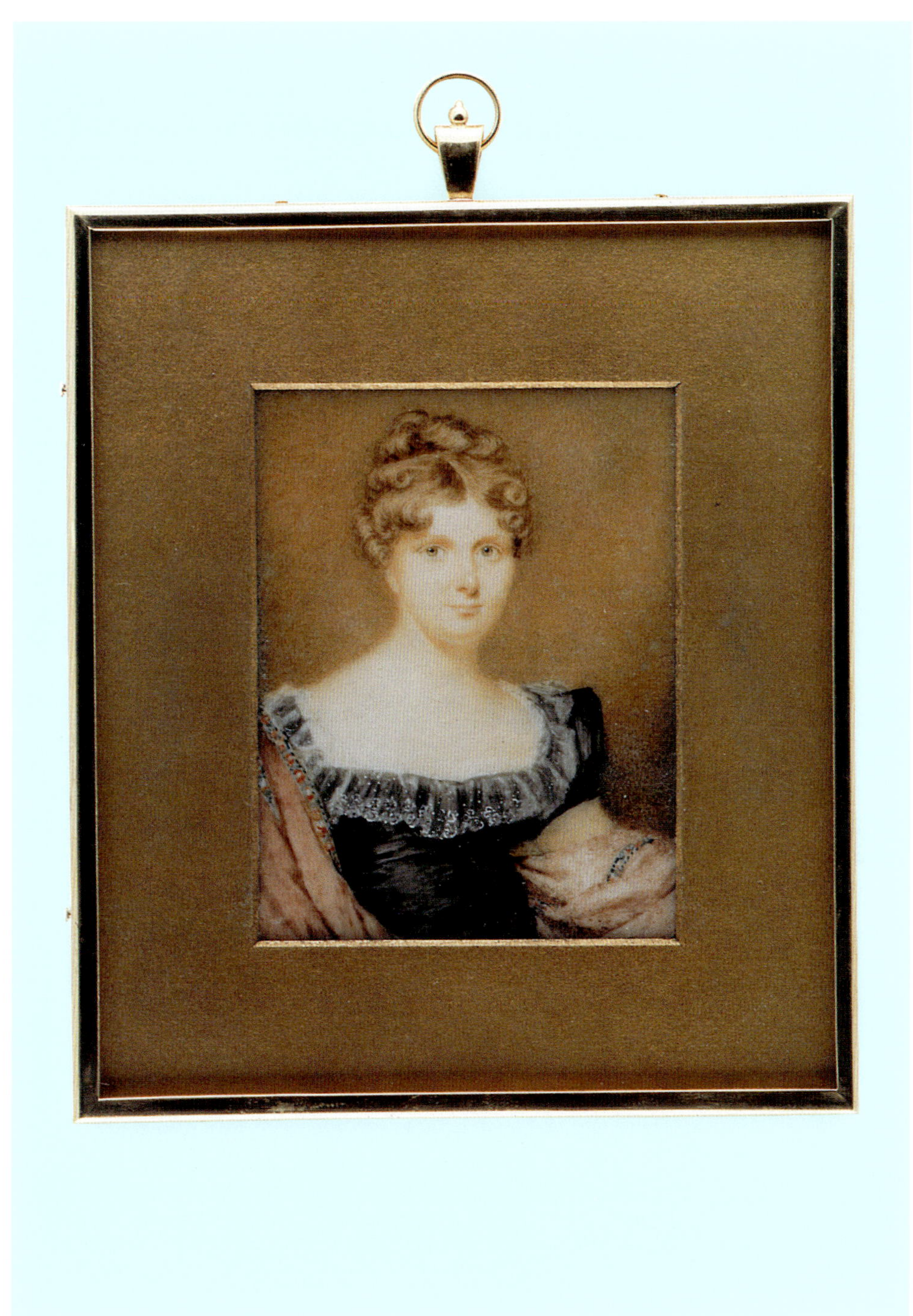

# Alfred Edward Chalon RA  (1780–1860)

Born in Geneva, of a French family, Chalon moved to England while young
and studied at the Royal Academy Schools under the Swiss artist L. A. Arlaud
from 1797. Both he and his brother were good draughtsmen and founded
their own sketching society in 1808. He exhibited paintings and drawings as
well as miniatures at the Royal Academy and British Institution and was taken
up by the royal family. He eventually became painter in watercolours to
Queen Victoria. Chalon was made an Academician in 1816 and enjoyed the
patronage of society from his home and studio in the fashionable district of
Kensington.

### 103  Unknown Woman
Watercolour on ivory; modern gilt metal frame. Signed top right
with monogram *C* around *AE. R.A.*
Rectangular,  8.6 x 6.9 cm

?The Gell family, Hopton; by descent to Lt-Col Chandos-Pole; Sold
Christie's, Newnham Hall 11 July 1994; purchased by the Draper
estate; given to Kenwood, 1994  (88029826)

The sitter's clothes and hair date this portrait to the early 1820s.
Her simply coiled hair and low-cut black dress with lace trimming
contrast with the elaborate coiffure and richly decorated dress
found in many contemporary portraits. Landscape backgrounds
became popular again in the early nineteenth century and were
often used to evoke romantic associations.

Chalon has successfully portrayed the liveliness of the young
woman's face, although he does not appear to have paid much
attention to her dress or provided much background detail. This
would have been reflected perhaps in the price he charged his
customer. There is some retouching on the right-hand side of the
miniature.

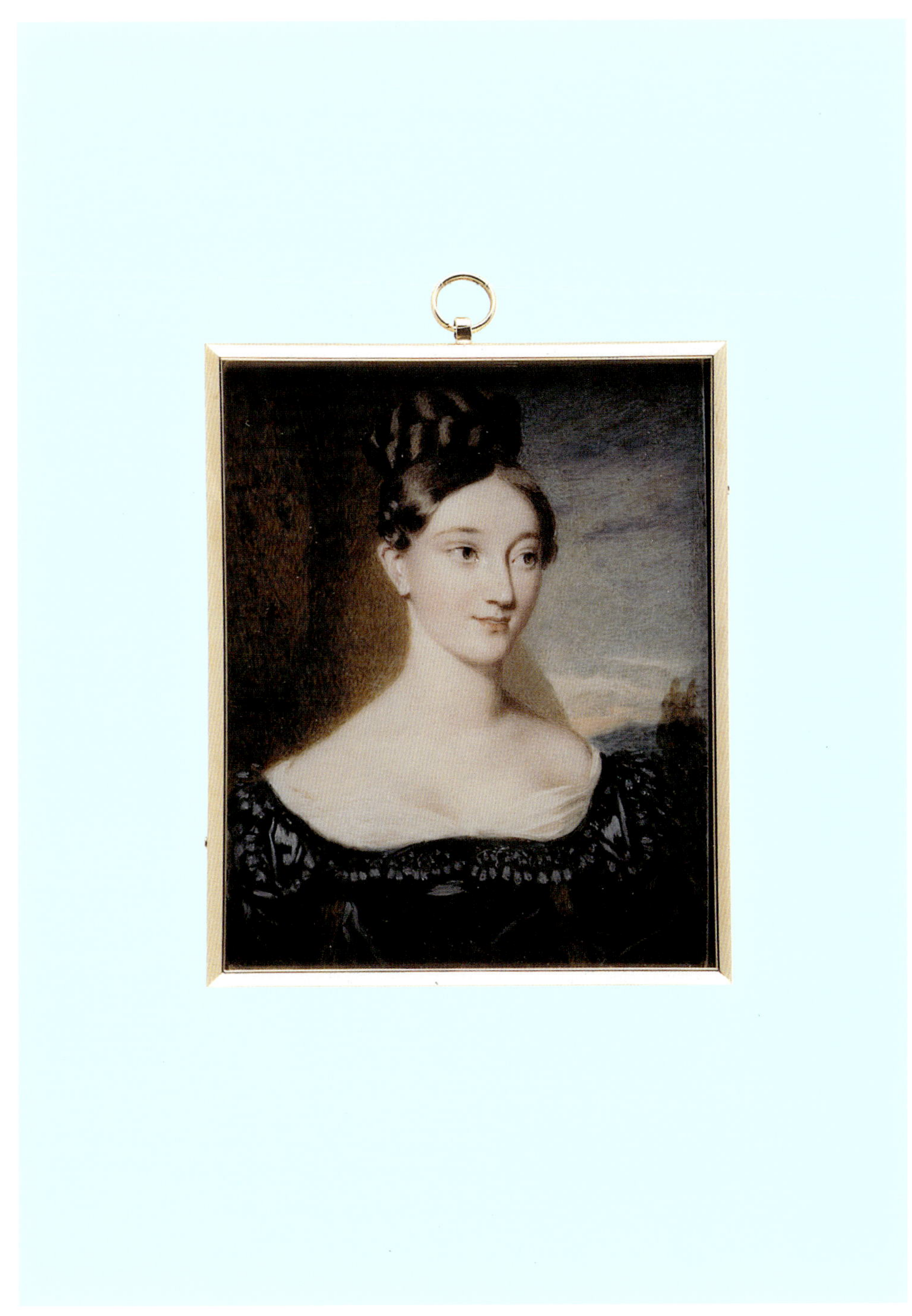

# Sir William John Newton  (1785–1869)

Born in London, Newton trained as an engraver under his father, James, but turned to painting miniatures. He entered the Royal Academy Schools in 1807 and was exhibiting there from the following year. His ability to draw well and use strong, clear colour found favour with wealthy and influential clients as well as other artists. In 1833 Newton was appointed Miniature Painter to William IV and Queen Adelaide. This success was crowned with appointment to the post under Queen Victoria, together with a knighthood in 1837, the first year of her reign.

Newton produced many miniatures, which vary enormously according to the care with which they were painted. At his best they compare with those of W.C. Ross, the leading miniaturist of the period. Like many of his contemporaries, he experimented with larger-sized ivory, but his attempt to create a work some three foot long, using joined pieces, was not a success. In addition to miniatures, Newton also worked in watercolour and chalk.

### 104  Miss Cuppage

Watercolour on ivory; gold card mount in leather case. Signed left side, *W.J. Newton 1832*. Signed on backing paper, *Miss  Cuppage / Wm J Newton / Pinxt / Miniature Painter in /ordinary to their / Majesties / 6 Argyll Street/ 1833*  [*sic*]
Octagonal, 4.6 x 3.8 cm

Christie's 10 July 1991 (162); purchased by the Draper estate; given to Kenwood, 1991  (88029869)

Newton had already exhibited portraits of Burke and Mrs Cuppage at the Royal Academy in 1829 and 1830 when he came to paint this child. (George Engleheart had previously painted another member of the family, one Colonel Cuppage – now in the Victoria and Albert Museum.) As with other portraits of children in this collection, the girl is painted full face in order to emphasise her childhood innocence and to create a more sentimental image.

The soft stipple and brush strokes of Newton's technique suit this simple subject very well. He almost makes the face and background blend together, creating a rather hazy effect to the miniature. His typically warm colouring, with just a little blue colour used to model the face, can be seen here.

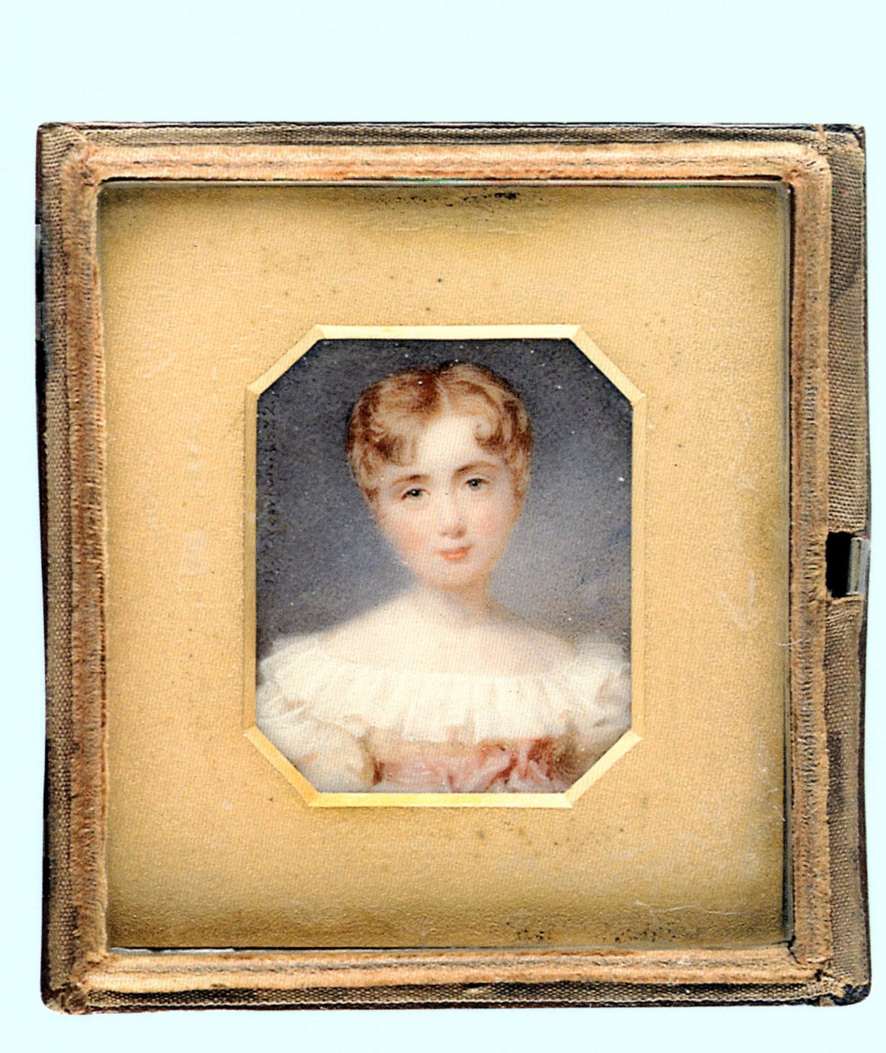

# Sir William John Newton

## 105  Eliza Petrie, Baroness Rouen des Mallets

Watercolour on ivory; gilded composition frame (not illustrated) with cats 50 and 72. Inscribed on backing paper: 1. *A Lady/ Wm. J. Newton/ Pinxit/*
*8 Argyll St./ 1828* and 2. [later] *Eliza Petrie daughter of [ ] Petrie / and his wife. Married 1st Nathaniel Parker Forth/ 2nd Baron Rouen des Mallets*
Rectangular, 7.9 x 6.1 cm

By descent; Capt. Noel Rouen de Forth; purchased by English Heritage for Kenwood, 1992  (88029237)

The sitter is reputedly the first wife of Lord Stormont's agent in France, Nathaniel Parker Forth (cat. 72). If this is correct, then she must have married him when he was very old, as he was born in 1740 and she is quite young-looking in 1828. Her father is shown in a portrait in the manner of Andrew Plimer (cat. 50).

Although the signature seems authentic, this portrait is rather average for the artist. He has spent some time on the face with closely hatched strokes, but the hair and clothes are dashed off without much care.

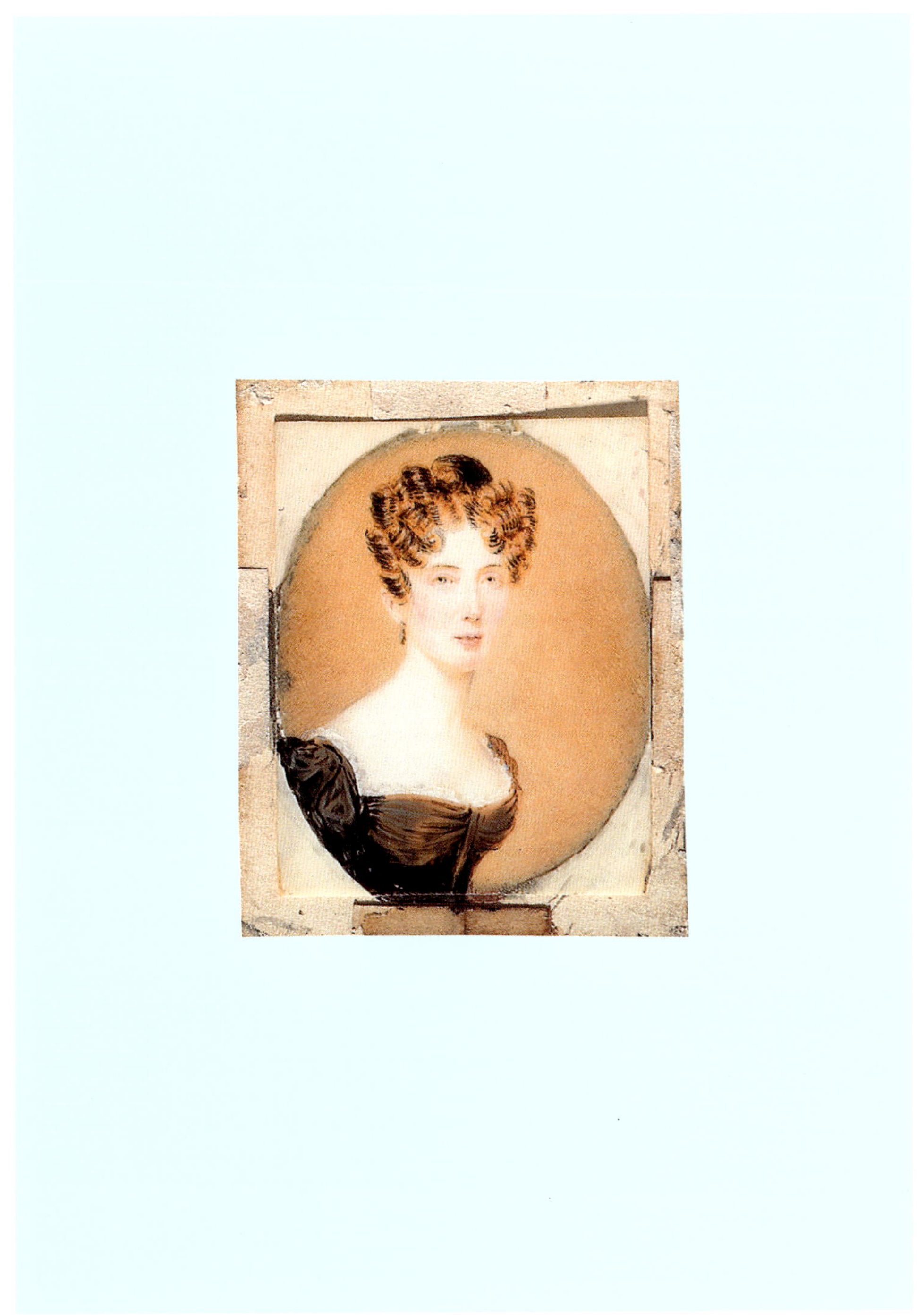

# Andrew Robertson  (1777–1845)

Robertson came from a family of artists from Aberdeen whose father was an architect. His youthful talent was recognised by wealthy patrons who helped him to study with the landscape artist, Alexander Nasmyth. Robertson's elder brother Archibald also instructed him, and Andrew attracted the attention of the leading Scottish portraitist, Henry Raeburn, who had a strong influence on his style in miniatures. His journey to London for a brief period of instruction, at the Royal Academy, extended to a lifetime spent between Scotland and London. He exhibited in London from 1802 onwards. A patriotic Scot, he painted his self-portrait in tartan, and, as a member of the Highland Society, was actively involved in the preservation of the traditional clan tartans.

Robertson was determined to overturn the dominance of Cosway's (and others') brilliant surface effects and return miniature painting to a more exacting art. To this end he mostly preferred large, square formats and built up a luminous surface with dense and minute brushwork. His works are notable for their lifelike poses,  using realistic shadow effects. These efforts paid off, for he not only attracted a clientele that included the royal family and leading artists, such as Lawrence and Chantrey, but changed the direction of miniature painting through his pupils and imitators. The former included W.C. Ross, Frederick Cruickshank and one of his sons, Edward. Andrew's brothers, Archibald and Alexander, both had successful careers as miniature painters in New York. His daughter Emily published his letters in 1895.

### 106  Unknown Woman
Watercolour on ivory; gilt card mount in a leather case.
Inscribed on backing paper *Painted by A. Robertson/ 33 Gerrard St/ 1816*
Rectangular, 8.8 x 6.8 cm

R.L. Bayne-Powell; Sotheby's 11 Oct. 1994 (132); purchased by the Draper estate; given to Kenwood, 1994  (88029833)

This very attractive miniature is painted in a manner that is strongly reminiscent of Raeburn, although Robertson's technique could not be further removed from that artist's broad brush. The sitter's dress is a development of the Grecian manner of the early nineteenth century, with the arrival of more frills and puffed sleeves that were soon to become very prominent. The transparent black gauze stole is especially well painted.

Robertson has given his sitter a very plausible setting, placing her in a chair seen from a low view point, to provide a simple backdrop of a sky with high cloud. The shadow on her face and throat looks like actual daylight, not merely a studio convention. The painting is deceptively simple looking. In fact, every texture is carefully rendered using very fine stipple and fused brush strokes. Robertson was known to expect up to nine sittings, and sometimes more.

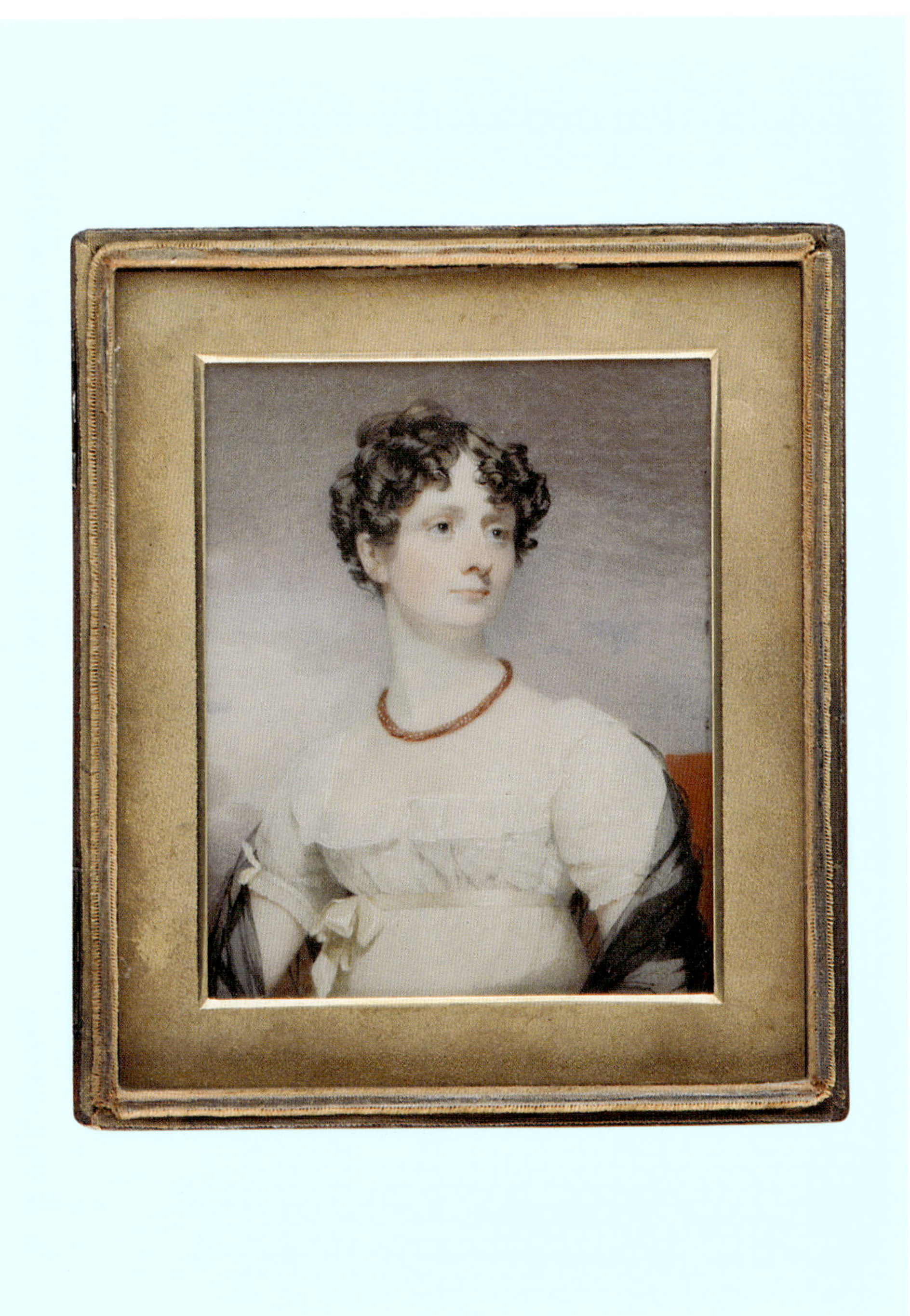

# Andrew Robertson

## 107  H.J. Danbury

Watercolour on ivory;  gilt card in modern papier mâché frame.
Inscribed on backing paper *H.J. Danbury Esq at 23 Painted by A. Robertson 19 Berners St London Dcr. 1836*
Rectangular, 8.4 x 6.9 cm

Limner Antiques, London; purchased by the Draper estate, 1990; given to Kenwood, 1990  (88029849)

This sitter is given a rather arresting appearance by the artist's choice of a sky background, in front of which his head seems to stand out with his high collar and stock. The coat is much more fitted than in earlier examples shown in the collection, as can be seen at the shoulder. Mr Danbury's large blue cravat is rather showy against the dark coat.

Robertson's later technique is a little less refined than in cat. 106, relying on pose and colour for effect, rather than perfectly rendered surface textures. The colours blended in the face are quite contrasting, which gives the sitter a somewhat florid appearance, perhaps correctly.

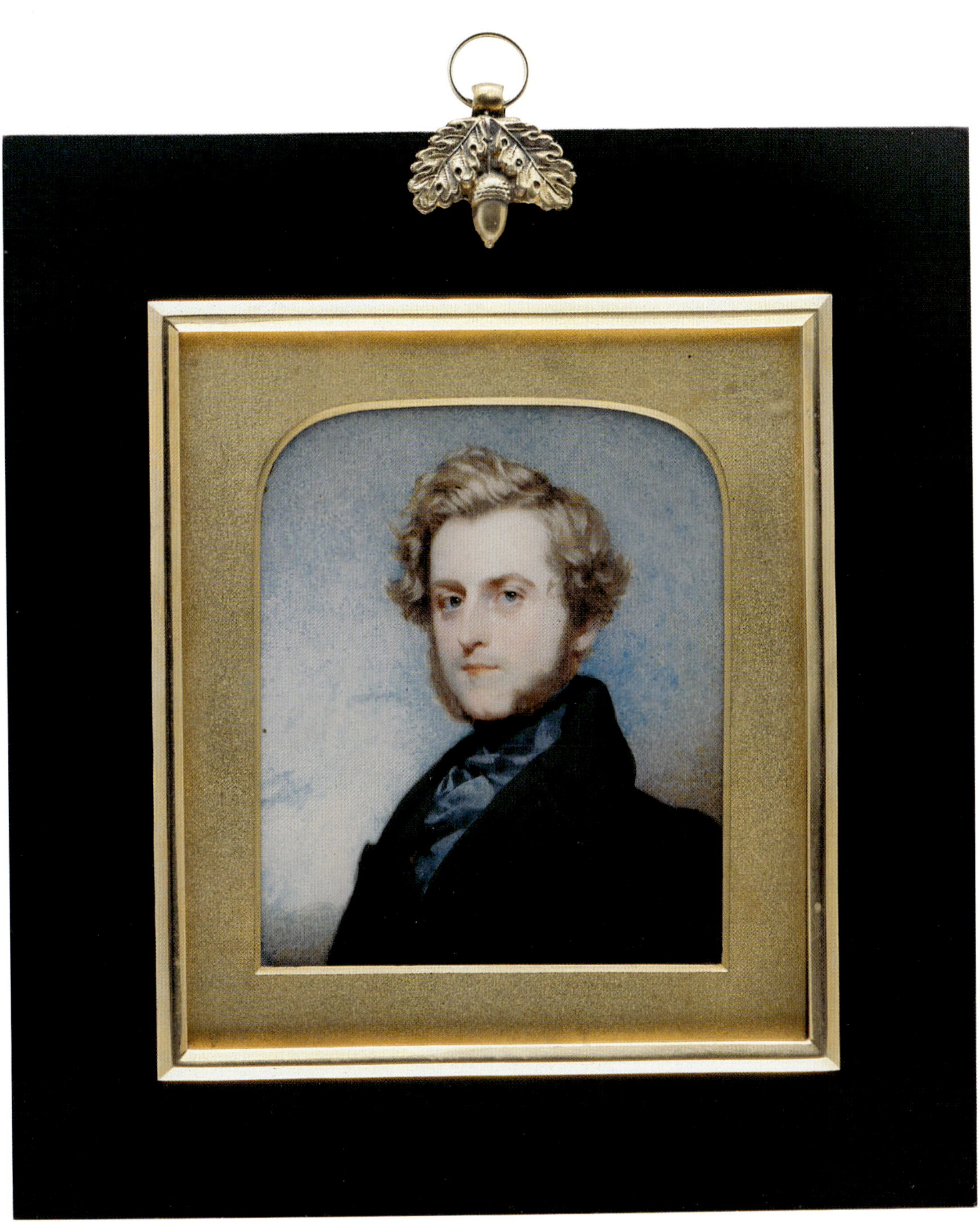

# William Egley  (1798–1870)

Born in Doncaster, Egley worked with a London publisher until he managed to build himself a career as an artist, being self-taught. In spite of a lack of formal training, he was technically rather able and worked in a style similar to William Charles Ross (see cat. 109), without matching the latter's suavity and brilliance. Egley established himself a well-to-do circle of clients and lived at a series of addresses around the then fashionable streets north of the Bayswater Road and Oxford Street. His son, William Maw Egley, also painted miniatures.

Egley senior's works have a high finish and can be rather hard-edged. He used neat, soft brush strokes but did not attempt a wholly smooth paint surface.

### 108  Milner Marcus

Watercolour on ivory; gold locket frame with hair verso
Oval, 5.2 x 4.0 cm

Limner Antiques, London; purchased by the Draper estate; given to Kenwood, 1990  (88029850)

Nothing is known about this fashionable young man, painted in the 1840s. The oil in his hair matches the sheen on his black silk cravat, and his plain brown coat is enlivened by the edge of a multi-coloured waistcoat that just shows beneath.

Egley uses strong colours, such as red and blue on the face, to build up his image. Most of the surface is comprised of short brush strokes, blended together, and the paint is fairly opaque, with much gum in it.

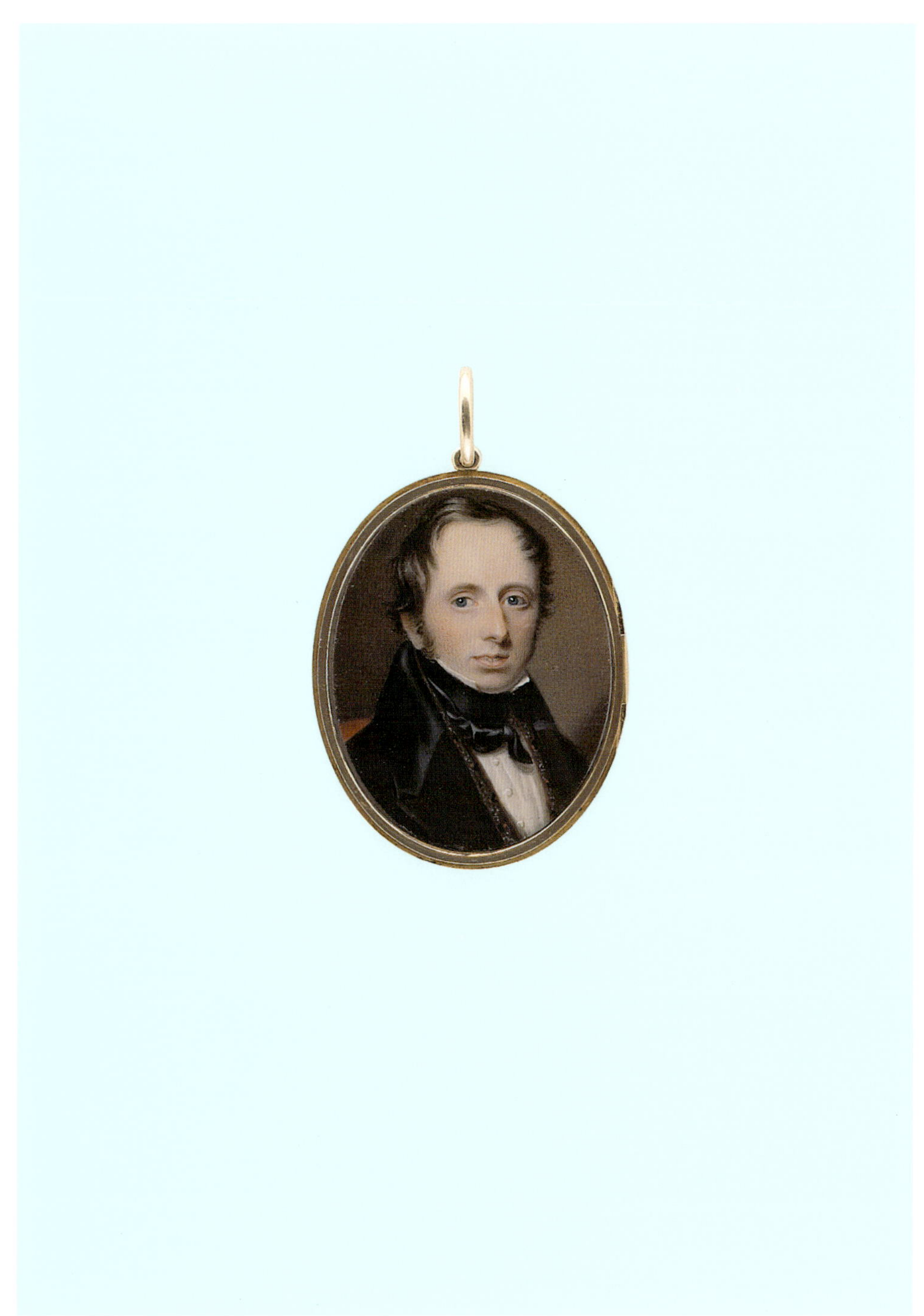

# Sir William Charles Ross RA (1794/5–1860)

Probably the greatest and certainly one of the most successful miniaturists of the nineteenth century, Ross came from a family of miniature painters and was winning prizes for his drawings at an early age. A great influence on his work came from a period spent as an assistant to Andrew Robertson (cats 106,107), whose innovations had changed the direction of the art early in the century. Ross became a full Royal Academician and was knighted in the same year, 1842. His sitters included Queen Victoria and Prince Albert, and Louis Philippe of France, as well as members of the French, Portuguese and Belgian royal families.

Ross was remarkable for his fine draughtsmanship and colouring. This mastery of technique allowed him to adapt many of the trends in full-scale portraiture to his large miniatures, which were made of several pieces of ivory on occasion. He was a prolific artist in a period when standards of miniature painting demanded considerable application.

### 109  William Ross (d after 1842)

Watercolour on ivory; gilt metal frame, bearing inscription *Mr Ross. by Sir W. Ross R.A.* Oval, 11.5 x 6.5 cm

Miss Ross (?Magdalena Ross), 1860; Jeffrey Whitehead, 1889; Sotheby's 21 June 1956 (50); R.L. Bayne-Powell; Sotheby's, 11 Oct. 1994 (163); purchased by the Draper estate; given to Kenwood, 1994  (88029834)

Exhib.: Society of Arts, London, 1860; Burlington Fine Arts Club, London, 1889; Edinburgh, 1965; Holburne Museum, Bath, 1994

William Ross was the father of W.C. Ross and a miniaturist himself. He came from a Ross-shire family and had three children, all of whom painted miniatures, including Magdalena (later Mrs E. Dalton) who was presumably the Miss Ross described as the first owner of this portrait. W.C. Ross also drew his father in chalk in 1842 (the drawing is now in the Victoria and Albert Museum), the year he received his knighthood. It is likely that this miniature was painted in, or not long after, that year, especially if the inscribed frame is contemporary.

This portrait is a masterly and touching portrait of an artist's father, one that goes beyond the usual limitations of miniatures. Ross senior is shown in dignified, dark dress with a touch of colour in his multicoloured (maybe plaid) waistcoat.

W.C. Ross has lit his subject from a high source, which makes the sitter's white hair and craggy face loom out of the dark background. The younger artist's technique is a mixture of fine stipple and brush strokes on the face, with delicate line work in the hair. The surface is carefully built up with opaque paint, only employing a watercolour technique on the areas of dress.

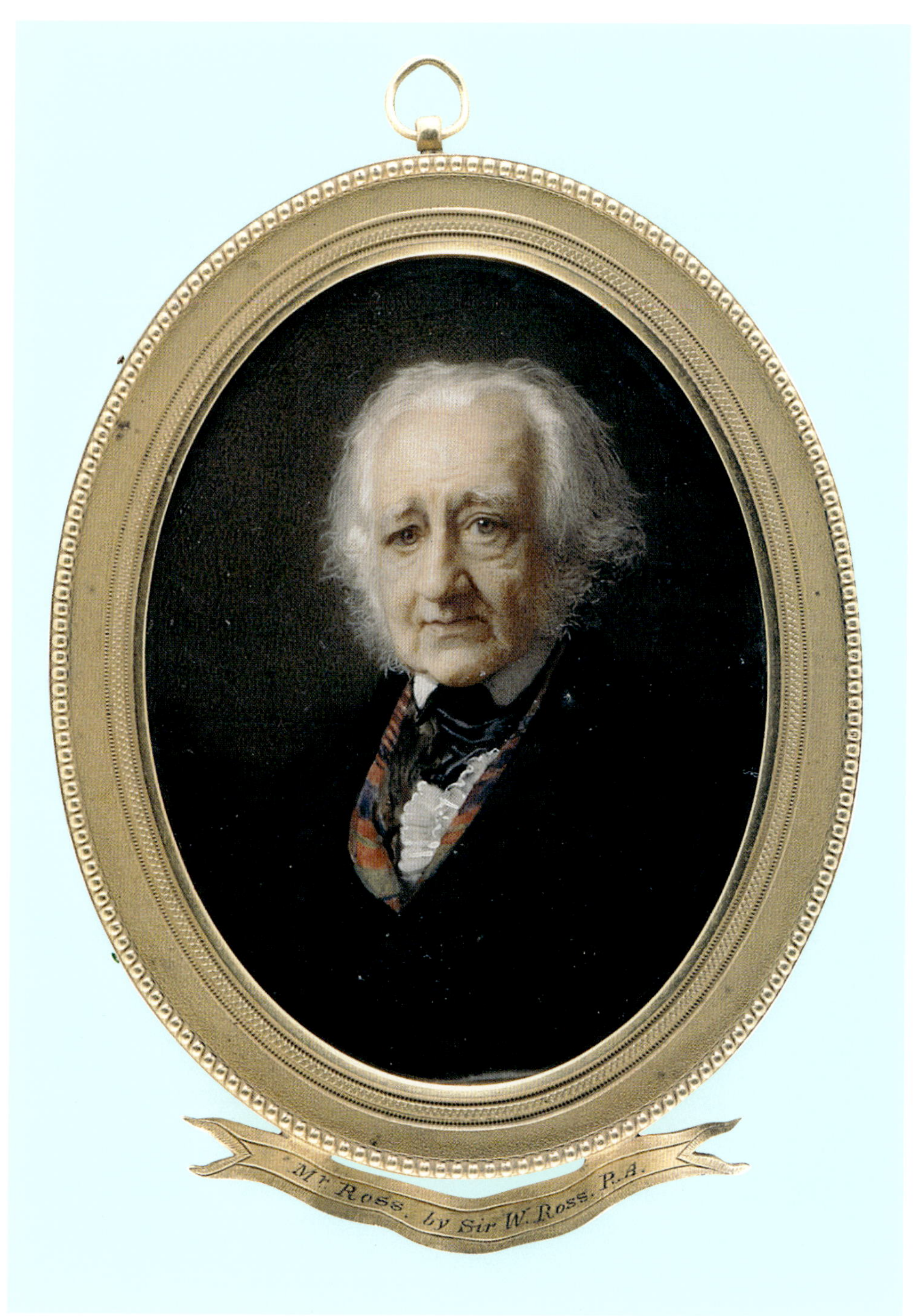


Mr Ross. by Sir W. Ross. R.A.

# Indian School (Delhi), nineteenth century

### 110  ? Emperor Bahadur Shah Zafir II (1775–1862)

Watercolour on ivory; gold brooch frame with mother-of-pearl verso
Oval, 3.9 x 3.1 cm

Joseph Bonnar (Jeweller), Edinburgh; purchased by the Draper estate; given to Kenwood, 1994  (88029821)

Lit.: (for comparison) M. Archer, *Company Drawings in the India Office Library*, London, 1972

The sitter is reputedly the last Mogul Shah in India. He was deported in 1858 by the British to Rangoon for his part in the Indian Mutiny at Delhi, where he was proclaimed leader.

A school of indigenous artists painting on ivory developed in Delhi from the late eighteenth century. Sometimes known as 'Company paintings', after their East India Company clientele, portraits were produced for both the local and European markets. Portraits of the great Mogul leaders, paricularly Bahadur Shah Zafir, were collected by the British after their eventual demise.

The anonymous artist of this miniature has evidently studied a European miniaturist's techniques and materials, but retained a traditional approach to the portrait itself. The application of the many jewels of the Mogul's dress is curiously reminiscent of Hilliard's use of raised points of colour and gold.

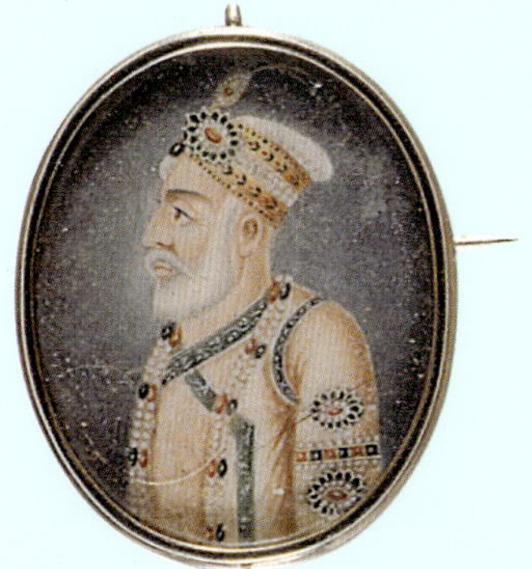

# Rosalba Carriera (1675–1757)

Born in Venice, Rosalba Carriera was to be of seminal importance as a painter
of both miniatures and pastels. As a pastellist, she represented the standard to
which later artists such as Mengs and, in Britain, William Hoare and Francis
Cotes aspired. A visit to her studio became one of the essential components of
the Grand Tour for British aristocrats visiting Venice, and portraits by her made
their way back to England to influence artists there. Her place in the history of
miniature painting is assured through her discovery of the advantages of bone
or ivory as a base on which to lay thin washes of paint allowing the base to
show through. The resulting luminosity accords well with the delicacy and
apparent spontaneity of her pastel portraits, although the background and
dress details were still painted in opaque colours. Failing eyesight led to a
falling-away in production of miniatures in the artist's later years.

Rosalba appears not to have visited England, and the credit for introducing
her innovation to this country lies with Bernard Lens.

### 111  General Jasper Clayton (d 1743)

Watercolour on ivory; mounted with rectangular ormolu slip, in the base
of a red leather travelling case (not illustrated).
Oval, 9.5 x 6.9 cm

Bonham's 21 November 1996 (24); purchased by the Draper estate; given
to Kenwood, 1996 (88009882)

Jasper Clayton, a distinguished officer, served as Captain in what became
known as the 9th Foot, in 1696; he was made colonel in 1713 and Lt.
General in 1739. He fought under George II at Dettingen, the last battle in
which British forces were commanded by their monarch in person, and
was killed there in 1743. It is in the role of Lt. General that Rosalba has
portrayed him here, in a swaggering style surely influenced by the military
portraits of Hyacinthe Rigaud and Largilliere, both of whom Rosalba knew
personally as a result of a triumphantly successful period of residence in
Paris from 1720 to 1721.

The portrait must have been painted around 1740, at a time when she
had already virtually ceased from painting in miniature, no doubt because
of difficulties with her eyesight. Certainly the softness of Rosalba's earlier
style seems here to have given way to something a little harder-edged.
However, the brilliance of colour, luminosity, and painterly handling of the
gilded armour, blue drapery and soft, full-bottomed wig still testify to her
virtuosity.

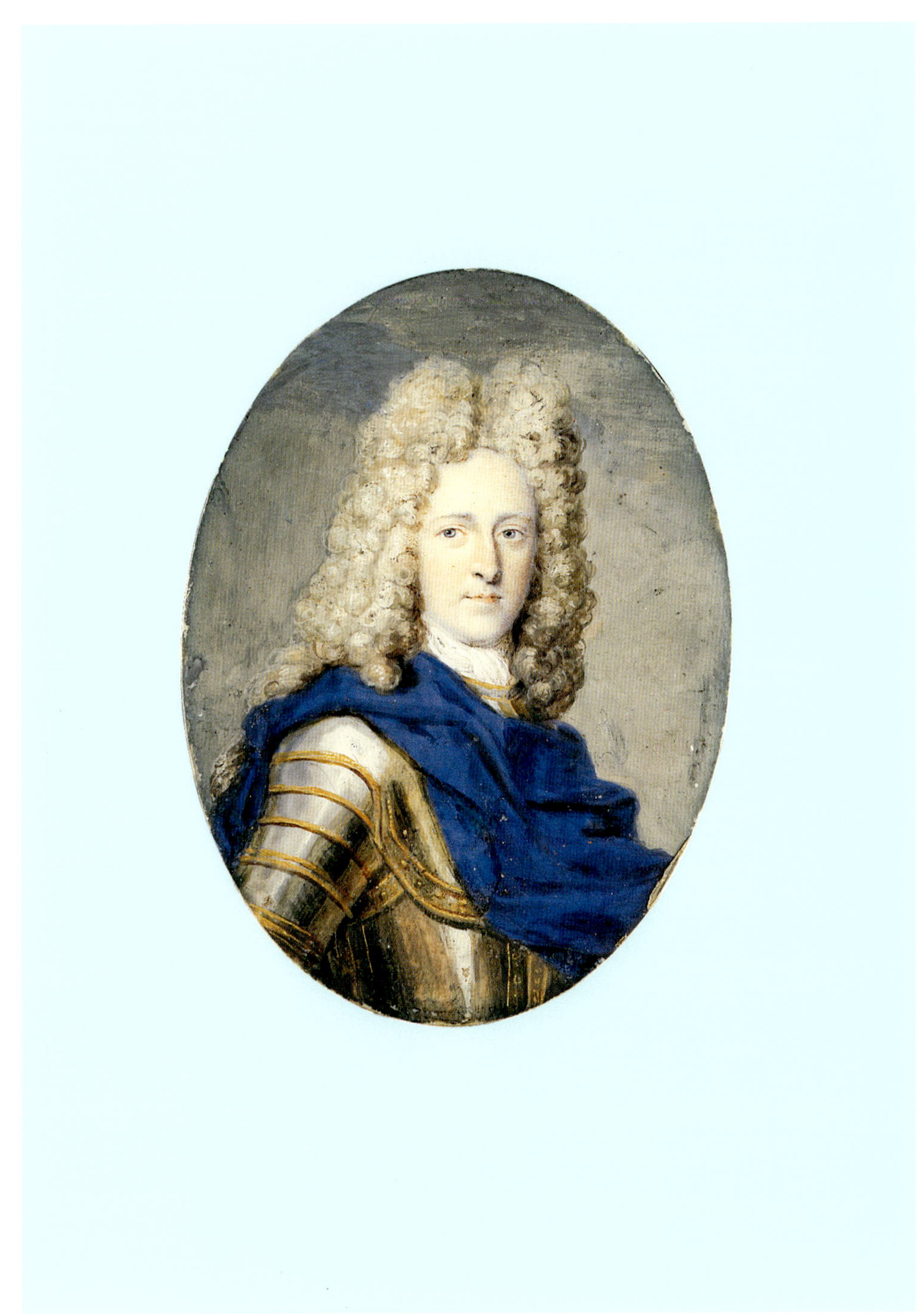

# Select Bibliography


Bayne-Powell, Robert L. *Catalogue of Portrait Miniatures in the Fitzwilliam Museum*, Cambridge, 1985.
Foskett, Daphne. *Collecting Miniatures,* Woodbridge, 1979.
Foskett, Daphne. *Dictionary of British Miniature Painters*, London, 1972.
The above two re-published together as:
Foskett, Daphne. *Dictionary and Guide*, Woodbridge, 1987.
Foskett, Daphne. *John Smart*, London, 1964.
Lloyd, Stephen. *Richard and Maria Cosway: Regency Artists of Taste and Fashion*, Scottish National Portrait Gallery, Edinburgh, 1995.
Murdoch, John et al. *The English Miniature*, London, 1981.
Murrell, V.J. *The Way Howe to Lymne*, London, 1983.
Reynolds, Graham. *English Portrait Miniatures*, London, 1952, 1988 (revised).
Strong, Roy. *The English Renaissance Miniature*, London, 1983.
Walker, Richard. *Miniatures in the Collection of H.M. the Queen: the Eighteenth and Early Nineteenth Centuries*, Cambridge, 1992.

Regular auction sales catalogues, illustrated in colour, are produced by Bonham's, Christie's and Sotheby's auction houses.


## Other collections to visit which are regularly open to the public

Ashmolean Museum, Oxford
Fitzwilliam Museum, Cambridge
Holburne Museum and Crafts Study Centre, Bath
National Portrait Gallery, London
Victoria and Albert Museum, London
Wallace Collection, London.

# INDEX